Economic Terms and Beyond: Capitalising on the Wealth of Notions

Linguistic Insights

Studies in Language and Communication

Edited by Maurizio Gotti,
University of Bergamo

Volume 176

PETER LANG
Bern · Berlin · Bruxelles · Frankfurt am Main · New York · Oxford · Wien

Catherine Resche

Economic Terms and Beyond: Capitalising on the Wealth of Notions

How Researchers in Specialised Varieties of English Can Benefit from Focusing on Terms

PETER LANG
Bern · Berlin · Bruxelles · Frankfurt am Main · New York · Oxford · Wien

Bibliographic information published by die Deutsche Nationalbibliothek
Die Deutsche Nationalbibliothek lists this publication in the Deutsche Nationalbibliografie; detailed bibliographic data is available on the Internet at ‹http://dnb.d-nb.de›.

British Library Cataloguing-in-Publication Data: A catalogue record for this book is available from The British Library, Great Britain

Library of Congress Cataloging-in-Publication Data

Resche, Catherine.
Economic terms and beyond : capitalising on the wealth of notions : how researchers in specialised varieties of English can benefit from focusing on terms / Catherine Resche.
pages cm. – (Linguistic insights – Studies in language and communication ; v. 176)
Includes bibliographical references and index.
ISBN 978-3-0343-1435-0
1. English language–Variation–English-speaking countries.
2. English language–Study and teaching–English-speaking countries.
3. Business communication–Cross-cultural studies.
4. English language–Globalization. I. Title.
PE1066.R45 2013
428.0071–dc23
2013028867

ISSN 1424-8689 pb.
ISBN 978-3-0343-1435-0 pb.
ISSN 2235-6371 eBook
ISBN 978-3-0351-0589-6 eBook

Hochfeldstrasse 32, CH-3012 Bern, Switzerland
info@peterlang.com, www.peterlang.com, www.peterlang.net

Contents

To my family

Acknowledgements

I wish to express my thanks to the many people who supported me throughout the development of this book.

I would particularly like to thank the anonymous reviewers of the manuscript for their insightful comments and suggestions; Maria Teresa Cabré, Rita Temmerman and John Humbley for their support from the very beginning; Rosalind Greenstein who so carefully proof read the manuscript; my colleagues Jacqueline Percebois, Shaeda Isani, Marie-Hélène Fries and Michel Van der Yeught, for their friendly support and my doctoral students Fanny Domenec, Caroline Peynaud and Séverine Wozniak who regularly expressed their interest in hearing how the project was progressing. They unknowingly helped me to go forward as I could not let them see when I had moments of doubt as to its viability.

Thanks also to the editorial staff of Peter Lang for their help and support; I owe a personal debt of gratitude to Adrian Stähli, commissioning editor and production manager at Peter Lang's, and of course to Maurizio Gotti, the director of the *Linguistic Insights* series.

I am especially grateful to my unfailingly patient, understanding, supportive and loving husband Marc, for accepting to give up so many family weekends, as well as winter, spring and summer holidays and to our daughter Anne-Sophie for her *joie de vivre* and reassuring optimism. I can truly say that this book could never have been written without them.

1. Introduction

This book is aimed at researchers in and teachers of English as a foreign language (EFL) in the field of specialised domains. Though the focus is on the field of economics in its broad sense, encompassing finance and management, the approach offered here can be adapted to many other areas of specialised knowledge. It can therefore be regarded as a case study and guide for the researchers and foreign language lecturers and professors who wish to acquire further knowledge in a specific domain and to understand the historical context beyond terms and expressions that are used in a given field. Underpinning this approach is, of course, my training as a linguist and my experience of teaching English for economics in a French university for well over two decades now. The point is that, since any specialised discipline or professional field is based on theory or practice that are expressed through language, language can serve as a starting point for further investigation into specific domains and specialised communities, and into their culture and discourse. Having the privilege to teach and do my research in the same field, i.e. English for economics, management and finance, I[1] have studied the domain systematically, from terminology and neology through phraseology to corpus-based genre and discourse analyses, always approaching language as a living, evolutionary process. All the paths I gradually explored were suggested by the terms I came across over the years for, as will be illustrated here, terms convey much more than the concepts they denote.

Devoting time and energy to tracking and studying terms most certainly does bring return on investment, to borrow from the terminology of finance, hence the second part in the title. The choice of "notions" rather than "concepts" was of course dictated by the allusion

---

1 Although I am French, I have chosen to write the book in English in order to make it easier for researchers in specialised discourse and domains and teachers of specialised varieties of English as a foreign language to understand my approach, whatever their mother tongue.

to Adam Smith's well-known contribution to economic theory through his study of the Wealth of Nations (1776). It should be noted, however, that for a long time the French translations of ISO standards seemed to waver between "*notion*" and "*concept*", though the English versions used "concept" from the start. Since 2001, "*concept*" has been used more consistently in the French translations. Nevertheless, I took the liberty of using "notion" in the title in order for the allusion to Adam Smith to make sense, hoping to be forgiven by the proponents of "concept", which has been adopted in the rest of the book.

As announced in the subtitle, the focus is clearly on research – not teaching – even though ideally research and teaching should be mutually enriching, provided the researcher's centre of interest matches her teaching activities. The decision not to use the term "ESP" was deliberate, since it is too often associated with analysing the needs of the workplace and devising tasks to prepare learners to communicate in an international professional setting. For reasons that are explained at greater length in the second part of Chapter 2, the phrase "Specialised Varieties of English" (hereafter referred to as SVE) was chosen in preference to ESP. The intended message is that, for a researcher in SVE trained as a linguist, the object of research is of course language – or more precisely specialised discourse actually used in a given field – but the ultimate goal is to provide as detailed and comprehensive a description as possible of a given specialised field through language as an entry point. As language is rooted in culture, whether pertaining to a discipline, an occupation, or any other specific activity, the work of the researcher implies understanding the various players, the specialised milieus, their origins, history and conventions: terms cannot be dispensed with and the multiple questions they raise are a perfect starting point for such investigation.

"Terminology" also needs to be defined, especially for younger researchers opting to investigate a specialised domain. In today's fast-advancing technical and scientific world, more and more people seem to be aware that the needs for terminological resources are growing. The use of the word "terminology" is currently widespread, even among ordinary citizens. Yet it seems that many of those who have added the word to their existing stock only have a vague idea of what "terminology" actually refers to: they mostly use it either as a synonym for "lexicon" or for "jargon". The main difference between a lexical and a terminological unit can be apprehended through the way they are defined. The definition of a terminological unit is the definition of the linguistic expression of a concept which is itself related to other concepts in a specialised field. Admittedly, the meaning of "terminology" can be confusing for the layperson as terminologists themselves seem to use the term in various ways, depending on whether they are referring to theoretical research or practical aspects (Humbley 1997). Bergenholtz (1995: 52) lists four meanings while de Bessé mentions five (1994: 136). It is true that it is not uncommon to read "terminology" instead of "terminography" to mean "the recording, processing and presentation of terminological data acquired by terminological research" (ISO 1087). Apart from this, terminology can correspond to any of the following definitions:

- "A theory, i.e. the set of premises, arguments and conclusions required for explaining the relationships between concepts and terms" (Sager 1990: 3). This body of theoretical knowledge is also referred to as "Terminology science" or "the scientific study of the concepts and terms found in special languages" (ISO 1087: 1990).
- The discipline dealing with the theory defined above. According to Sager again (1990: 3) "Terminology is also an interdisciplinary field of research because it is highly influenced by the activities and methods of the areas it serves".
- A field of activity "concerned with the collection, description, processing and presentations of terms, i.e. lexical items belonging to specialised areas of usage of one or more languages" (Sager 1990: 3).
- "A set of terms representing the system of concepts of a particular subject field" (ISO 1087: 1990). It is sometimes used to describe an author's idiolect or that of a school of thought (as in 'Marxist terminology').

In addition, terminology has become a specialised aspect of computational linguistics and information science. It can also find specific applications in standardisation and language planning, in specialised translation as well as in information retrieval.

In the circles of researchers and teachers in the field of SVE, terms should be considered as the core elements of specialised discourse in specific domains; unfortunately, too few colleagues seem to pay enough attention to terms as such and especially to the wealth of information that they can provide. To take an example that is familiar to me, it is also regrettable that, at the present time, students of English in higher education in France – and especially future teachers of and researchers in English – are not introduced to terminology through some theoretical and practical classes in the course of their studies, especially as more and more of the would-be teachers and researchers will be working with students specialising in domains other than languages. As statistics have shown, the number of students studying towards foreign language degrees[2] *per se* in French universities has been falling steadily in the past decade, while the number of students who need foreign languages related to their particular branch of studies has been rising substantially. In the fields of legal English, English for economics, medicine, physics, or biology, for example, demand has been growing lately for English teachers willing to become more knowledgeable about the subjects their students have chosen to study. The coming generation of foreigh language teachers in higher education – and especially teachers of English as a foreign language – will need to orient their research accordingly if they are to find jobs. If researchers and colleagues only realised what a wonderful resource terms can be, they would be more willing and would find it easier to explore specialised domains and milieus in order to broaden their horizons. And as anyone who has ever endeavoured to delve into a new field of knowledge knows, this can turn out to be a worthwhile, fascinating experience.

Major differences exist in the way foreign language researchers approach and investigate a specialised domain, depending on the traditions and research paradigms of the countries and circles they work in. For many, and it is to be deplored, terminology remains a vague concept. For some, terms are only interesting for their definitions. But the

2 i.e., traditionally enrolling in courses such as English or American literature, English linguistics, and cultural studies (known as "*civilisation*"in French, in a somewhat different approach).

point is that terms are just the tip of the iceberg and they have a lot more secrets to reveal about their origins, their creators, and the historical, cultural and scientific environment that motivated them, especially in a discipline like economics which is highly social and political. It is the duty of researchers to unveil those secrets. Metaphors provide a good example: though surface metaphors found in the specialised press may attract people's attention and be worthy of interest in some cases, theory-constitutive metaphors – expressed by metaphorical terms – should not be overlooked. As root metaphors, they may actually have inspired metaphors used for popularisation purposes, but their specificity lies in the great stories they can tell us about the influence of one science over another or about the prevailing paradigm at a given period. In this respect, theory-constitutive metaphors are pure gems and metaphorical terms can be a gateway into a specialised field of knowledge. Likewise, terms created by theorists and great figures in a specific field can be seen as signposts that guide the linguists' steps on their way to discovering more about how theories were born, why they emerged at a particular period of time, how they developed and came to be challenged.

Based on the lessons of several decades of research into the domain and the discourse of economics, this book is meant to show how, by choosing terms as a starting point, a language teacher of and researcher in SVE can explore promising avenues of research. Choosing the example of a soft science, I wish to highlight a different approach to terms as a multi-faceted source of information. Not only do they enable us to discover and understand how concepts are interrelated and how a domain is structured, but they can also open up new vistas on the history of ideas, on current developments, and on the preoccupations of a society at different points in time. They can also serve as signposts and draw our attention to potential paradigm shifts and scientific evolution. In this respect, terms can be considered as both mirrors and motors of change.

At this point, the reader who might only be familiar with the Vienna School and Wüster's recommendations – and might have overlooked more recent approaches to terminology – might rightly feel destabilised as the above-mentioned approach to terms seems to challenge several principles that lie at the basis of the General Theory of Terminology (GTT). After all, suggesting a focus on terms to discover the concepts they denote – in other words giving priority to a semasiological approach – means diverging from Wüster's onomasiological approach or "conceptual perspective" (L'Homme 2004: 24). Likewise, suggesting that terms evolve over time and should be interesting for what they tell us about the way concepts can be called into question in a given domain implies considering a diachronic perspective whereas Wüster advocated focusing on synchrony. A synchronic perspective is not, however, excluded for all that in the approach offered here. What is more, metaphorical terms – as well as euphemistic, oxymoronic or indeterminate terms – seem to contradict the idea that terms should be devoid of connotation or ambiguity. Obviously, the approach to terminology and language that is offered here reflects more recent strands in terminology and is thus based on a descriptive rather than a prescriptive stance. In this perspective, terms are observed *in vivo* and *in situ*, not *in vitro*, which means in their linguistic and discursive context, taking into account the situation in which they are produced, not to mention their social and historical environment. Again, such a position clearly diverges from Wüster's principles, but is in accordance with more recent corpus-based approaches to terminology: all the examples quoted in the various chapters of the book result from the corpus-based terminological investigations which I have been conducting for close to two decades now.

The above notwithstanding, the perspective offered here should not be interpreted as a total rejection of Wüster's tremendous contribution. As chapter 2 reminds the reader, his most-cited principles have left many of his insightful comments in the shadows, probably because too few people could read German. Although, at some time and in some circles, his recommendations were severely criticised for being too rigid and unrealistic, one should bear in mind that he paved the way for future approaches, and broke new ground in distinguishing between the terminological unit and a mere lexical item. It is also important to recall the context in which Wüster worked and his motivations. Obviously, a soft science like economics cannot be compared to an exact science or to a technical field, nor can it be approached by the layperson from the same angle as that which a domain-specialist would choose; the purpose is also very different, since research here is not guided by concerns for standardisation. Wüster's principles, however, have been very helpful through the many questions they triggered whenever economic terms struck me as anomalies and stimulated further research. Whatever the researcher's approach and motivation may be, terms remain fascinating insightful guides into any unfamiliar specialised domain.

The organisation of the book

Chapter 2 provides background on Wüster's contribution to terminology science and practice – beyond the five most-cited principles that have ignited criticism – with a view to highlighting his purpose and the circumstances in which he worked, and to doing justice to his writings. It introduces more recent approaches and explains the stance that has been adopted in this book. It also explains the difference between ESP and SVE, and clarifies these different strands. Finally, it offers an overview of the various approaches to research in SVE, with a discussion of such notions as specialised community and specialised discourse.

Chapter 3 is intended as a reference for the reader to better understand the following chapters. It should be noted that much of the information provided here resulted from investigations prompted by terms. Chapter 3 offers a brief summary of the evolution of economics, from social philosophy through political economy to economics. It highlights the quest for scientificity in the nineteenth century, hence the adoption of methods borrowed from physics and mechanics, and the heavy reliance on mathematics. Alongside the physics envy, it also reviews the biological analogies that have tempted a number of economists as an alternative to mechanical physics. It relativises the notion of economics as a science and stresses the specificity of economics as a soft science.

Chapter 4 focuses on the role of neology. It first analyses a number of economists' concerns with concepts and definitions. It then provides examples of key terms in economics and management whose origins can be dated and associated with the people who coined them: they can be seen as milestones and barometers of the evolution of scientific postures. The case of the 2008 housing and financial crises is also studied to evaluate the neonyms that emerged at the time and the insight that can be gained from examining them more closely. Economics and terminology seem to share a parallel development in terms of an orthodox set of theoretical assumptions that has since been questioned and enriched by a number of new approaches. A review of recently created branches of economics and their new names echoes the new branches in terminology described in Chapter 2. The example of green economics is studied at length to show how new terms can translate major changes and possibly signal paradigm shifts.

Chapter 5 explains how metaphorical terms can provide an entry point into the history of economic thought as introduced in Chapter 3. Metaphors can play different roles: there are heuristic metaphors, pedagogical metaphors, etc. Emphasis is laid on theory-constitutive metaphors – root metaphors, dormant metaphors – that help us understand how theory evolved and what influenced economics, and serve as indicators of turning points in the history of economic thought. Metaphors can also be seen as mediators or even revolutionaries when introducing new perspectives and can be analysed as mirrors of social changes. This approach calls for metaphors to be monitored, which would help the community of researchers detect new trends.

Chapter 6 broadens the perspective by taking into account the discursive context. Paradoxically, terms adapt to their textual environment and can be said to be at the service of discourse. The specificity of economic discourse is analysed at length in order to account for variability, concept fuzziness, loose meaning, vagueness and ambiguity. Terms naturally evolve along with concepts and ambiguous terms are no coincidence. Uncertainty being an essential feature of economics, this gives rise to euphemistic terms. In this respect, euphemistic as well as oxymoronic terms are to be analysed for what they tell us about the doubts, conventions and expectations of a given period. Examples of terminological correctness in economics are also provided. Another advantage offered by extending the observation of terms to their textual and discursive environment is that paying attention to how frequently they are used and to any sudden changes in their frequency may well alert us to imminent problems or new preoccupations.

Chapter 7 expands on the idea of interface terminology, opening borders and multi-, inter- and transdisciplinary fields and analyses the phenomenon of cross-fertilisation of economics and other sciences. It provides examples of three different categories of interface terms through the analysis of the fields of neurofinance, green management and the applications of chaos theory to various domains, including sub-fields of economics. Finally it suggests exploring the notion of interface terms further on the diachronic axis, as a means to trace the movement of intellectual trends through various disciplines, and to have a more holistic view of their influences. This means adopting a broader approach to terminology, against a background of scientific and technological progress that seems to introduce new assumptions, new sets of ideas and a new philosophy across disciplines. Interface terms remain the most reliable signals of such changes.

Understandably, the decision to devote separate chapters to neonyms, metaphors, indeterminate and interface terms may seem artificial since these categories are not mutually exclusive, and the same term could justifiably have a place in each of the chapters. However, for the purposes of clarity and precision, it seems necessary to highlight one particular phenomenon at a time, even if this means running the risk of analysing a topic in one chapter and then returning to it in another. In each case, the examples are chosen with a view to providing additional, complementary information or concentrating on a sub-field from a different angle so that, for example, economists' preoccupations with clear terms are mentioned in Chapter 4 when dealing with economists as wordsmiths and again in Chapter 7 when discussing clarity vs. indeterminacy in economics. Each time, these points are illustrated by different examples which highlight a different approach. Likewise, environmental considerations are used to illustrate the emergence of new branches of economics and identify potential paradigm shifts in Chapter 4; they are mentioned again in Chapter 7 through a different focus on the corporate world to underline the influence of environmental considerations on this sub-field. The same principle underpins the introduction of the chaordic metaphor in management in Chapter 5 and the choice of chaos theory and its concepts to illustrate cross-disciplinary interface terms in Chapter 7. It is to be hoped that the various angles and the echoes from one chapter to the other can help the reader have a more holistic view of the knowledge that can be gleaned by focusing on terms that may once have seemed anomalous.

2. Terminology and ESP/SVE

The real journey of discovery consists not in seeking new lands, but in seeing with new eyes.[3]

Marcel Proust

A la recherche du temps perdu (1918)

The way to do research is to attack the facts at the point of greatest astonishment.

Celia Green

The Decline and Fall of Science (1972)

Terminology, like any field of knowledge, cannot be dissociated from the social and political environment that triggered its emergence. If today's approach to terminology differs somewhat from the original recommendations that were made by Wüster in a specific context, it would nevertheless be unfair and unrealistic to disregard his foundational approach: today's researchers owe a lot to the pioneers in the field and the distance that has been taken by some in the past decades only translates the necessary evolution in the needs for and applications of terminology. Hence the great many possible approaches, methods and uses that depend precisely on people's activities, purposes, fields of interest and needs. Undoubtedly, a member of a standardisation committee, a translator, a trainee for a particular job, a student in a specific scientific or technical field, or in translation, interpretation or communication (Nuopponen 1996), a researcher in a given domain, a journalist reporting on a special topic or contributing

---

3 Translated from the French by C. K. Scott Montcrieff (Vol. 5 *The Captive*); original text in French: *Le seul véritable voyage, [...] ce ne serait pas d'aller vers d'autres paysages, mais d'avoir d'autres yeux [...].*

to the popularisation of techniques or science, or any citizen just practising a particular sport or leisure activity all have different purposes when it comes to terminology: they simply do not and cannot share the same perspective.

It is obvious from the above-mentioned list that not all the people are subject-specialists in the fields they are dealing with, so that they cannot be expected to be familiar with the concepts and the conceptual structure of a given field right from the start. Terms can then become a way in to further investigate a field, if need be. The same applies to researchers in and teachers of Specialised Varieties of English (SVE) whom this book addresses primarily: not only are they unlikely to all have a background in the specialised domain they are investigating, but very few of them have really been exposed to terminology theory and / or practice in the course of their studies. Therefore, they may well have a vague and simplified idea of terminology and terms, which makes it necessary to offer them a cursory overview of past and present approaches to terminology in this chapter. To this end, Section 1 describes Wüster's original perspective and position, before mentioning the various branches of terminology that have arisen since. Section 2 begins with a discussion of ESP and SVE and goes on to define the specificity of SVE. Several possible approaches to SVE research are analysed in order to show how a focus on terms may be useful for SVE researchers.

2.1. From Wüster onwards

Wüster's preoccupation with recording the names assigned to objects or the designations of concepts and organising them into tree structures was not altogether new: the need for scientific knowledge "to be organised around systems of technical concepts arranged in strict hierarchies of kinds and parts" (Halliday & Martin 1993: 6) emerged in the seventeenth century with Leibniz's[4] interest in classifying sciences and languages – not to mention ancient and medieval classifications[5]. However, the first major attempts at rigorously recording and classifying objects date back to the late eighteenth century with Linnaeus's [6] binomial nomenclature of minerals, plants and animals, Guyton de Morveau's[7] chemical nomenclature and Lavoisier's [8] classification of elements. The term "taxonomy" itself is said to have been coined by Swiss botanist Augustin Pyramus de Candolle in his 1813 *Traité élémentaire de la botanique.* As for "terminology", it was first used in the nineteenth century by W. Whewell[9] in his *History of the Inductive Sciences* (1837). It was then reused in international scientific conferences by botanists, zoologists and researchers in chemistry.

For all that, the former attempts have little to compare with the research and activity that took place at the end of the nineteenth century and, above all, in the first half of the twentieth century, when industrial development called for a consensus on definitions. Terminology soon emerged as a separate field, as technical progress and increased international exchanges triggered concern for unambiguous interna-

4 Gottfried Wilhelm von Leibniz (1646-1716) was a German mathematician and philosopher.

5 It must be noted that Dürer (1471-1528) had also worked on mathematics, and Vesalius (1514-1564) on anatomy.

6 Carl Linnaeus (1707-1778) was a Swedish botanist.

7 Louis Bernard Guyton de Morveau (1737-1816) was a French chemist who published a method aimed at systematically basing chemical nomenclature on the chemical components of compounds. Before that, chemical elements used to be named after the people who had discovered them, after places or any enigmatic property.

8 Antoine Laurent de Lavoisier (1743-1794) was a chemist, a philosopher and an economist (1743-1794).

9 Charles Whewell (1784-1866) wrote extensively on a number of subjects (mechanics, mineralogy, geology, astronomy, political economy, etc.). Many scientists such as Charles Darwin, Charles Lyell and Michael Faraday frequently turned to him for terminological assistance. He invented the terms "anode," "cathode," and "ion" for Faraday. Upon the request of the poet Coleridge in 1833, Whewell invented the English word "scientist"; before this time the only terms in use were "natural philosopher" and "man of science". (adapted from the *Stanford Encyclopedia of Philosophy* <http://plato.stanford.edu/entries/whewell>)

tional professional and scientific communication. In those days, Wüster was not alone in showing interest in the discipline and the Vienna school was one of three schools of terminology to be involved in terminological research and practice: the other two were the Czech and Russian schools. Although Wüster was not the only researcher to be interested in terminology, his efforts to have terminology recognised as a communication tool between specialists paid off and the role he played at the International Standardisation Organisation (ISO) and as the director of UNESCO's INFOTERM Centre in Vienna was prominent. He also worked hard towards achieving recognition of terminology in the academic sphere – which turned out to be a much greater challenge – but he eventually succeeded in creating and teaching a general terminology course at the University of Vienna, a course that still exists today. Later, the School of Vienna greatly contributed to the development of the General Theory of Terminology (GTT) and interpreted Wüster's ideas, thus helping to spread his influence.

Wüster's concern with terminology was born out of the need felt by technicians and scientists to harmonise and unify the concepts and their designation by terms in their respective fields. Wüster espoused the dreams of Esperantists and his multilingual dictionary (*The Machine Tool. An Interlingual Dictionary of Basic Concepts*, 1968) led him to systematise the methods for compiling terminological data. From his own practical experience, he later derived theoretical and methodological recommendations in the hope that they would ensure flawless international technical communication.

Although many researchers have already synthesised Wüster's principles (Cabré 1998: 30-32; Temmerman 2000: 5; L'Homme 2004: 24-26), it seems impossible to deal with terms – whatever one's approach or goal – without providing an overview of the main aspects of his contribution to the field of terminology, before mentioning more recent developments in the field. The following remarks are meant to remind the reader why he is considered as a founding figure of terminology studies. Actually, as pointed out by Cabré (2003: 165-166), he never himself used the word "theory" in the many articles he wrote or in the lectures he gave. Instead, he preferred *Terminologielehre*, which translates his concern for practical applications and knowledge transfer. It is only after Wüster died that Felber gathered his lecture notes and published them under the title *Einführung in die allgemeine Terminologielehre und Terminologische Lexikographie* in 1979. The expression General Theory of Terminology (GTT) was only coined later to refer to Wüster's legacy.

2.1.1. *Wüster's most-cited recommendations*

The following recommendations will be discussed below in the context of Wüster's activities and goals.

1) Terminology starts with concepts which are given priority over terms in an onomasiological perspective, translating a preference for systematic ordering.
2) Concepts are defined clearly and belong to a conceptual system; the one-term/one-concept – one-concept/one-term rule, also known as bi-univocal relationship, is most important in order to guarantee stable definitions (monosemy and mononymy).
3) Terms must be studied on the synchronic axis.
4) Priority should be given to written registers.
5) Terms should be standardised to ensure efficient communication and international forms of designation should be preferred.

Starting with the primacy of onomasiology, it is to be remembered that, as a trained engineer, Wüster had a thorough knowledge of his domain; thus, he naturally considered that only the field-specialist was in a position to be familiar with the conceptual structure of his field and able to find the appropriate terms to name those concepts. Understandably then, field-specialists were in the best position to cater to the needs of their peers in search of normalised terms in their own fields and of their equivalents in foreign languages. Wüster brought evidence of this by compiling his *Machine Tool Dictionary*. Consequently, a prescriptive approach was the natural outcome: terms were to be seen as tools to facilitate communication between specialists. Clearly delineated concepts were to be expressed by terms with stable definitions for communication to be free of misunderstanding; logically, fuzziness, variability and connotation were to be banned. In this respect, it is worth keeping in mind that the Latin root "term" (*terminus*) shares the idea of limit or boundary with that of "definition" (*finis*). Wüster's wish to avoid ambiguity or variability led him to advocate a synchronic approach – disregarding historical or textual context – and to erect barriers between domains or fields. The ultimate goal was to endow each scientific or technical field or sub-field with sets of terms systematically recorded in multilingual glossaries and accompanied by precise definitions respectful of international norms.

Wüster's recommendations were derived from his personal experience and goal, so that seen in the light of the constraints of the dictionary genre, they seem quite logical. Obviously, the approach adopted to compile a dictionary cannot be expected to take into account a number of real-life exchanges between experts, which explains why oral communication was ignored, for example. Working on a dictionary also greatly limited his consideration for any textual or social environment. Given the restricted frame that served as a basis for Wüster's recommendations, his "traditional" theory has been blamed for being reductionist. Criticism was first levelled at the overall conception of the terminological unit and its strictly denominative role. The fact that neither the syntactic aspect nor the communicative nature of terms was envisaged was considered as another flaw. In addition, Wüster's failure to acknowledge that concepts as well as terms could be subject to variation was condemned. Admittedly, many aspects of Wüster's prescriptions, when taken literally, can be – and have been – questioned but it is worth mentioning a number of points that show that he was aware that his principles could not always be heeded; the spectrum of his considerations was much broader than the few points on which criticism seems to have crystalised.

2.1.2. Another approach to Wüster's writings

The researchers who could read the original German version of his writings (Humbley 2004; Budin 1998) made a point of insisting that he qualified his position, conscious as he was that his recommendations were but an ideal to aim at. According to Candel (2004: 19), although he strongly insisted that his principles be implemented, he resorted to such verbs as *anstreben* or *trachten* (aim at) several times, as if he knew that the goal he had set would not always be easy to reach. For example, Candel (2004: 23) quotes his tolerance of a certain kind of synonymy as regards abbreviated forms: "*Gelegentlich kann es von Nutzen sein, eine ausführliche und eine kürzere Form nebeneinander als Synonyme zur Verfügung zu haben (...)*[10] *(47)*". Wüster recommended the longer, more transparent form when addressing people who are less familiar with the domain; when specialists communicated with their peers, the longer form was also to be preferred when first used in a text, as an introduction to the concept, and then to be replaced by its abbreviated form in the rest of the text.

Those who have only had access to a second-hand, simplified version of his main ideas should realise that Wüster did not altogether reject phraseology or context (Antia 2001; Humbley 2004): he even stated that in specialised dictionaries, information about phraseology was too limited. Furthermore, he did not refuse to take some oral aspects into consideration, insisting, for example, that indications concerning the pronunciation of abbreviations in various countries should be provided. Still, pronunciation has little in common with consideration for oral exchanges and their impact on the terminology actually used. His position as regards metaphor also seems to have been caricatured. Evidence of his awareness that his principles could not always be implemented as rigorously as would be necessary is brought to us by the following quotation: "*Auch in der Terminologie muss das Verlangen nach vollständiger Eineindeutigkeit ein frommer Wunsch bleiben*"[11]. More broadly, Antia (2002: 103) draws our attention to the fact that Wüster's contribution should not be confined to terminology. He was "an early contributor to modern linguistics thought, particularly synchronic semantics, and a pioneer of LSP who also tried to claim a place within linguistics for LSP research". Antia (2002: 105) stresses that he was also a pioneering figure in German Applied Linguistics: "Wüster writes that he was the first to use the term '*angewandte*

10 [Occasionally, it can be useful to have a shorter form next to the longer term as synonyms]. My translation

11 [Even in terminology, the desire to achieve a perfect one-term/one-concept – one-concept/one-term relationship is to be considered as wishful thinking]. My translation

Sprachwissenschaft' (applied linguistics) in his 1931 book". Though he was an engineer, he was quite familiar with linguistics and many of his articles were actually published in linguistics journals or in the proceedings of linguistics conferences. It is a great pity that an English version of many of his writings should not have been available earlier: many researchers who suggested other paths for terminology would then have realised that he had anticipated a number of questions that have been raised in the past two decades. By bringing together texts that would otherwise have been hard to access, Picht and Schmitz (2001) have shown how broad the scope of Wüster's preoccupations was.

Whatever his critics' arguments, Wüster's contribution is undeniable in the field of terminology and specialised language (Van Campenhoudt 2006). He raised the numerous questions linked with technological changes and the linguistic needs they brought about, with new concepts and the elaboration of technical language, with knowledge transfer, with international technical communication. Any multilingual perspective implies analysing concepts and defining them precisely. Wüster drew people's attention to the fact that, prior to translation, it is important to agree on the concept, as reality can be apprehended differently from one language to another. He also insisted on the importance of the concrete object: in technical fields, for example, it is easy to add a drawing of the object being described to make sure everyone is referring to the same physical part. Of course, this is not possible with more abstract fields of knowledge, which makes translation more difficult. But even in monolingual terminological research, depending on the domains under scrutiny and the perspective adopted by the researchers, Wüster's goals may seem unattainable. This has given rise to a number of new branches in terminology that should be mentioned before explaining the approach underlying this particular book.

2.1.3. More recent approaches

It might be confusing for the layperson to encounter, among other designations, "textual terminology" (Slodzian 1994, 1995), "socioterminology" (Gaudin 1993, 2003), "terminochrony" (Møller 1998), a "Communicative Theory of Terminology" or "CTT" (Cabré 1999), "sociocognitive terminology" (Temmerman 2000), "termontography" (Temmerman & Kerremans 2003), "pragmaterminology" (De Vecchi 2004), "terminometrics" (Quirion 2003, Resche 2004*a*), or "ontoterminology" (Roche 2007). Such a list translates a number of new positions among researchers in the field of terminology and is restricted to the designations that still include terminology or the "term/termino" root.

According to Myking (2001: 55), researchers in terminology fall into three categories: (a) moderate and loyal, (b) radical and subversive, and (c) radical and loyal. The moderate and loyal position (a), represented by Picht and Myking himself, is in favour of bringing terminology and linguistics closer, explaining and analysing the classical theory "without abandoning the established methodological and theoretical tenets – such as, in particular, the onomasiological approach to conceptology". The radical and subversive (b) position, as the adjectives imply, is much different as it "seems to reject traditional terminology completely", maintaining the divide "between *traditional* terminology and *current* linguistics". This position is exemplified by socioterminology and socio-cognitive terminology. Position (c) seems to combine some aspects of positions (a) and (b), advocating changes but not calling into question the foundations: it expresses its "explicit intention of analysing Wüster on the background of his historical context – hence the label 'loyal'". Among the radical and loyal, Bertha Toft (2001) is often quoted as stating that the Wüsterian tradition needs adjusting, for example through cognitive and functional approaches, but she insists that this does not require complete rejection of Wüster's position. Myking's categorisation seems somewhat rigid and perplexing: I must admit I do not really know which category I belongs to. Can one be at once loyal, acknowledging Wüster's contribution and the historical context that motivated his principles, and, at the same time, be "subversive", adopting a semasiological, diachronic, descriptive stance?

A short explanation of the main alternative approaches will help understand what motivated the sometimes diverging paths taken by researchers. Textual terminology, as the term implies, is linked with the idea that the application of terminology should mostly be based on textual analysis under the principle that the specific knowledge of an expert community is contained in the texts it produces and is thus accessible through this very source. Whatever the goals being pursued, analysing text corpora is required (Pearson 1998; Bourigault, Jacquemin & L'Homme 2001) – whether one is involved in translation, terminological extraction, indexation, bilingual or multilingual term alignment, or automatic and semi-automatic retrieval of information from texts or the web. Textual terminology involves text mining and computational terminology: terminology must emerge from texts to better return to texts (Bourigault & Slodzian 1999: 30; Slodzian 2000). This approach, which avoids confining the extraction of terms to noun forms, thus distances itself somewhat from the classical approach where noun forms only were considered as the norm: verbs, adjectives, etc. can be taken into account and larger units as well. The textual approach is descriptive, and challenges the idea that the term is a sort of tag assigned to a concept; it also rejects the principle of a preexisting conceptual system and considers that terms and concepts appear simultaneously.

Socioterminology, as a term, was born in the early 1980s, associating sociolinguistics and terminology. It stems from the realisation that the classical approach, influenced by Leibniz's logic and the vision of a perfect universal and artificial language, failed to reflect the social dimension and richness of language. It called into question a number of principles laid down by Wüster, pointing out that domains or fields cannot be clearly delineated since knowledge has flexible borders and is often interdisciplinary. As progress is made, a lot of overlapping takes place. Specialised discourse comes under various guises, depending on whether scientists address their peers, or engineers, technicians, students, politicians, etc., so the terminology used cannot be considered as a fixed set. Furthermore, language cannot be cut off from its historical roots: likewise, terms are connected to their creators and must be analysed from the point of view of diachrony; polysemy and synonymy are a natural part of a living language. Socioterminology also insists that definitions cannot be static since theories evolve. Language itself evolves and, in the context of language planning, it is important to observe whether users accept or reject new terms and to relate the data to their social or professional status.

Like socioterminology, sociocognitive terminology differs from the traditional standardisation-oriented and concept-centred approach: it can be defined as a communication-oriented and discourse-centred approach (Temmerman 2000). It suggests a pragmatic and realistic description of terms, inspired by the cognitive sciences. Logically, it maintains that synonymy and polysemy are functional in language and cannot be artificially excluded from specialised areas. It advocates combining semasiological and onomasiological approaches; it underlines the fact that cognitive models play a role in the development of new ideas, insisting for example that metaphorical models are worth analysing. It thus considers that concepts and terms should be studied diachronically. In addition, it states that the form and content of definitions are not set in stone and can vary depending on the user's needs.

Ontoterminology is claimed to offer "a new paradigm for terminology" (Roche *et al.* 2009: 1-3) although it shares its onomasiological approach with classical terminology. The proponents of ontoterminology have observed that whenever communication problems occur – especially in technical domains – experts turn to "technical diagrams or formulae rather than texts or standards". They conclude that "experts agree on concept definitions when they are written in a formal (logical) or semi-formal (e.g. conceptual graph) language. These definitions are objective since their interpretation is ruled by a formal system". Consequently they insist that "terms i.e. the 'verbal definition of a concept' [ISO 1087] need to be separated from concept names since they belong to two different semiotic systems": a linguistic system on the one hand and a conceptual one on the other. Once the definition of the term (its linguistic explanation) is separated from the definition of the concept, it is then possible to account for the use of different words to denote the same concept. In this respect, ontoterminology diverges from the GTT.

Termontography is described by Temmerman and Kerremans (2003: 3) as a result of "cross-fertilisation between the disciplines of ontology engineering and terminology". It is therefore a multidisciplinary approach combining the theories and methods pertaining to the sociocognitive approach (Temmerman 2000) with the methods and recommendations of ontological analysis. The idea of combining the two research fields derives from the realisation that the methodologies used by terminographers and ontologists share common points: both groups first define their goals, identify the domain that is at stake and then analyse the users' needs and the amount of knowledge needed to perform their tasks well.

Pragmaterminology focuses on the world of organisations and more specifically on the corporate world. It seeks to account for corporate sociolects as the reflection of corporate culture. Such terminologies are not always easy to access as they may hide secrets, but they are a priceless source of information for the researcher. Having observed that each company will describe reality in its own way through its own corporate sociolect, using its own terminology and thereby reflecting its own culture, needs and purposes, De Vecchi (2004) revisited the notion of domain to account for the fact that Peugeot and Renault, for example, do not use the same terms, though they are both carmakers; the same holds for Air France and Air Canada whose terminologies and sociolects differ. De Vecchi is interested in the dynamic function of terms, and in understanding their *raison d'être* at a given period of time. As the term implies, pragmaterminology takes into consideration the pragmatic aspects of terminology but not only. It can be said to borrow from cognitive linguistics, sociolinguistics, and terminochrony.

Terminochrony (Møller 1998) is to be understood as a special application of the focus on diachrony in order "to study how time can affect terms and concepts in different ways, changing either meaning or form or both and to various degrees" (Resche 1999: 619). It seeks to understand the origins of terms and their evolution and can provide useful information on the development of new techniques and ideas, on the life-cycle of terms, on the coexistence of synonyms until one is preferred over the others which will be abandoned, and on the reasons for such phenomena.

Terminometrics is quite recent as a branch of terminology (Quirion 2003). It measures terminology usage in specialised subject fields, relying on software programmes such as Barçah, which was developed at the Language Technology Research Center in Gatineau

(Quebec, Canada). Terminometrics can help achieve various goals: research can be conducted to measure synonymy, but also to assess the implantation of specific terms within a subject field in a given population and thus evaluate the success of terminology management. A different application, which corresponds to sentiment analysis, has also been referred to as terminometrics: for example, measuring how often a term like "recession" is used in a corpus of texts related to analyses of the economic environment over a number of months can provide information on the general state of mind of the population and its fears of recession. Thanks to this type of approach, it may be possible to know ahead of time whether recession is to be expected and at what stage of the economic cycle one is (Resche 2004). In a field where data have to be revised several times before the official announcement of the beginning and end of a recession is made public, it seems that terminometrics can help: language can serve to gauge society's reactions.

Among the approaches that have just been reviewed, some depart more clearly than others from the classical approach. Many share common choices, advocating a diachronic perspective and a semasiological approach, for example. Obviously, the evolution of linguistics and computer science, increasing interest in corpus linguistics and the opportunities afforded to analyse large corpora have played a role in inspiring these new approaches. They came as a reaction to the fact that the classical theory could not provide answers to the questions that were raised by the data the researchers had gathered or the goals they were pursuing. To solve the problem, a broader view of terminology needed to be considered, otherwise the risk was to have a multiplicity of competing approaches and interpretations, each meeting particular needs, without any common theoretical ground. In his report on the concluding remarks made by the participants in the Round Table of the Second International Terminology Conference[12] (CIT 2003), Blanchon (2004) underlined the fact that

> […] theoretical approaches that have often been considered as contradictory are in reality as complementary as the users' needs and should be reconciled,

12 The theme of the Conference was "Terminology: The State of the Theories"

> especially in view of the current and future evolution of terminology linked with the ever growing importance of information technologies. Thus onomasiology and semasiology, linguistics and terminology, must reunite and the different countries, different kinds of research, different kinds of practices, must share their knowledge in order to take advantage of an ambitious and robust theory, and provide continuous feedback. (Blanchon 2004: 340).

One major contribution has been left out of this cursory overview so far, i.e. Cabré's Communicative Theory of Terminology (CCT), and her "theory of doors" (2000); what it does is offer a means to reconcile different approaches under the umbrella of a more integrated theory. It is now time to examine it more closely as it will help clarify the perspective adopted in this book.

2.1.4. Cabré's Communicative Theory of Terminology, her "theory of doors" and the perspective adopted in this book

The idea behind Cabré's integrated theory is that terminology as a discipline requires a broader methodological and theoretical framework than Wüster's recommendations, which were derived from – and constrained by – his own preoccupations and intended applications in a context of international intra-professional communication. Wüster himself (1974) described terminology as an interdisciplinary field at the crossroads of linguistics, logic, ontology, computer science and technical sciences ("*ein Grenzgebiet zwischen Sprachwissenschaft, Logik, Ontologie, Informatik und den Sachwissenschaften*"). Still, given the context in which he worked, his GTT could not account for term complexity. By contrast, the CTT advocates studying terms in a situation of natural communication and from a social perspective, "providing [...] terminological data in their natural environment in discourse, with variations according to the different functional registers of specialized communication, [...]" (Cabré 2003: 178).

Cabré (2000) insists that "as well as being interdisciplinary, terminology is multi-functional". A broad theory must then provide researchers and users with the opportunity to approach terminology from different angles and meet their different objectives. In this respect, terms themselves can be approached from different angles. Cabré describes them as polyhedrons, or multi-faceted units, with three main components: one is of a cognitive nature, the second refers to the linguistic dimension and the third one is related to socio-communicative aspects. They reflect the three characteristics of terms as units of knowledge, of language and of communication. These multi-dimensional units therefore offer different entry points, hence the metaphor of "doors". If we consider that terminological units, as used by specialists, are not isolated but are inserted in sentences, texts and exchanges, they should be observed in their natural, authentic environment, i.e. in discourse. Obviously, even in specialised discourse, specialists can use synonyms, and terms will tend to be less mono-referential than they are made out to be in a specialised dictionary. The broader theoretical framework offered by the "theory of doors" therefore includes semantics and pragmatics.

The approach proposed in this book, which results from my research in the field of the language and discourse of economics over the last few decades, has found an echo in the theory of doors and seems to be validated by it. It has always seemed natural to me, as a linguist – not an economist – by training, not to start with concepts but with terms and to observe these terms in their textual and discursive contexts, taking into consideration the circumstances in which they are used. Terms were thus the starting point of all the paths investigated here in the context of economics and can be used in the same way by any observer in the process of discovering a new specialised domain.

Terms can of course be considered as guides to concepts and the conceptual structure of sub-fields, but their cognitive characteristics can be exploited to further explore the diachronic axis, tracking neonyms and studying the evolution of terms and/or concepts. In addition, metaphorical terms offer a wonderful opportunity to conduct investigations as to their origins, and to identify root metaphors and their branches. In this respect, they provide a much more holistic view of a field of knowledge than just surface metaphors, so much so that each entry point can lead to a room that branches out into several corridors allowing access to ever more rooms. From a linguistic point of view, terms can be studied in combination with other items in the context of phraseology; they can also be analysed from the angle of syntax, especially when diverging uses are observed between general and specialised discourse. A terminological unit can, at times, be seen to leave the terminological sphere and change into a lexical unit (Meyer & Mackintosh 2000), as has been shown by corpus-based approaches in terminology; instances of this phenomenon are most interesting for the information they provide as regards the impact of the popularisation of science on the general public, and the shifts in society's preoccupations at a given period of time. Lastly, the observation of terms in their discursive context helps to verify how terms are actually used by some specialists when conveying specific messages: in such circumstances, they are subject to the conventions of milieus and genres and used with the target public in mind. By carefully choosing his terms to match a more subtle discursive environment such as a speech on monetary policy, a central banker can actually talk his targeted public into reacting as he intended them to, which might save him the trouble of implementing aggressive measures that would take months to have any effect anyway. Euphemistic, terminologically-correct terms as well as vague terms cannot escape the careful observer's scrutiny; even in specialised discourse, rhetorical considerations most certainly affect the choice of terms. Disregarding discourse and the way terms are used in their natural linguistic environment would clearly deprive the researcher in SVE of a wealth of information.

Returning to the introductory remarks, it is now necessary to explain and justify the decision to coin a new acronym, SVE, and to show why it is preferable to ESP.

2.2. ESP vs. Specialised Varieties of English (SVE)

Much confusion exists among researchers when one refers to ESP and it is important to clarify the distinction between ESP and SVE and to describe the type of research that can be conducted in the field of SVE.

2.2.1. A reminder of ESP's preoccupations over the years

ESP stands either for English for Specific Purposes or English for Special Purposes and is clearly focused on teaching even when connected with research. It seems to have become one of the most important areas of EFL (English as a Foreign Language). The reasons for the sudden demand for ESP have been traced back to the post WW2 period: not only was it a period "of enormous and unprecedented expansion in scientific, technical and economic activity on an international scale" (Hutchinson & Waters 1987: 6), but it also coincided with the emergence of the United States as an economically powerful country and of English as an international language. Hutchinson and Waters identify another period that may have contributed to the pressing demand for ESP courses, namely the oil crisis of the early 70s, when money and knowledge started flowing into oil-rich countries, with English as a vehicle for knowledge transfer. Ever since, increased pressure has been exerted on language teachers to deliver courses that would be tailored to people's needs.

Two other factors came into play: linguistics started focusing on language as used in real communication situations and, in addition, the psychological aspects of language learning became a focus of interest. Thus, more attention was paid to the ways learners could be motivated and to the strategies they used. Logically, ESP is defined by its learner/learning-centred and "goal-directed" approach (Robinson 1991: 2). Still, there seems to be some disagreement as to what ESP really refers to. The British Council's definition reads as follows:

> ESP (English for Specific Purposes) has been referred to as "applied ELT" as the content and aims of any course are determined by the needs of a specific group of learners. ESP is often divided into EAP (English for Academic Purposes) and EOP (English for Occupational Purposes). Further sub-divisions of EOP are sometimes made into Business English, professional English (e.g. English for doctors, lawyers) and vocational English (e.g. English for tourism, nursing, aviation or bricklaying).[13]

13 <http://www.teachingenglish.org.uk/transform/teachers/specialist-areas/english-specific-purposes>

Reading this definition, some people will consider that ESP can be interpreted as the teaching of English for any purpose that can be defined as specific, while others will counter that ESP should be understood as an umbrella term for more targeted branches such as EAP and EOP, but also English for Vocational Purposes (EVP), English for General Business Purposes (EGBP), English for Science and Technology (EST), or English for Social Studies (ESS), to name but a few examples. These different branches echo the ELT tree Hutchinson and Waters drew back in 1987.[14] Before them, Carter (1983) had also mentioned a branch called English with Specific Topics, underlining that, in this particular case, the emphasis was no longer on purpose but on topics. However, when read more closely, this branch was still based on learners' needs, such as future scientists' needs to attend conferences or work abroad. In no way does this branch focus specifically on the scientific content.

In an attempt to make things clearer, Dudley-Evans and St John (1998) offered a revised and broader version of Strevens's definition (1988), maintaining the distinction between absolute and variable characteristics, as summarised in table 1.

	Strevens (1988: 1-2)	Dudley-Evans & St John (1998: 4-5)
Absolute characteristics	ESP consists of English language teaching which is: designed to meet specified needs of the learner; related in content (themes and topics) to particular disciplines, occupations and activities; centred on the language appropriate to those activities in syntax, lexis, discourse, semantics, etc., and analysis of this discourse; in contrast with General English	ESP is defined to meet specific needs of the learner; makes use of the underlying methodology and activities of the discipline it serves; is centred on the language (grammar, lexis, register), skills, discourse and genres appropriate to these activities;

14 In Hutchinson and Waters's ELT tree, ESP was broken down into three branches: English for Science and Technology (EST), English for Business and Economics (EBE) and English for Social Studies (ESS); each branch was then sub-divided into EAP and EOP.

Variable characteristics	ESP may be, but is not necessarily: restricted as to the language skills to be learned (e.g. reading); taught according to any preordained methodology.	ESP may be related to or designed for specific disciplines. may use, in specific teaching situations, a different methodology from that of General English; is likely to be designed for adult learners, either at a tertiary level institution or in a professional work situation. It could, however, be for learners at secondary school level; is generally designed for intermediate or advanced students. Most ESP courses assume some basic knowledge of the language system, but it can be used with beginners.

Table 1. Absolute and variable characteristics of ESP

One major change introduced by Dudley-Evans and St John is that they have removed Strevens's fourth absolute characteristic which defined ESP as contrasting with General English. However, it is clear that ESP remains essentially focused on meeting learners' needs and on adapting the activities that are offered to the tasks the future professionals will have to perform.

Classes in ESP may well be made up of various, sometimes heterogeneous participants, which may also explain why broader types of skills are targeted. Accordingly, much of the research conducted in the area of ESP revolves around second language acquisition, needs assessment and discussing how to devise the appropriate syllabuses. The following description of what topics are deemed relevant to ESP research as understood by the *English for Specific Purposes* editors is quite telling:

> Authors are encouraged to submit articles and research/discussion notes on topics relevant to the teaching and learning of discourse for specific communi-

> ties: academic, occupational, or otherwise specialised. Topics such as the following may be treated from the perspective of English for specific purposes: second language acquisition in specialised contexts, needs assessment, curriculum development and evaluation, materials preparation, discourse analysis, descriptions of specialised varieties of English, teaching and testing techniques, the effectiveness of various approaches to language learning and language teaching, and the training or retraining of teachers for the teaching of ESP. In addition, the journal welcomes articles and discussions that identify aspects of ESP needing development, areas into which the practice of ESP may be expanded, possible means of cooperation between ESP programs and learners' professional or vocational interests, and implications that findings from related disciplines can have for the profession of ESP. The journal also carries reviews of scholarly books on topics of interest to the profession.[15]

Although discourse analysis and descriptions of specialised varieties of English are mentioned, they seem to be outnumbered by pedagogical preoccupations and it is thus not clear what exactly they refer to.

More generally speaking, if and when specialised content is mentioned in the area of ESP research, it is only in the rarer cases when student or learner audiences are more homogeneous; besides, it is considered as a marginal aspect, for subject expertise is explicitly deemed the realm of professionals or the students themselves who are said to know more about the specialised domain they have chosen to study than the language teacher does. This remark should not be taken to mean that, by contrast, researchers in SVE can ever compete with field specialists; still, they may have become more knowledgeable about one specialised field through the type of research they do, as the major differences between ESP and SVE that are underlined in the next section will show.

2.2.2. The specificity of SVE research

Unlike ESP research, SVE research is not primarily focused on teaching and meeting learners' needs, and can even be conducted without teaching in mind. A major difference is also that ESP practitioners

15 <http://www.elsevier.com/journals/english-for-specific-purposes/0889-4906/guide-for-authors>

seem to take only the synchronic axis into consideration, while SVE researchers are also increasingly interested in the insights afforded by a diachronic approach. As language specialists, researchers in SVE naturally rely on language as a gateway to a specific domain, but language as such is not the sole object of research: beyond language, researchers investigate the domain's origins, history, culture, features, heroes and principal players, as well as their particular discursive habits. Not being restricted to just linguistic investigation, research conducted in SVE along the lines just mentioned enables researchers to become more knowledgeable about the field under investigation.

Incidentally, if the SVE they are investigating corresponds to the disciplinary field of the students in their EFL classes, researchers will be able to draw their attention to specific root metaphors or to the origin of some terms and the historical context that generated them, which might prove helpful: when provided with such information, students are more likely to retain sets of terms and to approach the language used in their field in a more logical and enriching way. Furthermore, it broadens their own views on their chosen field of study and provides them with a cultural background they are often lacking, unfortunately. Still, SVE research is not primarily concerned with teaching. For SVE researchers, language is the path to and vehicle for specialised knowledge but not only: it also reflects and translates ways of thinking, acting and being. As language and culture are closely linked, the point is to use language as a starting point in order to gain insight into the organisation of specialised communities, into their conventions and habits and into the way language is used as discourse in a given specialised domain and context.

The language and communities that can be analysed and studied may belong to a number of specialist or professional spheres which correspond to academic disciplines, such as law, economics, medicine or physics but not exclusively so. Other professional communities have their own culture and language, as is the case for craftsmen, for example, or mountain guides. For some activities to survive, it is essential that the field specialists be able to transmit their culture and language to the next generation and the SVE researcher can help record such heritage. Alongside more obvious categories of SVE, a third one might also draw our attention, as Sager *et al* point out (1980: 3):

Special languages, or more precisely special subject languages, are usually thought of as the means of expression of highly qualified subject specialists, like engineers, physicians, lawyers, etc. and are often derogatively referred to as 'jargon'. The fact that humbler occupations like nursing, book-keeping and cooking and even hobbies also involve special areas of human interest and therefore also require and indeed have their own special languages is much less often acknowledged.

'Humbler occupations or activities' that have their own conventions, terminology, culture and history – such as cricket in England – certainly deserve the SVE researchers' attention, for they are testimony to a way of life, and are closely connected with either a country, a people, a community or a *savoir-faire.*

It was therefore important to coin a new phrase and think of its abbreviated form to refer to this type of research. Before adopting SVE in this book, a number of options were considered and explored such as STE (Special Topic English), ESC (English in Specialised Contexts) or Domain-Specific English (DSE). However, SVE (Specialised Varieties of English) seemed to be more appropriate to describe an approach that can be applied to a wider range of situations, referring to either academic settings or specific professional – or other – communities with traditions and a rich background. STE risked being interpreted too narrowly while ESC was somewhat vague about the type of contexts concerned. As for DSE, it seemed to suggest that domains were clearly defined and distinct, which does not seem to be the case, as evidenced by overlapping or trans-disciplinary domains. And so, for want of a better term, SVE was preferred.

2.2.3. SVE researchers' different approaches

By now the reader will have understood that SVE research can be said to be at the crossroads of terminology, linguistics, discourse and genre analyses, history and cultural studies. As Russell ([1992] 1994: 4) insists, "the discursive practice of each field is [...] embedded in the texture of its disciplinary activity" – and, one might add, its professional or occupational activity – so that, while research in SVE starts with a focus on the type of English used in specialised contexts, it can soon branch out into other areas, depending on the researcher's purpose and background. A "theory of doors", to echo Cabré's suggestion for terminology, could be relevant to illustrate the idea that a specialised field can be analysed from different, complementary angles. The following suggestions are just meant to give an idea of a number of focuses adopted by various researchers in SVE.

It seems natural for a trained linguist to start with what is logically considered to be the core element of any specialised field, i.e. terms, and to broaden her scope to include and observe the typical associations of terms and other words that form specialised clusters or chunks, which means dealing with phraseology. Terms or phrasemes are a first step towards researching into SVE and, in this respect, corpus linguistics and the sophisticated software that is now available are reliable aids to help researchers retrieve useful data. However, as Hoffmann[16] (1979: 14) highlighted when examining the elements of a methodology of LSP analysis, "the isolation of words results in an obvious neglect of syntactic and textlinguistic features that cannot be missed in a complex analysis of LSP". Of particular interest are the special use of syntax in a given field or sub-field and the divergences from common use in general language. Semantics should not be neglected either. To Hoffman, who insisted on a broader approach to LSP than that which is often adopted by some LSP practitioners, "LSP analysis [should] reveal the interrelation(s) between reality, thinking and language in specialised fields of human activity". Of course, the English used in specialised domains remains English all the same; still, it may be worth highlighting the linguistic and stylistic features of this or that field. Hoffmann's tentative definition of LSP reads as follows (1979: 16): "By LSP we understand a complete set of linguistic phenomena occurring within a definite sphere of communication and limited by specific subjects, intentions, and conditions". In order to identify these linguistic phenomena, and the specific intentions and

16 Although Hoffmann dealt with LSP and not SVE, his position is much different from that of the ESP researchers quoted in the previous sub-section (1.2.2); the former were student- and teaching-oriented, while his position is much closer to mine in LVE. For this reason, he is quoted here to support my views.

conditions that are at play and to become familiar with a definite sphere of communication, it is therefore essential to go beyond isolated terms and consider broader contexts.

Going one step further, some researchers focus on how a specialised variety of English is actually used in specific domains, illustrating Saussure's distinction between *langue* and *parole.* Such concerns have translated into analysis of different types of register, discourse and genres that may help to better understand a given community's preferred forms of expression. From a diachronic perspective, it is possible to observe how genres have evolved, through the circumstances that have led to this. But the synchronic axis should not be disregarded: providing an accurate map of the different types of discourse encountered in one domain at a given period of time would undoubtedly be useful, though it may prove a challenging task if onc considers that some domains include both disciplinary and professional sub-fields. In fact, two main categories of researchers can be identified in SVE: those researchers who spend years investigating the same domain from different angles, be it the law, medicine or economics, and those who focus on particular aspects of discourse across domains, as is the case with Swales (1990, 2004) who dealt with the research article and its different moves, or scholars who studied hedging in specific genres or across genres and disciplines.

Beyond the linguistic or discursive features, SVE researchers are also interested in analysing and understanding cultural aspects. As Hofstede (1991: 7) insisted, culture is a multi-layered concept and it can be approached from different angles. Hofstede identifies four levels – symbols, heroes, rituals, and values – that can be seen "as the skins of an onion". On the outer layer are *Symbols*, i.e. pictures, gestures, objects or dress that are meaningful only to those who share the culture. Words and jargon belong to this layer. The next layer includes *Heroes* who are considered as models for behaviour. They may be living or dead, real or imaginary. The third layer consists of *Rituals*, such as ceremonies or conventions that represent collective activities. Though they are not indispensable to achieving a community's goals, they are regarded as essential. The three outer layers, through which values can be expressed, can be subsumed under the term *Practices.* At the core of the onion lie *Values* that form the most hidden part of culture. Outsiders can only infer them from the way people act and the choices they make in various situations. Obviously, Hofstede's "onion" needs adapting to learn more about a specific professional community, a branch of industry or a type of activity in an English-speaking setting. In the field of economics and management, for example, heroes may well be prominent figures in economics, or charismatic managers; rituals may be understood as a company's Annual General Meeting, a Semiannual Report on Monetary Policy by the Chairman of the Federal Reserve or a plenary lecture by a leading economist. For us, linguists, it is interesting to note that Hofstede's notion of *Practice* that cuts through the three layers around the core values shares the same root as the word 'Pragmatics' in late Latin (Pragmaticus) and in Greek (πραγματικός / pragmatikós). As Tatsuki (2001: 3) points out, in both Latin and Greek,

> [the terms mean] "practical" and are used to describe customs, conventions, norms or traditions of behavior. In linguistics, pragmatics-as-use looks at ways people use language (and other signs, rituals or symbols) to accomplish communication goals. In addition, pragmatics-as-effects includes research into the effects on listeners as well as the effects on those who learn and use a particular language and the cultural views embedded in it. Researchers into pragmatics begin by making observations of language in use and then look for patterns, rituals and connections that lead to understanding of the values that underlie them. The basic unit of analysis is usually an utterance or speech act. So pragmatists start with what can be directly observed and try to build up their understanding of how patterns in these observations offer insight into the underlying values. So to summarize, culture is learned human behavior specific to a group in which values are shared and expressed through various practices. These practices depend very heavily (although not exclusively) on language.

Capitalising on their training as linguists, a number of researchers in SVE have therefore chosen to analyse symbols, heroes and rituals in order to further investigate specialised communities with a view to understanding their core values. Analysing cultural aspects in SVE often means working with the specialised milieu, meeting its representatives, conducting interviews and surveys, and adopting methods used in anthropology and sociology. Research along those lines has already been conducted in such fields as the US Army (Trouillon

2003; Saber 2006), Wall Street (Van der Yeught 2009a), the system of higher education in Britain (Detourbe 2011), or communities such as engineers (Laffont 2006) or American mountain guides (Wozniak 2011). Ongoing research in the sciences and more precisely in the field of nanotechnologies (Fries 2011), in the American journalistic milieu and its discourse (Peynaud 2011) and in the corporate culture and discourse of industries involved in biotechnologies and oil (Domenec 2011) highlights the growing interest of researchers for SVE.

From the confrontation of these different approaches, a number of questions have arisen as to how to define a specialised community, specialised discourse, and how to identify an SVE. Each of these points deserves some attention.

2.2.4. Specialised communities and specialised discourse

When discussing specialised communities and specialised discourse, one cannot avoid thinking about the notion of "discourse community", a term that was coined in 1982 by the sociolinguist Nystrand. It was later defined by Swales (1990: 24-27) when working on academic writing styles. According to him, a discourse community:

1) has a broadly agreed set of common public goals;
2) has mechanisms of intercommunication among its members;
3) uses its participatory mechanisms primarily to provide information and feedback;
4) utilises and hence possesses one or more genres in the communicative furtherance of its aims;
5) in addition to owning genres, has acquired some specific lexis;
6) has a threshold level of members with a suitable degree of relevant content and discoursal expertise.

Porter (1992: 106) also insisted on the existence of "a textual system with stated and unstated conventions, a vital history, mechanisms for wielding power, institutional hierarchies, vested interests, and so on". Whatever the definition, it is important to realise that, unlike the members of a speech community who have inherited their language by birth (Australian English, Glaswegian or Geordie English), the members of a discourse community can only join a discourse community through training, once they have become familiar with its standards, expectations and interpretive conventions.

In 1998, Swales reconsidered his initial description of a discourse community based on written communication and introduced the term 'place discourse communities' which referred to communities united by both written and spoken communication. However, Borg (2003) questions the accuracy of Swales' shared goal criterion to define a discourse community and mentions another term used by Wenger (1998: 78): 'community of practice', more precisely associated with such notions as 'mutual engagement' and 'joint enterprise'.

Researchers in SVE will probably feel more comfortable with Gotti's approach (2003: 24): to him, the term 'specialised community' should be taken in a broad sense to encompass "the academic, the professional, the technical and the occupational areas of knowledge and practice". He defines 'specialised discourse' as "reflect[ing] more clearly the specialist use of language in contexts which are typical of a specialised community". Clearly, he considers that "for specialised discourse to develop", three factors are necessary, namely "the type of user, the domain of use, as well as the special application of language in that setting". It is therefore essential to keep in mind the need for shared norms. Different levels of specialisation must of course be taken into consideration, since "the mere presence of a specialist is not sufficient to ensure specialised use of a language, and this in turn is not limited to peer-communication alone" (Gotti 2003: 25). Specialists may indeed address other specialists, which is the typical example of expert communication. They may also address non-specialists to explain specialised notions, as do authors of textbooks, for example. This type of communication can be considered as semi-specialised. Specialists can also address a lay audience, using common language to introduce specialised concepts, relying on their audience's experience of everyday life to make up for their lack of specialised knowledge. The latter form of communication is typical of the popularisation of science or technology. Obviously, this type of discourse cannot be considered as specialised.

Still, a few more questions require closer examination, especially when one seeks to define an SVE. For example, is the presence of terms – or a given number of terms – a necessary condition for discourse to be deemed specialised? Are there any established criteria that can help us determine whether a specific area can really be said to be specialised? Since 'otherwise specialised' areas have been mentioned, apart from disciplinary or professional fields, how can we be sure that they deserve to be considered as such and worthy of our attention? Is it possible to consider an SVE without looking for its birth certificate in the form of a glossary or some written document that proves that, at some point, the need was felt to bridge the gap between a specialist community's terminology and the layperson's familiar idioms, thereby acknowledging the specialised status (Van der Yeught 2009b: 58)? Much research has been done so far in many disciplinary or professional areas, but it seems that it is necessary to use the researchers' findings in order to build a theory of SVE. Such work on the specialised status of SVE is in progress and will obviously require more time before it is stabilised.

Petit (2011) suggests a broader view of a specialised community as being any group defined by a specific activity whose end and conventions as well as the particular competences it requires from its members make it possible to identify its place and role in society. Its specific structure and organisation should also make it possible to differentiate it from other communities. In order to illustrate his definition, Petit quotes the example of clearly identifiable domains and their specialists – medicine and doctors, history and historians, journalism and journalists – and insists that if one is to describe such domains, one must take into account their complex organisation, their rules, the way their specialists are trained, the brochures, journals and magazines they publish, etc. A major point is that it is only because a domain has been established and identified as a specialised domain that the discourse it produces can be said to be specialised; it derives its specialised character from the fact that it stems from a specialised field and not the other way around.

For the purpose of this book, the specialised domain that has been chosen, economics, is clearly identifiable as such: the point is not to provide a thorough description of the many sub-domains which make it up, nor of all those who have played or still play a role in the economic sphere. It would probably take an encyclopedia to do so. As mentioned in the introduction, the aim is to offer an approach that will show how terms, beyond their primary function, can help researchers become more familiar with a disciplinary field, its traditions, history and worldview. Of course, this approach can be applied to other domains and other languages than English.

3. From 'social philosophy' to 'economics': the specificity of economics

Every science begins as philosophy
and ends as art.

Will Durant
The Story of Philosophy (1926)

To know the history of science is to
recognize the mortality of any
claim to universal truth.

Evelyn Fox Keller
Reflections on Gender and Science (1995)

Traditionally, terminology is an obvious vantage point from which to consider a new area of knowledge: terms provide information on the conceptual structure of the field through their position in networks and relations with other terms belonging to the same sub-field. However, the title of this chapter has been chosen to highlight a different way of approaching terms, as witnesses to the way the field evolved over time and an expression of the influences that came to be exerted upon it.

The information provided in this chapter was gathered thanks to the questions raised by all the economic terms that appeared to be anomalies, i.e. in contradiction with the traditional view of terms according to the GTT as described in the first section of Chapter 2 but in accordance with the notions of interdisciplinary knowledge and diachronic approach advocated by socioterminologists and sociocognitive terminologists. The choice of offering such general information on the origins and evolution of the domain to start with was made deliberately: the reader, who may not be well-versed in economic matters, will be able to refer back to this chapter when reading the following ones. The point is to make it easier for anyone to understand why neonyms from various periods of time are so helpful in terms of the insights they offer (Chapter 4), where theory-constitutive metaphors stem from and why they are so meaningful (Chapter 5), or why, due to the specificity of economics, economic concepts and terms cannot always be set in stone. The need for terms to match the discursive features of economics, as analysed in Chapter 6, will also be easier to apprehend, as will the interface terms resulting from the increasing interconnections between economics and other disciplines described in Chapter 7.

This chapter first offers a brief overview of the evolution of economics, from its Greek origins as *SOCIAL PHILOSOPHY* through *POLITICAL PHILOSOPHY*, *MORAL PHILOSOPHY* and *POLITICAL ECONOMY* to *ECONOMICS* as we know it today, if only to underline that historical contextualisation cannot be dispensed with if one is to understand the theoretical underpinnings. The simplified summary that is offered here shows how ideas that emerged at any point in the past were a product of a wide range of factors: social interests, dominant views on some notions, generally accepted criteria for science, prevailing scientific concepts, technical possibilities available at a given time, not to mention individual personalities.

Economists' concerns with scientificity are then discussed in order to explain some of their choices and the impact those choices had on the discipline's concepts and terms. Alongside the physics envy, biological analogies are reviewed before going on to identify the specificity of economics and the way this influences discourse; this is discussed at greater length in Chapter 5.

3.1. From philosophy to economics

Even before the economy was considered as a specific domain and economics was born as a discipline, many thinkers reflected on and felt concerned about economic issues. For these reasons, it is essential to look closely at the various terms used over time for referring to such issues, as represented in the timeline below (Fig.1), if only to realise how much information can be collected from this perspective:

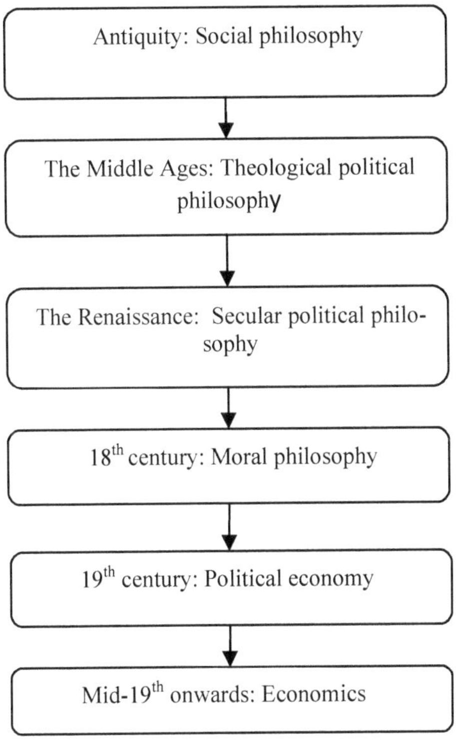

Fig.1. Terms denoting preoccupations with economic matters over time.

3.1.1. *From* SOCIAL PHILOSOPHY *to* THEOLOGICAL POLITICAL PHILOSOPHY

Economic considerations first originated as SOCIAL PHILOSOPHY. The Greek roots for 'economy' are *oikos* (οἶκος) and *nomos* (νόμος). The former refers to the house, household or estate and the latter to law, rule or code. What we now call ECONOMICS was then considered the art of establishing rules for the house or, in other words, of managing the household, which, according to Xenophon[17], one of Socrates' students, was women's responsibility. The meaning and scope of economics then evolved, in Plato's *Republic*, to become the fairest possible management of goods and people in the ideal city. With Aristotle, a distinction was made between economics and chrematistics, or the art of getting richer through the accumulation of wealth for wealth's sake. Chrematistics was of course condemned for its dehumanising aspect, while exchanging goods and services was valued for strengthening social links. Preoccupations with economic matters thus date back to ancient times, but they were then part of a much broader framework of philosophical reflection.

Medieval economic thought was mainly concerned with ethical questions pertaining to wealth and property, money, commerce, the just price and usury. Typically, the economy was seen as part of a larger social body, and thinkers were influenced by the theory of "Humours" which dominated medical thinking at the time. The body was said to contain four kinds of Humour – blood, black bile, yellow bile, and phlegm – which, for an individual to remain healthy, were to be maintained in a state of balance. Borrowing from the medical beliefs of the time, Oresme (1956: 43-44) suggested applying the theory of Humours to government and the distribution of riches:

> The state or kingdom, then, is like a human body and so Aristotle will have it in Book V of the Politics. As, therefore, the body is disordered when the Humours flow too freely into one member of it, so that that member is often thus inflamed and overgrown while the others are withered and shrunken and the body's due proportions are destroyed and its life shortened; so also is a commonwealth or kingdom when riches are unduly attracted by one part of it. For a commonwealth or kingdom whose princes, as compared with their subjects, increase beyond measure in wealth, power, and position, is as it were a monster, like a man whose head is so large and heavy that the rest of his body is too weak to support it. And just as such a man has no pleasure in life and cannot live long, neither can a kingdom survive whose prince draws to himself riches in excess".

This approach seems to have inspired various theorists who endeavoured to balance private rights and the common good. The extraordi-

17 In Oeconomicus.

nary expansion of trade and markets prompted monetisation of the economy from 1100 onwards and theorists were eager to defend the integrity of coinage. Usury, often associated with commerce, triggered anti-usury measures that were especially intensified in the later Middle-Ages. Scholars like Thomas Aquinas, for example, were mainly concerned with how to guarantee the just price, which meant ensuring normal market conditions. For businesses, selling goods at a just price became a moral obligation. It is to be noted that medieval economic thought was the preserve of academe, which was wholly scholastic, i.e. Christian, and so it was considered as *THEOLOGICAL POLITICAL PHILOSOPHY*.

3.1.2. From THEOLOGICAL to SECULAR POLITICAL PHILOSOPHY

During the Renaissance, *SECULAR POLITICAL PHILOSOPHY* began to emerge. After feudalism in the Middle-Ages, economic thought evolved toward mercantilism which became the dominant economic theory of the late Renaissance, based on the idea that people were motivated by self-interest. This translated into strict protectionist measures meant to promote national interest: the goal was to maximise exports and minimise imports from other nations by means of taxes, regulations or price controls.

In reaction to mercantilism, the Physiocrats advocated *laissez faire:* they felt that letting individuals do as they please would naturally result in economic growth. They also considered that a nation's wealth lay in the size of its net product rather than in its gold and silver stocks. For them, the source of wealth was to be found in agriculture. It is to be noted that the Physiocrats were certainly influenced by advances that were being made in natural science and anatomy at that time, i.e. the end of the seventeenth and the beginning of the eighteenth century. For example, their notion of a circular flow of income through the economy owes much to the discovery of blood circulation through the human body. It was presented by François Quesnay (1694-1774) in his *Tableau économique* (1759). Quesnay, who incidentally trained as a doctor, insisted that agricultural surpluses, by flowing from sector to sector through the economy in the form of rent, wages and purchases, were the real stimulating forces of the economy. According to the Physiocrats, once these income flows had achieved a state of "balance", the economy would enjoy a "natural state" and would reproduce itself again and again.

3.1.3. From SECULAR POLITICAL PHILOSOPHY through MORAL PHILOSOPHY to POLITICAL ECONOMY

It was only in the eighteenth century that economic thinking started becoming autonomous. Adam Smith is generally credited with laying the foundations of POLITICAL ECONOMY with his seminal book *An Inquiry into the Nature and Causes of the Wealth of Nations* published in 1776, which analyses wealth, growth and the allocation of riches within a nation. Though he is often referred to as the father of modern economics, Adam Smith was not an economist in the modern sense of the term. His training as a philosopher cannot be ignored. In the eighteenth century, economics was one of the branches of MORAL PHILOSOPHY which dealt with social sciences, as opposed to 'natural philosophy' – the realm of 'physical' sciences. But on the eve of the industrial revolution, which was to introduce major changes in the economy in terms of technological progress and global exploration, POLITICAL ECONOMY emerged and Smith's writings were most influential. After Smith, classical economists such as Thomas Malthus, David Ricardo and John Start Mill were interested in how national riches were produced and distributed in society and how population or international trade affected national output.

3.1.4. The emergence of an economic science: ECONOMICS

The nineteenth century was marked by the recognition as an academic discipline of what was then still known as POLITICAL ECONOMY. In December 1825, Oxford University founded a chair of political economy which was first held by Nassau William Senior (1790-1865) for five years. From the start, teaching was conceived along two main lines: on the one hand, a theoretical course inspired by exact sciences that served as a basis for reasoning, and on the other hand, a more applied branch, as it were, meant to provide recommendations for political economy after taking the historical context into account.

The term *POLITICAL ECONOMY* was defined by Senior ([1850] 1854) as "the Science which treats of the Nature, the Production, and the Distribution of Wealth". However, he noted that the term had been given various meanings depending on the authors who used it:

> Our readers must be aware that that term has often been used in a much wider sense. The earlier writers who assumed the name of Political Economists avowedly treated not of Wealth but of Government. [...] The modern continental writers have in general entered into an equally extensive inquiry. [...] The modern writers of the English school have in general professed to limit their attention to the theory of Wealth; but some of the most eminent among them, after having expressed their intention to confine themselves within what appears to us to be their proper province, have invaded that of the general legislator or the statesman (Introduction §1.1: Definition of the science).

The different meanings reviewed by Senior are summed up in Table 2 below.

AUTHOR	DEFINITION OF POLITICAL ECONOMY	*REFERENCES*
Pierre-Paul Le Mercier de la Riviere (Government)	[Political economy means to propose an organisation] "which shall necessarily produce all the happiness that can be enjoyed on earth."	*The Natural and Essential Organisation of Society (Discours Préliminaire,* vi.)
James Steuart (Government)	"The principal object of the Science is to secure a certain fund of subsistence for all the inhabitants, to obviate every circumstance which may render it precarious, and to provide everything necessary for supplying the wants of the society."	*An Inquiry into the Principles of Political Economy.*Vol. I. p. 2.
Heinrich von Storch (Government)	"Political Economy is the Science of the natural laws which determine the prosperity of nations, that is to say, their wealth and their civilisation."	*Cours d'économie politique, ou exposition des principes qui déterminent la prospérité des nations.* Vol. I. p. 21.

Jean-Charles Léonard Simonde de Sismondi (Government)	"The physical welfare of man, so far as it can be the work of government, [can be considered] as the object of Political Economy."	*Nouveaux Principes d'Economie Politique,* Bk. 1. ch. 2
Jean-Baptiste Say (Government)	"Political Economy is the economy of society; a Science combining the results of our observations on the nature and functions of the different parts of the social body."	*Cours Complet,* Vol. I. pp. 1, 2.
John Ramsey M'Culloch, (Wealth) (Law and government)	"The Science of the laws which regulate the production, accumulation, distribution, and consumption of those articles or products that are necessarily useful or agreeable to man, and possess exchangeable value." "Its object is to point out the means by which the industry of man may be rendered most productive of wealth, to ascertain the circumstances most favourable to its accumulation, the proportions in which it is divided, and the mode in which it may be most advantageously consumed."	*Principles,* p. 1. *Principles*, p. 8.

Table 2. Definitions of political economy

Senior's definition announced the shift from POLITICAL ECONOMY as interested in government and law to a science interested in the production and distribution of wealth. A century after Adam Smith's description of political economy as a tool for improving the well-being of mankind, the notion of 'well-being' was transformed into that of 'utility'. "The economist need not envelop his own science in the hazes of ethics, psychology and metaphysics", Irving Fisher insisted ([1892] 1965: 23). The shift in ideas, which can be considered as a form of revolution in economics, took place in the 1860s. The Marginalist school (embodied by Léon Walras from France, Carl Menger from Austria and Stanley Jevons from Great Britain) was part of a broader group described by the umbrella term 'Neoclassical economists'.

Other economists were Vilfredo Pareto, known for the theories of general equilibrium and optimality, Alfred Marshall, and Arthur Pigou, as well as Austrian economists Eugen von Böhm-Bawerk and Friedrich von Wieser from the Vienna school.

Characteristically, the term *ECONOMICS*, to be understood as a concise term for 'economic science' became popular thanks to neo-classical economists like Alfred Marshall who was one of the most influential economists of his time. While Jevons' *Theory of Political Economy* (1871) still retains the term *POLITICAL ECONOMY* in its title, some of the works by Léon Walras (*Elements of Pure Economics,* 1874) or Carl Menger (*Principles of Economics,* 1871) clearly adopt the term *ECONOMICS*. The nineteenth century can be considered as a turning point in the methods and in the discipline since it clearly translated a shift to more scientific considerations, with the concept of energy in physics serving as a model for the concept of utility in economics. The phenomenon must be considered against the background of the scientific environment of the nineteenth century and the fact that many of the economists in those days were no longer philosophers but trained engineers. Economics was to be considered as a "calculus of pleasure and pain" (Jevons [1879] 1965: vii), "a mechanics of utility", a "*physique sociale*" (Moore 1914: 85). The shift from the formerly used term *POLITICAL ECONOMY* to *ECONOMICS* also translated the influence of mathematical methods on economics. Neoclassical economics was also later referred to as *ORTHODOX ECONOMICS* and served as a basis for modern *MAINSTREAM ECONOMICS*.

3.2. The quest for scientificity: the physics envy

The turning point described above must be put into its historical context. The economists of the nineteenth century felt that the political economy of Enlightenment writers was unscientific, lacked conceptual precision and that their style was too flowery. The main preoccupation was to have economics recognised as a science, which meant that economists should take their cue from exact sciences. "A hierarchy of sciences was proclaimed, with Newtonian astronomy at its head" (Morrell and Thackray 1981: 267), while Whewell (1833: xiii) even referred to astronomy as "the queen of sciences": quite naturally economists started dreaming of economics as social physics.

3.2.1. *Economics and the hierarchy of sciences*

The problem was that economics as such was not even mentioned in the hierarchy of sciences as revealed by the six sections suggested by the governing committee of the British Association for the Advancement of Science (BAAS) at its 1833 meeting (Henderson 1994: 522). The sections are presented below in their hierarchical order, with subsections indicated in brackets:

1) Mathematics and physio-mathematical sciences (astronomy, mechanics, hydrostatics, hydraulics, light, sound, heat, meteorology, and mechanical arts);
2) Chemistry, electricity, galvanism, magnetism, mineralogy, chemical arts and manufactures;
3) Geology and geography;
4) Natural history (botany and zoology);
5) Anatomy, medicine;
6) Statistics.[18]

The last section was actually founded by economists with a view to making economics more respectable in terms of scientificity and was later renamed "the section of Economic Science and Statistics". Although its creation had been controversial, and although it was often attacked for the unscientific papers that were presented at its meetings, it was maintained within BAAS, but somehow supervised by members of the Statistical Society of London, founded in 1834. In those days, some disagreement was voiced between the proponents of a deductive methodology and those of an inductive one, borrowed from natural

18 The sixth section became known as section F in 1835, when the sections established by the BAAS at its 1833 meeting were replaced with letters.

science, and supported by Whewell. Increasingly, the empirical element in economics seemed to be separated from the method of science (Henderson 1994: 504). As the latter was of course considered to be more important, economists chose to separate theory from its possible applications, which meant treading a somewhat different path than physics, as expressed by Jevons (1879: xvii):

> The present chaotic state of Economics arises from confusing together several branches of knowledge. Subdivision is the remedy. We must distinguish the empirical element from the abstract theory, from the applied theory, and from the more detailed art of finance and administration. Thus will arise various sciences such as commercial statistics, the mathematical theory of economics, systematic and descriptive economics, economic sociology, and fiscal science.

The separation of quantification and mathematical theorising translated into the need for the neoclassical economists to have their own organisation: The Royal Economic Society was founded in 1890, with its own *Economic Journal.* According to Stigler (1964: 40) the *Economic Journal*, the first editor of which was Edgeworth, was considered as the "first fully professional journal" in Britain, overshadowing the *Journal of the Statistical Society* which was considered as merely semi-professional.

3.2.2. Mechanical physics as a model for economics

Vilfredo Pareto's role in the struggle to establish economics as a science is also worth our attention and his case is quite telling: after training as a mechanical engineer and starting a career as a managing director in a business firm, he turned to economics in the early 1890s. He then devoted his time and energy to economics and became a leading researcher in the field of *MATHEMATICAL ECONOMICS*, concentrating his efforts on developing General Equilibrium Theory. Like many of his contemporary colleagues, he strongly believed that rational mechanics ought to serve as a model for shaping economic theory, and he made his beliefs very explicit in volume 2 of his *Cours,* published in French in 1911, through a table reproduced by Donzelli (1997: 3); the sentences in English I have inserted in the table are adapted from Finer's English translation (1966: 106-108):

Mechanical phenomenon / Phénomène mécanique	Social phenomenon / Phénomène social
Un certain nombre de corps matériels étant donnés, on étudie les rapports d'équilibre et de mouvement qu'ils peuvent avoir entre eux, en faisant abstraction des autres propriétés. *On a une étude de 'mécanique'.*	*Une société étant donnée, on étudie les rapports que la production et l'échange de la richesse suscitent entre les hommes, en faisant abstraction des autres circonstances.* *On a ainsi une étude 'd'économie politique'.*
Mechanics: the study of equilibrium and relative movement of a given number of material bodies, excluding other properties.	*Political economy*: the study of production and exchange relationships among a given collection of human beings forming a society, any other properties excluded.
Cette science de la mécanique se divise elle-même entre deux autres. On considère des points matériels et des lignes inextensibles. On a ainsi une science pure : la mécanique rationnelle, qui étudie d'une manière abstraite l'équilibre des forces et le mouvement. La partie la plus facile est la science de l'équilibre. Le principe de d'Alembert, en considérant les forces d'inertie, permet de réduire la dynamique à un problème de statique. *À la mécanique rationnelle fait suite la mécanique appliquée, qui ne considère plus seulement les corps élastiques, les liens extensibles, les frottements, etc. [...]*	*Cette science de l'économie politique se divise elle-même entre deux autres. On considère l'homo oeconomicus, n'agissant qu'en vertu des forces économiques. On a ainsi l'économie politique pure, qui étudie, d'une manière abstraite, les manifestations de l'ophélimité. La seule partie que nous commençons à bien connaître est la partie qui traite de l'équilibre. Nous avons pour les systèmes économiques un principe semblable à celui de d'Alembert (586); mais nos connaissances sur ce sujet sont encore des plus imparfaites. La théorie des crises économiques fournit pourtant un exemple d'étude de dynamique économique.* *À l'économie politique pure fait suite l'économie politique appliquée, qui se rapproche un peu plus de la réalité, en considérant l'homo oeconomicus, mais d'autres êtres se rapprochant plus de l'homme réel. [...]*

Mechanics can be further divided into two sub-domains: Pure mechanics: the study of a postulated set of material points and lines; an abstract study of the equilibrium of forces and of motion. The easiest part is the scienicence of equilibrium. Employing d'Alembert's principle and considering the forces of inertia, it is possible to consider dynamics as a mere problem of statics. Applied mechanics no longer considers such phenomena as elastic bodies, friction and the like.	Political Economy can be further divided into two sub-domains: Pure political economy: the study of Economic Man, an abstract study of economic phenomena arising under a maximization-of-utility principle (ophelimity). The only part we are starting tobe comfortable with is that which deals with equilibrium. A similar principle to that of d'Alembert can be used for studying economic systems, but knowledge of the field is far from perfect. Yet the helory of economic crises provides an example of how to study dynamic economics Applied political economy more closely approximates real human beings.

Table 3. Pareto's table: mechanics and political economy

Quite tellingly, a few years later, Irving Fisher drew up a concordance table of the principles and concepts of rational mechanics and economics in his 1926 doctoral dissertation. The resulting pairs, reproduced in Mirowski (1989: 224) are shown in Table 4:

Mechanics	*Economics*
A particle	An individual
Space	Commodity
Force	Marginal utility or disutility
Work	Disutility
Energy	Utility
Work or energy = force *x* space	Utility = marginal utility *x* commodity
Force is a vector.	Marginal utility is a vector.
Forces are added by vector addition.	Marginal utilities are added by vector addition.
Work and energy are scalars.	Disutility and utility are scalars.
The total energy may be defined as the integral with respect to impelling forces.	The total utility enjoyed by the individual is the like integral with respect to marginal utilities.
Equilibrium will be where net energy (energy minus work) is maximum; or equilibrium will be where impelling and resisting forces along each axis will	Equilibrium will be where gain (utility minus disutility) is maximum; or equilibrium will be where marginal utility and marginal disutility along each axis

be equal.	will be equal.
If total energy is subtracted from total work instead of vice versa the difference is "potential" and is a minimum.	If total utility is subtracted from total disutility instead of vice versa the difference may be called "loss" and is a minimum.

Table 4. Fisher's concordances (1926: 86-86)

3.2.3. The emergence of ECONOMETRICS

Another important contribution was that of Ragnar Frisch (1895-1973), another representative of a generation of economists who wanted to reform economics and turn it into a science modelled on physics, i.e. an experimental science. His 1926 article "On a Problem in Pure Economics" opens with a definition of *ECONOMETRICS* as a new branch of economics:

> Intermediate between mathematics, statistics, and economics, we find a new discipline which, for lack of a better name, may be called *econometrics*. Econometrics has as its aim to subject abstract laws of theoretical political economy or 'pure' economics to experimental and numerical verification, and thus to turn pure economics, as far as possible, into a science in the strict sense of the word. (p. 386)

A few years later, on 29th December 1930, during the annual joint meeting of the American Economic Association and the American Statistical Association in Cleveland, Ohio, the *Econometric Society* was founded. Its first president was Irving Fisher. The first paragraph of its constitution, which states its object, clearly echoes Ragnar Frisch's earlier definition of *ECONOMETRICS*:

> [to] promote studies that aim at a unification of the theoretical-quantitative and the empirical-quantitative approach to economic problems and that are penetrated by constructive and rigorous thinking similar to that which has come to dominate in the natural sciences. Any activity which promises ultimately to further such unification of theoretical and factual studies in economics shall be within the sphere of interest of the Society.

The Society created its own journal, *Econometrica*, whose first editor was Ragnar Frisch from 1933 to 1954.

3.2.4. Keynes and after

The first quarter of the twentieth century was marked by the 1929 Wall Street Crash that put an end to the roaring twenties. The ensuing Great Depression brought about sharp rises in unemployment in the United States, the ripple effect of which was felt across the world. Under such circumstances, economic theory could certainly not be cut off from *APPLIED ECONOMICS*. Although orthodox economists advocated spending cuts until business confidence and the long run market equilibrium were restored, Keynes believed that the extraordinary conditions called for public sector action and advocated both monetary management and an active fiscal policy. After WW2, Keynes's economic theory was combined with statistical methods and mathematical representations and the resulting theory, developed by John Hicks (1937), was known as *THE NEOCLASSICAL SYNTHESIS*, a term coined by mathematical economist Paul Samuelson. The synthesis was "largely Keynesian" (Clark 1998) as regards *MACROECONOMICS* and neoclassical as regards *MICROECONOMICS*.

Samuelson's influential textbook, which was adopted on many US and foreign campuses, has helped to provide generations of students with an introduction to economics where economic theory is presented as a unified whole, in spite of the many divergent strands that have marked the evolution of economic thought. If the latest edition of the textbook mentions new trends in modern economics, such as *ENVIRONMENTAL* or *BEHAVIOURAL ECONOMICS*, the body of knowledge that is presented is still representative of mainstream economics, with general equilibrium theory at its core. Human beings are still seen as rational, informed individuals whose behaviour can be modelled by mathematical formulae and translated into graphs, and the image that is conveyed of economics is that of a mathematical science.

3.3. An alternative to mechanical physics: biological analogies

Alongside mechanical physics that seems to have inspired many economists with the general equilibrium theory since the nineteenth century, it must be noted that biological analogies have greatly influenced economic thinking too; in fact, such analogies date back to ancient times, and were also used in the Middle-Ages, as pointed out in section 3.1.1. They abound in the literature from Adam Smith to the present time, so that one could argue that economics has continuously hesitated between Newton and Darwin.

3.3.1. A long, winding itinerary through time

In fact, "biological and economic reasoning have been closely intertwined since the Scottish Enlightenment" (Schabas 1994: 322). Strikingly, shortly after Linnaeus had entitled a Latin tract *Œconomy of Nature* (1751), Adam Smith mentioned the "œconomy of nature" in *The Theory of Moral Sentiments* (1759). It is also often said that Darwin was strongly influenced by Thomas Malthus's work on population and by the writings of Adam Smith. Another case in point is Quesnay who, as mentioned in section 3.1, was inspired by Harvey's discovery of the circulation of blood, hence the analogy with the circular flow of income in his *Tableau économique*. Alborn (1994: 179) points out that the circulatory image was also used by Adam Smith ([1776] 1979: 675). Disapproving of the mercantilists' colonial policies, Alborn adds, Adam Smith

> compared the protected eighteenth-century trade route between England and the United States to a 'great blood vessel, which has been artificially swelled beyond its natural dimensions, and through which an unnatural proportion of the industry and commerce of the country has been forced to circulate'.

Implied in this analogy is "an alternative model of the economy as a healthy body with blood flowing freely and equally through all its veins" (Alborn 1994: 179). Christensen (1994: 249) reminds us that "physiology provided an obvious set of analogies. Nature, like the economy, was produced by the self-activity of living organisms". Let it be clear that he meant physiology as a science here.

The division-of-labour concept as presented by Adam Smith through the description of the pin factory naturally calls to mind the division of labour in nature and conjures up images of an ant colony or a beehive:

> One man draws out the wire, another straights it, a third cuts it, a fourth points it, a fifth grinds it at the top for receiving the head; to make the head requires two or three distinct operations; to put it on, is a particular business, to whiten the pins is another; it is even a trade by itself to put them in the paper; and the important business of making a pin is, in this manner, divided into about eighteen distinct operations, which, in some manufactories, are all performed by distinct hands [...]. (Adam Smith 1776; Book 1 Chapter 1)

Though, in this case, it is often said that Smith inspired Darwin and not the reverse, it is obvious that, in the making of economic thought, biological analogies have either inspired or tempted economists. It is particularly true as regards those who later worked on the theory of the firm. The most obvious illustration is the life cycle analogy whereby the creation, growth and disappearance of firms recall the birth, growth and death of organisms. The "survival of the fittest", a phrase coined by Spencer, and not Darwin, was undoubtedly exploited in the field of competition. Another sign of Spencer's influence is to be found in the impact his ideas had on evolutionary economists like Marshall and Veblen, more precisely through the concept of evolution, which he made popular (1852), and the idea of social Darwinism. In his well-known 1898 article "Why is economics not an evolutionary science?" Veblen explicitly criticised Marginalists for taking their inspiration from Newton and advocated opting for a new approach to economics influenced by Darwin.

> The premises and the point of view required for an evolutionary economics have been wanting. [...] Even if it has been possible at any time to turn to the evolutionary line of speculation in economics, the possibility of a departure is not enough to bring it about. [...]

> Under the stress of modern technological exigencies, men's everyday habits of thought are falling into the lines that in the sciences constitute the evolutionary method; and knowledge which proceeds on a higher, more archaic plane is becoming alien and meaningless to them. The social and political sciences must follow the drift, for they are already caught in it.

EVOLUTIONARY ECONOMICS actually offered a new framework for economics, questioning the fundamental theoretical concepts of the neo-classical school revolving around static equilibrium. By suggesting that both society and economics were caught in an evolutionary process, it also countered the view of economics as pure, abstract theory, cut off from history and society.

When considering the link between biology and economics, one name that unfailingly comes to mind is that of Alfred Marshall for his oft-quoted remark that "the Mecca of the economist is economic biology rather than economic dynamics". It is to be found in the Preface to his *Principles of Economics* where he adds, however, that:

> biological conceptions are more complex than those of mechanics; a volume on Foundations must therefore give a relatively large place to mechanical analogies, and frequent use is made of the term equilibrium which suggests something of a static analogy. (1920: 19)

Although Marshall acknowledged that mechanical analogies seemed simpler to use, his analysis of organisation is based on a biological analogy; clearly, such notions as the struggle for existence and the division of labour – or the "subdivision of functions" – are connected in his eyes, as evidenced in the following excerpt:

> Before Adam Smith's book had yet found many readers, biologists were already beginning to make great advances towards understanding the real nature of the differences in organisation which separate the higher from the lower animals; and before two more generations had elapsed, Malthus's historical account of man's struggle for existence started Darwin on that inquiry as to the effects of the struggle for existence in the animal and vegetable world, which issued in his discovery of the selective influence constantly played by it. Since that time biology has more than repaid her debt; and economists have in their turn owed much to the many profound analogies which have been discovered between social and especially industrial organisation on the one side and the physical organisation of the higher animals on the other. In a few

> cases indeed the apparent analogies disappeared on closer inquiry: but many of those which seemed at first sight most fanciful, have gradually been supplemented by others, and have at last established their claim to illustrate a fundamental unity of action between the laws of nature in the physical and in the moral world. This central unity is set forth in the general rule, to which there are not very many exceptions, that the development of the organism, whether social or physical, involves an increasing subdivision of functions between its separate parts on the one hand, and on the other a more intimate connection between them. Each part gets to be less and less self-sufficient, to depend for its well-being more and more on other parts, so that any disorder in any part of a highly-developed organism will affect other parts also. (1920, *Principles of Economics* IV, 8, 1)

However, even though Marshall saw the value of the biological analogy for economics, actually stating that economics "is a branch of biology broadly interpreted", there is a difference between recognition of this potential value and "full incorporation of an evolutionary theory in the sense of specified processes and criteria of selection" (Hodgson 1993: 406). It is important to realise that analogies can only be accepted when the time is ripe for them.

Another example of a biological influence is to be found in Joseph Schumpeter's[19] theory of creative destruction, associated with innovation and entrepreneurship. Schumpeter considered that the static approach chosen by economists aiming at equilibrium was a mistake. For him, economics resulted from a dynamic process of both creation and destruction, whereby obsolete firms were replaced by those whose creators imagined new products that met the consumers' expectations. In such a process, the entrepreneur played a major role.

3.3.2. *Disaffection and renewed interest*

After 1914, however, reluctance to use ideas from biology in the social sciences gained ground, probably under the influence of logical positivism. That some politicians and scientists should base their racist, sexist or imperialistic ideas on arguments borrowed from biology may also have played a role in distancing economic thinkers from

19 Joseph Schumpeter (1883-1950).

biology. It is only in the 1940s that the situation changed, when the "neo-Darwinian synthesis" emerged in biology. Interestingly enough, after WW2, as mentioned at the end of section 3.2, a *NEOCLASSICAL SYNTHESIS* also emerged in economics.

So, in the 1950s, Alchian revived the analogy between biology and economics, drawing parallels between organisms and firms, genes and imitation, mutation and innovation, selection and positive profits. For him, adapting meant optimising. Although his analogy was debated and criticised by Edith Penrose (1952), it did bring the biological alternative back to life in economics. At the same period, Kenneth Boulding (1950) declared that the economy was part of the ecosystem. In addition, a strong impulse also came from neoclassical Chicago economists like Gary Becker (1976). Another Chicago economist, Jack Hirshleifer, highlighted the isomorphism between economics and sociobiology:

> Fundamental concepts like scarcity, competition, equilibrium and specialisation play similar roles in both spheres of inquiry. And terminological pairs such as species/industry, mutation/innovation, mutualism/exchange have strikingly analogous denotations. (1970: 2)

It seems that from the 1980s onwards, the biological analogies have continued to draw the attention of researchers. Nelson and Winter (1982), acknowledging the influence of both Schumpeter and Alchian, underlined parallels between the evolution of firms and biological evolution, even considering routines as replicators (Rosenberg 1994: 404):

> The comparative fitness of genotypes (profitability of routines) determines which genotypes (routines) will tend to become predominant over time. However the fitness (profitability) clearly depends on the characteristics of the environment (market prices) confronting the species (collections of firms with similar routines). The environment (price vector) in turn depends, however, on the genotypes (routines) of all the individual organisms (firms) existing at a time – a dependency discussed in the sub-discipline called ecology (market theory). (Nelson and Winter 1982: 160)

It is to be noted, however, that references to biology on the part of an economist should not be taken to translate adherence to the idea that economics has much to learn from biology. Disagreement with – and skepticism of – biological analogies have often been voiced. Some of the arguments put forward by some critics (Foster 1997; Penrose 1952) concerned self-organisation which they saw as an alternative to such analogies. Hayek insisted that evolution is cultural, not biological. Another argument (Commons 1926) was that natural selection could very well find an alternative in "artificial selection" as regards socio-economics. These objections, however, have been said to stem from a restrictive interpretation of Darwinism. According to Hodgson (2002: 260),

> Darwinism contains a broader and more general set of ideas, whose application is not confined to biology. Darwinism involves a general theory of the evolution of all open, complex systems. Furthermore, Darwinism involves a basic philosophical commitment to detailed, cumulative, causal explanations.

Some economists (Kauffman 1993; Wicken 1987; Weber and Depew 1996) argued that self-organisation was not contradictory with selection. Although many economists did not come to the same conclusions, which gave rise to harsh debate and ended in the emergence of several separate strands, it is important to realise that the biological vein also runs through the body of knowledge that economics was built on.

The more modern approach which borrows from biology, taking into account the advances in the field, considers the economy as an ecosystem, i.e. a system of complex interactions where order emerges naturally rather than being imposed. It has led to the emergence of environmental economics and more heterodox branches that are presented in Chapter 4.

The debates that the physics envy or the biological analogies have triggered naturally raise the question of whether economics is more like physics or more like biology. Actually, economics is neither physics, nor biology and some people have even wondered whether it qualifies as a science or should be viewed as an art or a discipline.

Whatever the answer, its specificity is obvious and should be analysed more closely.

3.4. The specificity of economics

As pointed out in section 3.1., economics started as *SOCIAL PHILOSOPHY*, became *POLITICAL ECONOMY* and finally *ECONOMICS*.

3.4.1. The goal and nature of economics

Before examining its specificity, it will be helpful to compare the various definitions provided by economists themselves for the term ECONOMICS, from Adam Smith to modern times, keeping in mind that:

> The definition of a science must necessarily be progressive and provisional. Any extension of knowledge or alteration in the current opinions respecting the subject-matter may lead to a change more or less extensive in the particulars included in the science. (Mill 1941: 91)

Adam Smith (1723-90) *An Inquiry into the Nature and Causes and of the Wealth of Nations* (1776)	Wealth econom-ics	"Economics is the science of wealth" "The Science relating to the laws of production, distribution and exchange."
Nassau William Senior (1790-1864) *Political Economy* ([1850] 1854)	Wealth econom-ics	"The subject treated by political economics is not happiness, but wealth. (1854, Introduction; §1.3)
John Stuart Mill (1806-1873) *Principles of political economy* ([1848] 1909)	Wealth econom-ics	"Economics investigates the nature of wealth and the laws of production and its distribution including, directly or remotely, the operation of all the causes by which the condition of mankind, or of any society of human beings in respect to this universal object of desire, is made

		prosperous, or the reverse". (1909: 5)
Alfred Marshall (1842-1924) *Principles of Economics* (1890)	Welfare economics	"Economics is the study of mankind in the ordinary business of life; it examines that part of individual and social actions which is closely connected with the attainment and with the use of material requisites of well being". (1920, 8th ed.: 4) <http://www.econlib.org/library/Marshall/marP1.html#Bk.I>, Chapter 1
Arthur Pigou (1877-1959) *The Economics of Welfare* (1952)	Welfare economics	"Economics is the study of economic welfare; being described as that part of welfare that can be brought directly or indirectly into relation with the measuring rod of money". (1952: 11)
Lionel Robbins (1898-1984) *An Essay on the Nature and Significance of Economic Science* (1932)	Economics of Scarcity and Choice	"Economics is the science which studies human behaviour as a relationship between ends and scarce means which have alternative uses". (1935, 2nd ed.: 16)
George Stigler (1911-1991) *The Theory of Price* (1946)	Economics of Scarcity and Choice	"Economics is the study of principles governing the allocation of scarce means among competing ends when the objective of allocation is to maximize the attainment of the ends". (1946: 12)
Kenneth Boulding (1910-1993) "Economics as a moral science" (1969, American Economic Review, Vol. 59, n°1, 1-12)	Economics as a moral science	"Economics specialises in the study of that part of the total social system which is organised through exchange and which deals with exchangeables. This to my mind is a better definition of economics than those which define it as relating to scarcity or allocation, for the allocation of scarce resources is a universal problem which applies to political decisions and political structures through coercion, threat, and even to love and community, just as it does to exchange". (1969: 4)
Paul Samuelson (1915-2009) *Economics* (1976, 2005)	Growth economics	"Economics is the study of how people and society end up choosing, with or without the use of money, to employ scarce productive resources that could have alternative uses, to produce various commodities and distribute them for consumption now or in the future among various

		persons and groups in society". (1976: 3) "Economics is the study of how societies use scarce resources to produce valuable commodities and distribute them among different people". (2005: 4)
James M. Buchanan (1919-) "What Should Economists Do?" (1964, *The Southern Economic Journal*, Vol 30 n°3, 213-222)		"The study of the whole system of exchange relationships". (1964: 220)
Gary Becker (1930-) *Economic Theory* (1971)	Science of scarcity and choice	"The study of the allocation of scarce means to satisfy competing ends". (1971)
David Colander (1947-) *Economics*. 2006		"The study of how human beings coordinate their wants and desires, given the decision-making mechanisms, social customs, and political realities of the society". (2006, 6th ed.: 4)
Gregory Mankiw (1958-) *Principles of Economics* (2001)	Science of scarcity and choice	"The study of how society manages its scarce resources". (2001: 4)

Table 5. Definitions of economics

The common thread in the definitions listed in Table 5 is that economics deals with human wants and their satisfaction. Since wants are unlimited, but resources are limited, the question of choice arises. When resources are scarce, there is a price to pay for enjoying them, so money does play an important role in economics in that standards of living affect people's lives. Since wealth – any economic good that has money value – is meant to ensure human welfare, it is easy to understand that economics is concerned with the relationship between wealth and welfare. While the authors of the definitions in Table 5 do not all view economics from the same angle, they all consider society, which is made up of human beings. Whether to create wealth or to ensure well-being or welfare, it is necessary to make the best use of the scarce resources and to allocate them as efficiently as possible;

since economic agents are not the rational beings they were once thought to be, they are not always predictable. Measuring the outcomes of uncertain choices is thus a major challenge.

3.4.2. Economics as a soft science

Consequently, though conventional economics would like to think of itself as a hard science, "economics cannot be compared with the exact physical sciences for it deals with the ever-changing and subtle forces of human nature" (Marshall [1890] 1920: 5). Unlike physics that has always regarded theory as important and never separated it from experiment, economics does not enable researchers to conduct experiments in laboratories. There lies a fundamental difference between economics and physics. In order to solve this problem, economics has resorted to models, which obviously implies a risk of oversimplification, and thus inaccuracy. In this respect, economics has been said to suffer from methodological "softness". Unlike exact sciences like mathematics where the solution to a complex equation will not give rise to any argument, economics will seldom provide simple answers, hence the frequent disagreement between different schools of thought and the lack of consensus in approaches. Accordingly, economics is often called a "soft science" to indicate that its findings cannot be expressed as laws in the same sense as laws in physics, for they are not proven facts of nature.

As Fetter (1924: 520) insists, in economics, the term "law" itself should be "applied sparingly and used not at all where such terms as principle, hypothesis, doctrine, or theory, may serve to describe the character of generalisation attempted". Interestingly, as evidenced by the entries in *An Eponymous Dictionary of Economics* (2004), economists do not primarily choose the term "law" to refer to their own findings or those of their colleagues. Table 6 shows that "theorem" is the term of choice and that "model" is also preferred to "law", which only ranks third. "Theorem" would tend to confirm the mathematical bend of economists and their efforts to contribute to the recognition of their science as a rigourous one. "Model" underlines economists' need to reproduce reality as best they can to compensate for their inability to conduct real experiments. The choices of "test", "criterion", "condition", and "hypothesis" underline the researchers' cautious approach and their efforts to establish the reliability of their research by setting a frame and limits. The terms "principle", "rule", and "effect" are of course less general than "laws", but, as a group, they represent a greater number of occurrences.

TERMS	EXAMPLES	Number of anthroponyms including the terms listed in the first column
Theorem	Coase theorem, Heckscher-Ohlin theorem, Neyman-Ficher theorem	34
Model	Hicks-Hausen model, Sraffa's model	26
Law	Gresham's law, Say's law	20
Effect	Cantillon effect, Fisher effect, Keynes effect, Pigou effect	16
Test	Lagrange multiplier test	14
Paradox	Lauderdale's paradox, Leontief paradox	12
Principle	LeChatelier principle, Pontryagin's maximum principle	09
Criterion	Koopman's efficiency criterion	09
Index	Laspeyre's index, Suit's index, Theil index	08
Rule	Palmer's rule, Ramsey's inverse elasticity rule	06
Condition	Samuelson condition	06
Hypothesis	Clark-Fisher hypothesis, Friedman hypothesis	05

Table 6. How economists refer to the main findings in their domain (based on the entries in *An Eponymous Dictionary of Economics*)

It is true that economic laws, which are based on hypotheses and assumptions, can just indicate trends, but they cannot be expected to predict the future as accurately as one might wish. They depend on various factors, which is why the phrase "all other things being equal" or the Latin version *ceteris paribus* are so often used. Actually, such well-known economic laws as

> […] Gresham's law, the law of diminishing returns, of price, of supply and demand, of population are hardly more than general descriptive phrases to indicate problems, or at most broad explanations, which cannot be formulated in single propositions. Few of them approximate a precise mathematical form such as do laws of physical science: the laws of gravitation, falling bodies, expansion of gases (Boyle's Law), planetary motions (Kepler's Laws), and many others. (Fetter 1924: 520)

Marshall himself pointed out the imperfection of economic laws, insisting that they

> are to be compared with the laws of tides rather than with the simple and exact law of gravitation. For the actions of men are so various and uncertain, that the best statement of tendencies, which we can make in a science of human conduct, must needs be inexact and faulty (1890: Book 1, chapter 3).

Human beings, who are at the core of economics, cannot be reduced to matter. Thus, the laws of economics can never be as exact and inexorable as physical laws. Like other sciences, economics is interested in establishing cause-effect relationships, but it is by essence a social science.

Being a social science does not prevent it from being a science, however, even though physics seems to be the standard by which "scientificity" is assessed. McCloskey ([1994] 2000: 59) denounces the narrow definition of science which excludes most sciences and the "sneer" which

> attack[s] the appropriation of "science" in social science, judging economics […] as failing to measure up to a formula for Science. Science must enumerate; that excludes political philosophy as true Science. Science must be mathematical: that excludes most anthropology. Science must test hypotheses; that lets out history. Science must experiment: that excludes every social science except parts of psychology and tiny bits of economics, archeology and sociology. Science must be about the physical world: that excludes everything but the modern, English-speaking definition of the word.

Economics is related to many different disciplines including history, psychology, philosophy, sociology, politics, law and ethics. The very fact that early economists called their discipline *POLITICAL ECONOMY* provides ample evidence of the relationships between economics and politics. It stands to reason that a country suffering from political instability, for example, will not attract investors, which will hamper its economic development. Likewise, angry citizens dissatisfied with their living conditions or purchasing power will go on strike and demonstrate; they will cause social unrest, which will in turn weaken government. Historical, political and sociological factors are closely related and bear heavily on economic progress. The legal framework is also important: laws can be either an impediment or a stimulus for economic progress; taxes and employment legislation can make a real difference. Psychology also matters when analysing economic problems and making the right decisions. The law of diminishing marginal utility, for example, is based on psychology: it holds that as more and more of any one commodity is being consumed, its marginal utility declines, i.e. one derives less satisfaction out of consuming it. Self-fulfilling prophecies provide yet another example: the fear of recession might cause people to make choices that will precipitate recession.

Though it is now obvious that economics cannot rival the hard sciences, it aims nevertheless at being considered as the most scientific of the social sciences. Lazear's analysis (2000: 102) offers an explanation for the success of economics as a soft science:

> The power of economics lies in its rigour. Economics is scientific; it follows the scientific method of stating a formal refutable theory, testing the theory, and revising the theory based on evidence. Economics succeeds where other social sciences fail because economists are willing to abstract.

It is thus not surprising that economics should have aroused admiration on the part of other, more recent social sciences which have come to consider it as an example to follow. In the last two decades, there seem to have been growing exchanges between economics and other sciences such as anthropology, neuroscience, psychology and ethics. For example, the behaviour of the human brain has been analysed by borrowing resources from economics in the field of game-theory and decision-making. As for the links between economics and ethics, they can be illustrated by the difference between positive and normative economics. Positive economics is interested in analysing what is, while normative economics is concerned with what ought to be: advocates of the latter approach contend that economics is an ethical science.

The specificity of economics lies in its historical ambivalence: it remains a soft science though it has introduced methods borrowed from hard sciences in order to be taken more seriously. Its categorisation as a soft science is justified by its constant need to deal with uncertainty: history never repeats itself and people are unpredictable. Conditions change, to such a point that they may force theory to evolve, calling into question what used to be considered as widely-acknowledged rules. As concepts evolve, so do terms. New terms are coined to better suit a new, uncertain context. Conceptual structures may be altered by new findings and relationships between terms may therefore evolve. When measures are taken by policy-makers, their implementation takes time and their effects can only be felt months later so that the situation may continue to worsen for a while. Under such circumstances, economists and decision-makers have to handle their discourse very carefully and cannot afford to be too categorical if they want to remain credible. Understandably, discourse in economics, whether that of researchers or that of policy-makers, has to be hedged. Statements need to be softened, standpoints justified, ample evidence must be provided, explanations are expected, the pros and cons must be systematically weighed up. Terms are therefore naturally affected by the constraints of the discipline, as illustrated in the following chapters through the analysis of neonyms, theory-constitutive metaphors and instances of indeterminacy. All these categories of terms reflect the specificity of this soft science and provide precious clues for the researcher of the language and culture of economics.

3.5. Concluding remarks

The goal of this chapter was to provide the reader with background information based on the various terms that have been used in the past to refer to what we now know as economics. It was also an opportunity to show how a diachronic investigation of key terms can help understand the origins and evolution of an area of activity or a discipline. Much of the information was of course derived from analyses conducted over a number of years, always using terms as an entry point into the various sub-fields, as will be made clearer in the following chapters. As already mentioned, for purposes of clarity, each chapter focuses on specific themes dictated by the divergences from the basic principles of terminology discussed in Chapter 2, but many terms would no doubt qualify for an entry in several chapters: a metaphorical term can be both a neonym and an indeterminate or interface term. Hopefully, each chapter will help to piece together the jigsaw of how terms can be approached to investigate a specialised field of knowledge, its discourse and milieu and thus contribute to the bigger picture.

4. Insights from economic neonyms

> The genius of democracies is seen not only in the great number of new words introduced but even more in the new ideas they express.
>
> Alexis de Tocqueville
> *Democracy in America* (1840)

In specialised domains, neonyms are a source of information as to the vitality of the domain, since new concepts, objects or tools need to be assigned names for communication to remain possible. As the pace of technological progress or theoretical findings accelerates, so does the need to coin new terms. Analysing neonyms in the context of the period of time when they first appeared can therefore provide a chronicle of the evolution of a discipline or a science, much as the growth rings of a tree are indicators of the tree's life history and age. Neonyms can thus be approached as markers of culture and progress.

Accordingly, this chapter is not exclusively devoted to terms that have appeared recently, all the more so as the perception of neonyms is a problem in itself: what some consider to be a neonym, others do not. In addition, there is no objective criterion by which to decide how old a term must be to cease being considered a neonym. The point here is to underline what those terms that have come to enrich a field – and can be traced back to the specialist who crafted them, or to an event that prompted their emergence – can reveal about a given period of time and the stage of development of a specific discipline, science or specialised domain. Metaphorical terms, which are a form of neonym, are not commented on in this chapter but in the following one which is devoted to metaphors. Name attributes[20], or

20 The most frequent examples of terms named after economists are as follows: Arrow's impossibility theorem, Coase theorem, Edgeworth box, Fisher effect, Giffen goods, Gresham's law, Keynesian multiplier model, Kondratief cycle,

anthroponyms, which abound in economics, undoubtedly offer the layperson a way into economic theory, but there is no real consensus over their qualifying as terms or neonyms *per se*. Actually, Sager considers name attributes as "spurious items which are of no use to the terminologist" (1990: 131), and others (Picht, Draskau 1985: 39) fail to suggest any adequate terminology to deal with these units. However, positions have evolved in the past decades and those terminologists who study terms in context are not likely to overlook derived forms associated with the names of famous figures in a specific field. Actually, the use of anthroponyms, which bear the name of the person who either invented a solution, a process or an object, or who raised a problem, indicates that the notion thus designated is important. Particular cases of terms based on names may understandably draw the linguist's attention, especially when they underline the need to also consider adjectives as terms, after checking with the specialists. The creative potential around the name Pareto, for example, has given birth to noun forms such as *PARETO ANALYSIS*, and to such frequent instances of syntactically unusual combinations for a layperson as *PARETO-DISTRIBUTED*, *PARETO-EFFICIENT*, *PARETO-OPTIMAL* or *PARETO-COMPATIBLE*:

> This paper analyses the set of <u>Pareto efficient</u> tax structures. (Stiglitz 1982)

> Consider an economy with d commodities and n individuals. A pair (p, M), where p is a price vector and $M = (m_1, m_2, \ldots, m_n)$ is a set of n individual income levels, defines a set of individual budget constraints. It is known that such pairs provide a framework for duality-based investigations of <u>Pareto efficient</u> allocations and of equilibria. This paper employs this framework in a general setting, not requiring smoothness or boundedness of budget sets, to develop duals of the first and second theorems of welfare economics. Namely, under suitable assumptions: 1) the price-income pair associated with any equi-

---

Laffer curve, Leontief paradox, Lorenz curve, Lucas aggregate supply curve, Lucas critique, Marshallian cross diagrams, Nash equilibrium, Okun's law, Pareto efficiency, Pareto optimality, Phillips curve, Pigovian taxes, Say's law, Schumpeterian hypothesis, Schumpeterian profits, Solow model, Tobin tax, Ricardian equivalence, Veblen goods, Walras's law, Walrasian price. All the above-mentioned name attributes were recorded in three commonly-used economics textbooks: Lipsey and Chrystal (1999), Mankiw (2004) and Samuelson & Nordhaus (2005). In *An Eponymous Dictionary of Economics* (Segura & Braun 2004), 317 entries are listed.

librium is dual Pareto efficient, and 2) corresponding to any dual Pareto-efficient pair, there is an allocation which together with the given prices forms an equilibrium. Luenberger 1994, abstract)

Anonymity is usually expressed by means of a group of cyclic or Pareto-compatible permutations. (Lauwers 2009, abstract)

The distribution of compound sums of Pareto-distributed losses (Ramsay 2009, Title of the article)

As the excerpts show, such terms invite the observer to investigate further Pareto's contribution to the theory of distribution, to learn more about his 20/80 principle[21], which has found so many applications in business, risk-management, etc., and about the concept of Pareto efficiency. Disregarding such nouns and adjectives and not seeing the emergence of new ones to translate new concepts might well miss the mark. However, as examining anthroponyms in economics at length in this chapter would have been too long, I have chosen to devote a whole paper to them elsewhere (Resche 2013).

This chapter begins with an overview of the main sources for generating neonyms, based on examples of economic terms to illustrate the linguistic forms they can take. It goes on to underline the role played by economists and management figures as wordsmiths; the neonyms they contributed can be considered as signposts for the lay-person wishing to inquire into what stimulated their creation at the time. Section 3 examines more recent neonyms in the context of the 2008 subprime and financial crises resulting from the bursting of the housing bubble. Section 4 provides an analysis of the new terms which refer to new branches of economics and highlights the role of neonyms in signalling changes in standpoint. This particular focus

21 The 20/80 principle is not a law of nature, but stems from observation: 20% of a country's population will own 80% of the riches. The 20/80 princple has become a rule of thumb in business: 20% of the stock takes up 80% of a company's warehouse space and comes from 20% of its suppliers; 20% of its workers account for 80% of its production; 20% of its customers create 80% of its revenue; 80% of the sales come from 20% of the sales staff. A large majority of problems (80%) are produced by a few causes (20%). If those causes can be pinpointed, most problems can then be solved.

also underlines a parallel between terminology and economics: the GTT, as shown in Chapter 2, has been challenged and other approaches to terminology do exist; likewise, mainstream economics is no longer the only possible approach to economics and has been either enriched or challenged by a multiplicity of new branches. Section 5 studies the example of green economics at greater length to show how new terms can mirror a new approach to problems and perhaps indicate an ongoing paradigm shift.

4.1. Basic patterns for neonyms and their linguistic forms

If they are to have a chance of being understood and accepted, neonyms must show lexico-semantic adequacy and conform to morpho-syntactic rules. Algeo (1991) lists six basic processes for neonym generation: "creating, borrowing, combining, shortening, blending and shifting"; a number of sub-types obviously exist in some categories and have to be taken into account.

The first category – creating – is probably the least productive one as it means creating an altogether new term from nothing. Though *ex nihilo* creation is of course theoretically possible, it remains quite rare: it might result in onomatopoeic words imitating natural sounds, but no real example can be put forward in the economic sphere where most neonyms are inspired by existing terms or roots, whatever changes they undergo in the process.

The second option – borrowing from other languages – has proved a more common pattern, and can translate into three types of neologisms: simple loanwords that are adopted directly (*LAISSEZ FAIRE, ARBITRAGE, COUPON, ENTREPRENEUR, KAIZEN, KEIRETSU, NICHE, CAVEAT EMPTOR, EMBARGO, AGIO*); loanwords that are subjected to morphological, phonological or orthographic changes in order to be adapted to the English language (*ENTREPRENEURSHIP*); and calques or translations of borrowed words. In the latter category, the initial foreign phrase will sometimes coexist with its translation as is the case for *LET THE BUYER*

BEWARE and *CAVEAT EMPTOR*. In other instances, the foreign term will be translated in a very transparent way: Vilfredo Pareto's coinage of the term *OPHÉLIMITÉ* in French was translated directly into *OPHELIMITY*[22] in English. There exists yet another interesting option, when word-for-word translation is not possible, which consists in trying to render the meaning and cadence of the original term. For example, in the field of management ideas, the Japanese phrase *GENCHI GENBUTSU*[23] – which means "go and see for yourself" and is associated with the famous management system initiated by Toyota – has been translated into *GET YOUR BOOTS ON*, a phrase that echoes the rhythm of the original expression. It is also referred to as *MANAGEMENT BY WALKING ABOUT*, or *MBWA*.

The third process – combining – provides a much richer source of neonyms, for two types of combinations are possible, i.e. compounds and derivatives. Compounds result from combining two or more words or bases, as in *ECOLOGICAL ECONOMICS*, *STRUCTURED PRODUCTS* or *FLAT HIERARCHY*. Derivatives are composed of a base and one or more affixes. Lately, prefixes such as eco- (for ecology/ecological) or bio- (for biological) have proved popular, echoing current social preoccupations or centres of interest: *ECOMANAGEMENT*, which helps companies improve their environmental practices, and *BIONOMICS*, a new approach to economics, are cases in point. In the field of management, "shore"/ "shoring" has proved a productive base to express the idea of outsourcing abroad, leading to the use of *OFFSHORING* and *NEARSHORING* – depending on the distance between home and the foreign country where production and services are outsourced. When the process is reconsidered for quality concerns, *BACKSHORING* or *INSHORING* can provide a reasonable solution and bring manufacturing or services back home; in all cases, choice is crucial and *BESTSHORING* is the ultimate goal. Occasionally, the term "economics" itself has provided the

22 Translating the word in English was no problem as the noun is derived from the Greek *ophelimos* (ὠφέλιμος), which means useful; it was introduced into economics by Vilfredo Pareto (1848-1923) who preferred it to its equivalent "utility", or "the capacity to provide satisfaction".

23 This expression indicates that the best way to understand a problem is to go and see for oneself on the factory floor what the matter is.

"econ" prefix as in *ECONOSPHERE*[24] or *ECONOMETRICS*; it has also yielded the fruitful "n/omics" suffix. The latter generated the neonym *NIXONOMICS* in late 1969 to refer to the economic policies of President Richard Nixon. Since then the suffix has been added to every US President's name to describe their particular type of economic policies; hence, *REAGANOMICS*, *CLINTONOMICS*, and *OBAMANOMICS*. Whenever necessary, the vowel "o" has been inserted before the suffix to facilitate pronunciation as in *FORDONOMICS* or *BUSHONOMICS*. There seems to be no end to the use of this suffix. The pattern is not limited to Presidents' names, but has also given birth to *ENRONOMICS* during the Enron scandal to describe the company's *CREATIVE ACCOUNTING* practices – another neonym coined by the firm itself to downplay its reckless attitude. In addition, it was resorted to by *The Economist* that crafted *BURGERNOMICS* in 1986: it defines an alternative way of calculating Purchasing Power Parity (PPP) by comparing the price of a burger in a number of countries throughout the world. *BURGERNOMICS* offers a PPP index and has now entered the terminology of economics textbooks. More recently, during the financial crisis, *DEPRESSIONOMICS* also surfaced, underlining the creative potential of the suffix.

The fourth device – shortening – comes under various guises: clippings (fore-clipping and back-clipping), abbreviations or acronyms, as well as words including alphabet letters. Clippings, or the subtraction of one or more syllables from a word, can be illustrated by *COCOS*, which stands for *CONTINGENT CONVERTIBLES*.[25] Abbreviations can end up keeping just the initial letter of words as in *THE THREE C'S*, a term often needed recently to refer to the three criteria examined by creditors to determine creditworthiness: *CREDIT, COLLATERAL AND CHARACTER*.[26] Acronyms such as *TARP (TROUBLED ASSET RELIEF PROGRAM)* are

---

24 According to Craig Thomas (2009), the *ECONOSPHERE* describes "a living, breathing, global organism that choreographs billions of performers with breathtaking precision and can make life better for everyone. But the *ECONOSPHERE* works best if we understand what *nurtures* it and what *poisons* it".

25 A type of convertible bond where the stock price must reach a particular level before the investor can make the conversion.

26 *CREDIT* refers to a borrower's ability to repay based on income and current debt. Lenders want to make sure a consumer earns more than he owes. *COLLATERAL* refers to property or other valuables that can be sold to guarantee the

clearly associated with the recent subprime crisis, translating an effort to solve the problems. Of course, the choice of "troubled" must be understood as a euphemism for *TOXIC ASSETS*. The widespread use of electronic mail and the internet has also affected the business world and produced such neonyms as *E-COMMERCE*, *E-TAIL* (for electronic retail) and *E-BUSINESS*. The increasing recourse to initial letters can be explained by the natural trend towards an economy of language; SMS technology has also probably exacerbated an already popular habit of writing words phonetically whenever possible as in "Can B2BB4U?"[27] found in an advertisement in a management magazine; abbreviations like *B2B* (business-to-business) and *B2C* (business-to-customer) are now common currency. Many recent management ideas have been abbreviated and *CSR*[28], *CRM*[29], *SCM*[30], and *ERP*[31] have entered the language of the corporate world. The same holds true in the financial sector to refer to financial instruments: analyses of the recent financial crisis were littered with such abbreviations or acronyms as *CDO*s[32], *ARM*s[33] or *CDS*s[34], that were thus introduced to the general public. Alphabet letters are also used in combination with a full word either to avoid mentioning an unpleasant word as in the *R-WORD* (for recession) or as an economical way to describe the general movement of a line on a graph. Comments on the recent crisis and the probable kind of recovery that could be expected made ample use of this device: mention was made of *J-SHAPED*[35], *U-SHAPED*[36], *V-SHAPED*[37], *W-*

repayment of a loan. *CHARACTER* is assessed by looking into the borrower's past: his ability to handle past debt responsibly, to keep a job long enough, to keep a house or flat without foreclosure or bankruptcy.

27 Can "business-to-business" be for you?

28 *CORPORATE SOCIAL RESPONSIBILITY*

29 *CUSTOMER RELATIONSHIP MANAGEMENT*

30 *SUPPLY CHAIN MANAGEMENT*

31 *ENTERPRISE RESOURCE PLANNING*

32 *COLLATERALISED DEBT OBLIGATIONS*

33 *ADJUSTABLE-RATE MORTGAGES*

34 *CREDIT DEFAULT SWAPS*

35 A *J-SHAPED RECESSION* refers to a situation when, for some reason, recovery is unusually sharp, boosted, for example, by a new category of high-tech products.

SHAPED[38], or *L-SHAPED*[39] recessions. The letters refer to the general shape of the corresponding charts.

The fifth process – blending – results from the conflation of two words and represents a fruitful source of neonyms. Obviously, the necessary condition for portmanteau words is to enable the reader to trace the resulting blend back to the initial words. Blends are fashionable in everyday language and have become so in management and economics in general. Even the layperson will understand that *GLOCALISATION*[40] is a mix of globalisation and localisation, or that *STAGFLATION*[41] has to do with both stagnation and inflation; likewise, it seems rather obvious that *COOPETITION*[42] can be expanded as competition and cooperation. Logically, *FLEXICURITY*[43] stems from both flexibility and

---

36 A *U-SHAPED RECESSION* takes longer than a *V-SHAPED* one; the trough is less-clearly defined and the economy grows its way out of the recession very gradually.

37 A *V-SHAPED RECESSION* or *RECOVERY* refers to an economic situation where a severe downturn in the markets is met with an equally strong upturn in the markets. *V-SHAPES* are the normal shape for recession.

38 A *W-SHAPED RECESSION* generally starts out as *A V-SHAPED RECOVERY* but some other economic event may send the economy back down to previous lows; another rebound will be needed to finish off the *W-SHAPE. A W-SHAPED RECOVERY* is also called a *DOUBLE DIP*.

39 An *L-SHAPED RECESSION* describes a situation when an economy suffers a severe recession, translating into a very steep drop, followed by a long period of underperformance which prevents the economy from recovering; hence the flat line of the L. The L describes the most severe type of recessions.

40 More precisely, *GLOCALISATION* results from the idea that though the market for goods and services may be global, it is important to adapt goods and services to the local markets, tailoring them to conform with local laws and customs, and to consumer preferences and needs.

41 *STAGFLATION* describes a combination of slow economic growth and relatively high unemployment accompanied by a rise in prices, or inflation.

42 *COOPETITION* appeared as a neologism in the economics literature about a dozen years ago; it suggests that companies can cooperate with others on certain aspects of their business where they do not have a competitive advantage while competing in other areas.

43 The term *FLEXICURITY* was first coined in the 1990s by Denmark's Prime Minister Poul Nyrup Rasmussen. It was then adopted by the European Council to call on Member States to "[…] promote flexibility combined with employment security and reduce labour market segmentation, having due regard to

security and *PROSUMER*[44] results from the combination of producer and consumer. Of course, as economic terms, they will require closer examination and their exact definitions will have to be understood, but the process is now familiar to every reader. As already mentioned, it is important to always keep in mind the environment which gave birth to neonyms or try to trace the new term back to its origin in order to fully understand the reference. For example, anyone now encountering the portmanteau word *BILLANTHROPY*[45] will immediately think of Bill Gates who is well-known for his philanthropic penchant. But how will it be interpreted 60 years on? Will it have disappeared or will it have entered the common lexicon? If so, it might well be associated with corporate philanthropy while the reference to Bill Gates will be lost on the majority except for those interested in the story behind the terms! Alongside economic neologisms, in a somewhat different register, *FUNEMPLOYMENT* can also be quoted, though it cannot be considered as an economic term *per se*. Nevertheless, it provides a recent example of the influence of the economic sphere and environment on ordinary language. Its coinage and use translate the wish to hide one's financial difficulties under a veil of humour or a euphemism: unemployment can only be fun if you consider it to be limited in time and you know you have enough money to enjoy yourself and take advantage of the extra free time that is forced on you.

Finally, the sixth process – shifting – happens when an existing term is caused to evolve because of new discoveries or technological progress. Shifting can first refer to semantic shift that does not affect the form of terms; such a phenomenon, though more difficult to detect immediately than formal neology, is important as it may announce or

---

the role of the social partners". (Guideline n° 21 of the Integrated Guidelines for Growth and Employment)

44 The term 'prosumer' dates back to 1980 when Alvin Toffler coined it in his book *The Third Wave* by blending *producer* and *consumer*. In so doing, Toffler had in mind a possible future type of consumer who would be given a say in the design and manufacture of products. Thus, goods could better match consumers' needs in special niche markets. The term opened the way for the concept of 'mass customisation'.

45 It would probably be fair to imagine "Warrenanthropy" (for Warren Buffett) but I have not encountered the neonym yet.

translate a turning point in concepts, theories, trends or circumstances. Its origin may lie in a new discovery or situation that calls for reconsidering the established conceptual organisation. Consequently, room must be made for a new term that will help distinguish two formerly blurred concepts: the existing term will be stripped of part of its previous semantic surface and undergo a semantic shift and a new term will have to be coined. Examples are provided in section 4.2.2 when discussing the evolution of terms such as *CLASSICAL* and *NEOCLASSICAL ECONOMICS*. Shifting also includes words that change parts of speech without signalling the change by means of an affix. Thus, a noun can be converted into a verb and vice versa. For a while, the subprime crisis was so often mentioned in the media that *SUBPRIME* changed from adjective to verb status: in technical terms, it meant giving credit to the working poor at predatory rates, while in common parlance, it was loosely defined as the ability to play ostrich, i.e. to stick one's head in the sand, and then expect a bailout.

This overview of basic patterns for generating neonyms has underlined the ability of language to adapt and provide ways to coin terms to meet new needs. Analysing these neonyms for what they mean, but also tracing them back to the events that led to their creation or to their authors can provide useful information on different periods of time (Dury 1999) and different ways of dealing with problems. As far as economic theory is concerned, neonyms can be considered as a barometer of the prevailing ideas and preoccupations of a given period of time and reflect the history of ideas in the world of sciences.

4.2. Economists as wordsmiths

Science in the making requires naming new concepts, a challenging endeavour for scientists; the terms they coin may well not be the most appropriate ones, or they may rename an existing concept and introduce confusion merely because they want to leave their mark in the history of ideas. Economics is no exception.

4.2.1. Economists' preoccupation with clear concepts and terms

For communication between specialists to be unequivocal, terms should be agreed upon and proliferation of competing neonyms should be avoided as much as possible. Understandably, allowance must be made for variation that inevitably translates conceptual instability[46]. Variation may also translate a desire to stress a particular semantic trait, thus giving preference to one term rather than another. But specialists sometimes quarrel over slight shades of meaning and they should be encouraged to put an end to lengthy debates and refrain from coining new words for the same concept indefinitely. In this respect, it is not surprising that economists themselves should have been made aware of the need to adopt the most suitable terms and of the risk of confusion otherwise. Irving Fisher expressed his concern with this issue in his 1918 article "Is 'Utility' the Most Suitable Term for the Concept it is used to Denote?"

> In all sciences, and particularly in one like economics, which appeals to the general public and which uses concepts and terms already at least partially familiar, it is a matter of some practical importance to select a suitable terminology. The concept called 'final degree of utility' by Jevons, 'effective utility', 'specific utility', and 'marginal efficiency' by J. B. Clark, 'marginal utility' and 'marginal desirability' by Marshall, Gide and others, '*Grenznutzen*' by the Austrians, '*Wert der letzten Atome*' by Gossen, '*rareté*' by Walras, and '*ophélimité*' by Pareto, seems still in need of really satisfactory terms by which to express it.

It is important to note that the various economists quoted in the passage above as authors of different terms to describe the concept were all born in the first half of the nineteenth century, though they were not all British[47], and that they were familiar with one another's theoretical positions. The question of the most appropriate denotation for

46 Instability is dealt with in Chapter 6.

47 Heinrich Gossen was German and his one book was translated into French by Léon Walras; Vilfredo Pareto was born in Paris of a French mother and an Italian father. He went back to Italy to study and teach, and then to Switzerland. Charles Gide and Léon Walras were both French; Alfred Marshall was British and John Bates Clark was American.

the concept of utility provides an example of neology in the making before a single term is finally adopted and can make its way into scientific language. After continuing to examine potential substitutes for Bentham's *UTILITY* in the same article, Fisher rejected *DESIRABILITY*, though he admitted he used it himself several times, because of the ethical connotation it carried, and finally seemed attracted by *MARGINAL WANTABILITY*. He even suggested the neonym *A WANTAB* to refer to a unit of 'wantability', but was careful enough to ask his fellow economists for their opinion and suggestions: consensus is essential. However, as regards the utlity concept, it seems that these efforts at harmonizing terminology were vain (Resche forthcoming).

In the same issue of *The Quarterly Journal of Economics* (1918), Fisher drew his fellow economists' attention to the problems of competitive innovation in terminology, underlining the ensuing obstacles to fruitful exchanges and the damaging effects on theory construction and clear thinking:

> The issue is thus squarely presented whether the application of the term "capital" to "a stock of wealth existing at an instant of time" is good terminology, and, in particular, whether it is consistent with or in violation of former usage. To many this question, being one of words only, will not seem to merit extended discussion. [...] But it is evident from the foregoing criticisms, and others which might be mentioned, that the principal obstacle to the acceptance of the proposed definition and the conception which it carries with it is the belief that it is an innovation in terminology. [...]
>
> Be it said that this paper is written not in the interests of a purist nomenclature, but in the hope of removing certain verbal obstacles which now block the way to important ideas. What meanings are attached to the words "capital" and "income" would be of slight consequence were it not that the present usage (or lack of usage) prevents economists from exploiting the ideas of "stock" and "flow". Words and ideas usually move together, and it can scarcely be expected that those who feel obliged to define the word "capital" as a part of stock will nevertheless, like Marshall, proceed to treat the "problems of capital" with reference to the whole. It is simpler and less confusing to first square our words with our ideas.

Somewhat differently, Ragnar Frisch deserves mention here, not only because he was the first Nobel Laureate[48] in economics in 1969 – with Jan Tinbergen, another pioneer in the field of econometrics – and a respected Professor at the University of Oslo, but because he can be considered as one of the key individuals in the dramatic transformation of economics in the course of the twentieth century. As such, he was also a very productive creator of neonyms. Though some of his neonyms (*POLYPOLY, THE PARI PASSU LAW*) failed to really catch on, he is known for crafting many terms that are now commonly used in economics, among which *FLOW INPUT, POINT OUTPUT, IMPULSE* and *PROPAGATION*. Considering that he coined *MACROECONOMICS* and created and named the field of *ECONOMETRICS*, he was certainly in the best position to define new concepts within those fields and name them. He was certainly eager to give a clear definition of the discipline of econometrics and the term he had chosen for it, which he did in the introduction to the first issue of *Econometrica*, the journal he also created:

> A word of explanation regarding the term econometrics may be in order. Its definition is implied in the statement of the scope of the [Econometric] Society, in Section I of the Constitution, which reads: The Econometric Society is an international society for the advancement of economic theory in its relation to statistics and mathematics. [...] Its main object shall be to promote studies that aim at a unification of the theoretical-quantitative and the empirical-quantitative approach to economic problems. [...] But there are several aspects of the quantitative approach to economics, and no single one of these aspects, taken by itself, should be confounded with econometrics. Thus, econometrics is by no means the same as economic statistics. Nor is it identical with what we call general economic theory, although a considerable portion of this theory has a definitely quantitative character. Nor should econometrics be taken as synonymous with the application of mathematics to economics. Experience has shown that each of these three view-points, that of statistics, economic theory, and mathematics, is a necessary, but not by itself a sufficient, condi-

48 It is to be noted that the term "Nobel Prize" for economics is a misnomer as it is not one of the original Nobel Prizes created by the will of Alfred Nobel. Though is is awarded by the Royal Swedish Academy of Sciences, it was actually established and endowed by Sweden's central bank in 1968 on the occasion of the bank's 300th anniversary, in memory of Alfred Nobel. It is thus officially known as the Sveriges Riksbank Prize in Economic Sciences in Memory of Alfred Nobel.

tion for a real understanding of the quantitative relations in modern economic life. It is the unification of all three that is powerful. And it is this unification that constitutes econometrics. (*Econometrica*, (1933), 1, pp. 1-2)

It is most important to be able to trace terms to their creators and not to cut them off from their historical roots and socioterminologists insist on this point too. A linguist undertaking research into neonyms and their authors at different periods can thus acquire a lot of information on the prevailing concerns of the time, on the emergence of new paradigms, as well as on the theoretical debates that played a part in shaping economic theory as we know it today. The next section is devoted to economic neonyms crafted by famous economists to illustrate how such terms can highlight important themes and offer a bird's eye view of economic theory.

4.2.2. Economic neonyms coined by identifiable economists: an entry point into theory and the history of ideas

Even though Table 7 lays no claim to exhaustivity, it would still be a tedious exercise to comment on every single neonym in the list. The point here is to give a glimpse of the insight that can be gained from investigating the terms that have been crafted by economic figures over several hundred years of economic thought.

Neonyms (date of creation)	Creators
ABSOLUTE ADVANTAGE*[49]	Adam Smith (1723-1790)
AUCTION	Léon Walras (1834-1910)
CAPITALISM	Karl Marx (1818-1883)
CATALLAXY*	Friedrich von Hayek (1899-1992)
COMPARATIVE ADVANTAGE*	David Ricardo (1772-1823)
CONSUMER SURPLUS	Alfred Marshall (1842-1924)
CREATIVE DESTRUCTION	Joseph Schumpeter (1883-1950)
ECONOMICS*	Alfred Marshall (1842-1924)
ECONOMETRICS *	Ragnar Frisch (1895-1973)
ELASTICITY OF DEMAND	Alfred Marshall (1842-1924)

49 The terms followed by an asterisk explicitly refer to economic schools or branches of economics and are discussed at greater length in this section.

ENTREPRENEUR	R. Cantillon (1680s-1734); J-B. Say (1767-1832)
EVOLUTIONARY ECONOMICS*	Thorstein Veblen (1857-1929)
FLOW INPUT	Ragnar Frisch (1895-1973)
HEDONIMETER	Francis Ysidro Edgeworth (1845-1926)
HUMAN CAPITAL	Gary Becker (1930-); Jacob Mincer (1922-2006)
IMPULSE	Ragnar Frisch (1895-1973)
INVISIBLE HAND *	Adam Smith (1723-1790)
MACRODYNAMICS	Ragnar Frisch (1895-1973)
MACROECONOMICS*	Ragnar Frisch (1895-1973)
MARGINAL UTILITY	Alfred Marshall (1842-1924)
MARGINALISM *	John A. Hobson (1858-1940)
MARGINALISTS	John A. Hobson (1858-1940)
MERCANTILISM*	Marquis de Mirabeau (1715-1789)
METAECONOMICS *	Carl Menger (1840-1921)
MICROECONOMICS*	Ragnar Frisch (1895-1973)
NEOCLASSICAL ECONOMICS*	Thorstein Veblen (1857-1929)
OPHELIMITY	Vilfredo Pareto (1848-1923)
PLAYOMETRICS*	Ragnar Frisch (1895-1973)
POINT OUTPUT	Ragnar Frisch (1895-1973)
PROPAGATION	Ragnar Frisch (1895-1973)
REPRESENTATIVE MONEY	William Stanley Jevons (1835-1882)
SATISFICING	Herbert Simon (1916-2001)
STAGFLATION	Paul A. Samuelson (1915-2009)
TATONNEMENT	Léon Walras (1834-1910)
UTILITY*	Jeremy Bentham (1748-1832)

Table 7. Neonyms attributable to the economists who coined them

One particular category of neonyms can be singled out for discussion, namely the terms explicitly referring to economic schools or characteristics of branches of economics, starting with Smith's classical view of the self-regulating market expressed through his well-known metaphor of the *INVISIBLE HAND*[50]. His preoccupation with international trade, which translated into his *ABSOLUTE ADVANTAGE*[51] theory that coun-

50 [The] concept [was] introduced by Adam Smith in 1776 to describe the paradox of a laissez-faire economy. The invisible-hand doctrine holds that, with each participant pursuing his or her own private interest, a market system nevertheless works to the benefit of all as though a benevolent invisible hand were directing the whole process. (Samuelson & Nordhaus 2005: 742)

51 (In international trade). The ability of Country A to produce a commodity more efficiently (i.e. with greater output per unit of input) than Country B. Possession of such an absolute advantage does not necessarily mean thayt A

tered *MERCANTILISM*[52], was later refined upon by Ricardo with his concept of *COMPARATIVE ADVANTAGE*[53]. *UTILITARIANISM*[54] is also represented by Bentham's *UTILITY*[55] concept.

The term *ECONOMICS* itself is interesting as a neonym, as it marks a turning point from what was previously known as *POLITICAL ECONOMY*: as was pointed out in Chapter 3, it was first introduced by Alfred Marshall, signalling the field as a discipline in its own right. Likewise, the introduction of *ECONOMETRICS* in 1926 by Ragnar Frisch points out the desire to make economics more scientific. As for *PLAYOMETRICS*, it tells us another story: towards the end of his life, Frisch coined this derogatory term, implying that his work had been misused and misunderstood by econometricians: "I have insisted that econometrics must have relevance to concrete realities, otherwise it degenerates into something which is not worthy of the name econometrics, but ought rather to be called 'playometrics'" (Frisch 1970). All his other neonyms in the list, including *MACROECONOMICS* and *MICROECONOMICS*, are connected with his work on business cycles.

Veblen's coining of *EVOLUTIONARY ECONOMICS* in 1898 marks the beginning of a strand that was to influence the research agenda of generations of social scientists and is still alive today. Special atten-

---

can export this commodity to B successfully. Country B may stil have the comparative advantage. (Samuelson & Nordhaus 2005: 731)

52 A political doctrine emphasizing the importance of balance-of-payments surpluses as a device to accumulate gold. Proponents therefore advocated tight government control of economic policies, believing that laissez-faire policies might lead to a loss of gold. (Samuelson & Nordhaus 2005: 744)

53 (In international trade). The law of comparative advantage says that a nation should specialize in producing and exporting those commodities which it can produce at relatively lower cost and that it should import those goods for which it is a relatively high-cost producer. Thus it is a comparative advantage – not an absolute advantage – that should dictate trade patterns. (Samuelson & Nordhaus 2005: 734)

54 The political philosophy according to which the government should choose policies to maximize the total utility of everyone in society. Mankiw 2004: 834)

55 (also total utility). The total satisfaction derived from the consumption of goods or services. To be contrasted with marginal utility, which is the additional utility arising from consumption of an additional unit of the commodity. (Samuelson & Nordhaus 2005: 752)

tion should also be paid to *NEOCLASSICAL ECONOMICS*, a perfect illustration of how research on neonyms can open up new vistas on the evolution of a term from its creation to its later use and adaptation. The story of the evolution of the term *NEOCLASSICAL* is well documented by Colander (2000: 130), who calls it a "story of metamorphosis". But to understand the changes that the concept has undergone, it is necessary to start with the landmark term *CLASSICAL* crafted by Karl Marx in 1847 to refer to David Ricardo's formal economics, as opposed to "vulgar or romantic economics", by which he meant "economics close to the people". Colander points out that, in spite of some hesitation as to when the Classical period started in economics, most historians of economic thought seem to include Smith as a Classical economist, thus agreeing that the period when economics was based on the labour or cost theories of value started in 1776 and ended in 1870. The reason why the need was felt to introduce a new term to describe the period starting in the 1870s was to draw attention to a change in the way some economists approached economics: it was at this time that *UTILITARIANISM* and *MARGINALISM* started gaining ground, along with deductive models. Colander (2000: 131) explains how misleading the different uses of "neoclassical" have been over time:

> The term neoclassical was initially coined by Thorstein Veblen (1900) in his "Preconceptions of Economic Science." As Veblen used the term, it was a negative description of Alfred Marshall's economics, which itself was a type of synthesis of the marginalism found in Menger and W.S. Jevons with broader Classical themes in Smith, Ricardo, and J.S. Mill. Thus, from the beginning, the term was used by an outsider to characterize the thinking of another group.
>
> When Veblen coined it, it was not meant as a description of mainstream economics. In the early 1900s, economics was divided and, in the US at least, neoclassical thought was not mainstream; institutionalism was more embedded than neoclassical thought. Veblen's terminology caught on, and the term neoclassical came into general use and can be found in the writings of W.C. Mitchell (1967), J.A. Hobson (1925), and Eric Roll (1938, 1942).
>
> Hicks (1932, 1934) and Stigler (1941) extended the meaning of neoclassical to encompass all marginalist writers, including Menger, Jevons, and J.B. Clark. Most writers after John Hicks and George Stigler used the term inclusively.

> Thus it lost most of its initial meaning. Instead of describing Marshallian economics, it became associated with the use of calculus, the use of marginal productivity theory, and a focus on relative prices. As has been noted by a number of authors, while the neoclassical terminology makes some sense for Marshall, who emphasised the connection of his approach with the Classical approach, it makes far less sense for the others, such as Jevons, who emphasised the difference between his views and those of the Classicals. Some have suggested that anti-Classical would have been preferable.

When J.M. Keynes entered the economics arena, he chose to retain only one category, calling all economists Classicals. Henceforth, Classicals were contrasted with Keynesians, until Paul Samuelson (1955) developed *THE NEOCLASSICAL SYNTHESIS*, reconciling Keynes with Classicals but adding another layer of confusion as regards the concept of neoclassicism. Today the term neoclassical remains confusing as it either refers to the period of economic thought from 1870 to the 1930s, or describes modern *MAINSTREAM ECONOMICS* as opposed to heterodox thinking.

As was the case with classical and neoclassical economics, *MARGINALISM* was created by an outsider to the movement, i.e. after the marginalists themselves had made their contribution to economics. The explanation lies in the context in which the neonym appeared and what motivated it: "Hobson gave the word a disparaging tinge, since he found the concept faulty and its policy conclusions unwelcome" (Howey 1972: 281). Once again, this underlines the importance of considering the theoretical and historical setting of neonyms. Since then, of course, marginalism has lost its negative connotation and is used in a neutral way to refer to the school of thought mentioned in every economics textbook.

Another interesting term on the list, *CATALLAXY*, crafted by Friedrich von Hayek, translates the wish to rename economics as the science of exchange. In Hayek's words (1976: 108-109), *CATALLAXY* is "derived from the Greek verb *katallatein*[56] (or *katallasein*) which meant, significantly, not only 'to exchange' but also 'to admit into the community' and 'to change from enemy into friend'". He used it to describe the spontaneous order that is "brought about by the mutual

---

56 καταλλαττείν

adjustment of many individual economies in a market". As for *METAECONOMICS*, coined by Carl Menger in 1936, it should be understood in the context of the debate around logic and mathematics that took place in Vienna at the time: it is clear from the paper where he used the term for the first time (1979: 280):

> Following a suggestion of Hilbert, modern logisticians refer to the study of the logical relations between the statements of a theory as the corresponding *meta-theory*. In this terminology, the contents of the present paper can be described as a chapter in metaeconomics.

Menger felt that economists were trying to adopt a logical point of view based on deduction, but failed to also use inductive methods, hence the need for *METAECONOMICS*. The term later underwent a semantic shift to refer to the re-embedding of ethics into economics and it has been used by behavioural economists.

As can be seen from the remarks above, it only takes a few neonyms to cover a large spectrum of economic thinking and travel through time. The other terms on the list reflect the preoccupations of economists with themes such as money, prices, inflation and stagnation, demand and consumption, entrepreneurship and progress. Three items are of particular interest because, at different points in time, they re-introduce the human dimension. The first one is the *HEDONIMETER*, imagined by Francis Ysidro Edgeworth, against the background of preoccupations with the measurability of utility. Influenced by psychophysicists who were considered to be doing cutting-edge work at the time, focusing on "developing a sensory theory that related external stimuli to individual feelings", Edgeworth (1881 [1967]: 102) describes how his machine to measure hedonism would work:

> [...] let there be granted to the science of pleasure what is granted to the science of energy; to imagine an ideally perfect instrument, a psychophysical machine, continually registering the height of pleasure experienced by an individual, exactly according to the verdict of consciousness, or rather diverging therefrom according to a *law of errors*. From moment to moment the hedonimeter varies; the delicate index now flickering with the flutter of the passions, now steadied by intellectual activity, low sunk whole hours in the neighbourhood of zero, or momentarily springing up towards infinity. The continually indicated height is registered by photographic or other frictionless

apparatus upon a uniformly moving vertical plane. Then the quantity of happiness between two epochs is represented by the area contained between the zero-line, perpendiculars thereto at the points corresponding to the epochs, and the curve traced by the index; or, if the correction suggested in the last paragraph be admitted, another dimension will be required for the representation. The integration must be extended from the present to the infinitely future time to constitute the end of pure egoism.

The second item – *SATISFICING* – is to be considered in the context of the theory of bounded rationality dealing with decision-making. *SATISFICING* was coined by Herbert Simon who, unlike classical economists, considered that individuals do not always seek profit-maximisation and therefore are content with what is "good enough" or satisfactory and acceptable. Such behaviour can be observed when information is only partially available or difficult to process. It is important to understand that Herbert Simon was also interested in management theory, which may explain his "real-world" approach. The third item – *HUMAN CAPITAL* – is analysed at greater length in Chapter 5. Suffice it to say here that it translates the idea that investments in education, training and health are the most important investments in human capital since, unlike financial and physical assets, human capital cannot be separated from the person.

As the next section shows, the field of management theory abounds in neonyms that also offer the opportunity to observe how ideas emerged and cross-fertilised.

4.2.3. Management neonyms coined by identifiable management figures: signposts on the path to management ideas

The main neonyms listed in Table 7 were extracted from a corpus of papers and reports in the *McKinsey Quarterly*, the *Harvard Business Review*, the quarterly magazine *Strategy+business*, from *Knowledge@Wharton* from the Wharton School of the University of Pennsylvania, as well as two widely-acclaimed books: Tim Hindle's

2008 *Guide to Management Ideas and Gurus* and Art Kleiner's[57] 2008 "History of the radical thinkers who reinvented corporate management": *The Age of Heretics*.

Before discussing the neonyms in Table 7, it should be pointed out that management is not only a science but is also about motivating people, which explains why the management specialists who are the fathers of the concepts on the list come from different horizons. A minority of them studied economics (Bartlett, Christensen, Kotler), management (Sull, Prahalad, Moss Kanter, Pascale) or business (Hamel) from the outset; several were trained in mechanical engineering (Hammer, Krafcik), electrical engineering (Juran, Kaplan, Sloan) civil engineering (Champy), aerospace engineering (Senge) or held/hold degrees in physics (Ghoshal, Kahn); others studied sociology or psychology. Many turned to management later, either because they happened to work in organisations that were faced with problems awaiting solutions, or because they were studying for an MBA or writing their PhD in management. As a result, management ideas came from people who were polymaths: Levin studied psychology, medicine and biology; Kotler added mathematics and behavioural science to economics; Senge studied philosophy and management, in addition to aerospace engineering.

A good example of the cross-fertilisation of ideas can be found in the work of the Gilbreth couple because they symbolise two of the main strands of management thinking that were brought together in their research. Interestingly, Frank Gilbreth did not go into higher education; after high school, he began work as a bricklayer, before becoming a building contractor and setting up his own engineering consulting business. His wife Lilian, by contrast, studied literature and psychology, and she wrote a PhD dissertation on the psychology of management. Frank Gilbreth's experience as a bricklayer helped him to analyse the ways in which bricklayers performed their tasks and to

---

57 Art Kleiner is the author and co-author of several acclaimed business books; his articles have been published in a number of places like the *Harvard Busines Review, the New York Times Magazine, Wired or Fast Company*. He is a faculty member at New York University's Interactive Telecommunications Program and the editor-in-chief of the Quarterly magazine *Strategy+business*.

record each of the movements entering into a task. This gave birth to what was later called time-and-motion study: the motion camera he used was able to record movements in fractions of minutes and each movement corresponded to a unit called a *THERBLIG*, after his own name spelt backwards (except for the letters "th"). This aspect of his work could be thought to follow naturally from Taylor's scientific management but, combined with his wife's interest in psychology, it actually aimed at finding the best way to make work easier while increasing output, and showed more concern with workers' well-being than did Taylor's approach. The Gilbreths advised managers to always improve conditions in the workplace and opened the way for today's concerns about repetitive strain injury (RSI).

Neonyms	**Creators (date of creation)**
ACTIVE INERTIA / ACTIVE WAITING	Donald Sull (2005)
ACTIVITY-BASED COSTING (ABC)	Robert Kaplan (early 1980s)
BALANCED SCORECARD	Robert Kaplan (1990s)
BOTTOM OF THE PYRAMID (BOP)	C. K. Prahalad (2004)
BRAINSTORMING	Alex Osborn (early 1940s)
BUSINESS CLUSTER	Michael Porter (1990)
BUSINESS-PROCESS REENGINEERING (BPR)	Michael Hammer, James Champy (1990)
CORE COMPETENCIES	C. K. Prahalad, Gary Hamel (1990)
CORPORATE DNA	Ken Baskin (1998)
COMPANY-WIDE QUALITY MANAGEMENT (CWQM)	Joseph Juran (1951)
DISCONTINUOUS CHANGE	Charles Handy (1990s)
DISRUPTIVE TECHNOLOGY/ INNOVATION	Clayton Christensen (1997)
EMPOWERMENT	Rosabeth Moss Kanter (1990)
FEDERAL DECENTRALISATION	Alfred Sloan (1930s)
FORCE FIELD ANALYSIS	Kurt Levin (1940s)
FUTURE SHOCK	Alvin Toffler (1965)
GUERILLA MARKETING	Jay Conrad Levinson (1984)
HIERARCHY OF NEEDS	Abraham Maslow (1943)
INTRAPRENEUR / INTRAPRENEURSHIP	Reg Jennings, Charles Cox, Cary L. Cooper (1994)
KNOWLEDGE WORKERS	Peter Drucker (1969)
LEAN MANUFACTURING	John Krafcik (1988)
LEARNING ORGANISATION	Peter Senge (1990)
LEFT-BRAIN ORGANISATION	Christopher A. Bartlett & Sumantra

	Ghoshal (2005)
MANAGEMENT BY OBJECTIVES (MBO)	Peter Drucker (1960s)
MASS CUSTOMISATION	Joseph Pine (1993)
OBSOLEDGE	Alvin and Heidi Toffler (2006)
ORGANISATIONAL AGILITY	Richard Pascale (1984)
PROSUMER	Alvin and Heidi Toffler (1980)
PORTFOLIO WORKING	Charles Handy (1994)
RESILIENCE	Gary Hamel (2003)
SCENARIO PLANNING	Herman Kahn (1950s)
SHAMROCK ORGANISATION	Charles Handy (1990s)
SOCIAL MARKETING	Philip Kotler (1971)
SUSTAINABILITY SCORECARD	Robert Kaplan (2007)
THEORY X; THEORY Y	Douglas McGregor (1960)
THEORY Z	William Ouchi (1981)
THERBLIGS	Frank and Lilian Gilbreth (1912)
TOTAL QUALITY MANAGEMENT (TQM)	Edwards Deming Joseph Juran (1950)
TRIPLE BOTTOM LINE	John Elkington (1994)
VALUE CHAIN	Michael Porter (1985)

Table 8. Management neonyms attributable to management thinkers

The list of neonyms in Table 8 can be read in three main ways, which will give a more accurate picture of the evolution of management ideas. The first approach, choosing the dates when the neonyms were coined as pointers, can provide insight into the ideas that prevailed or coexisted at a certain time. For example, a focus on the seven neonyms born in the first decade of the twenty-first century would highlight preoccupations with sustainability, the need for a company to be proactive, creative, innovative, for looking for new potential consumers, for constantly updating its people's skills in order to survive in a faster-changing, more competitive and challenging environment. Allowance must be made, however, for pioneering ideas that may have taken decades before actually being implemented. The second approach entails organising ideas into different categories based on the disciplines that influenced them: psychology, biology, or physics. The third and last approach, which focuses on thematic lines, traces the evolution of positions in different sectors, such as production, consumption, marketing, working conditions, innovation, or strategy. Researching into the meaning of these neonyms, their authors' backgrounds and the theoretical and historical framework that prompted their emergence provides an opportunity to realise just how deeply-rooted in scientific and social evolution management ideas are.

Looking at the emergence of neonyms chronologically, it becomes clear that there have been many more of them since the 1980s, with a particularly productive decade in the 1990s. But again, caution is required as neonyms are not the only indicator of novelty in management practices; moreover, their number does not necessarily reflect the impact they had on the corporate world. For example, Sloan's FEDERAL DECENTRALISATION, the only neonym in the list dating back to the 1930s, has had enduring consequences: his reorganisation of General Motors into autonomous divisions controlled by a small central staff for whom financial and policy matters were the priorities has served as a template for nearly all corporate entities ever since. But when we look at the 1990s, we see that more and more attention is paid to people inside and outside the organisations: organisations were described as LEARNING ORGANISATIONS as if they were human beings, an analogy that also translated into CORPORATE DNA at the same period. LEARNING ORGANISATIONS are defined by Senge (1990: 3) as follows:

> Learning organisations [are] organisations where people continually expand their capacity to create the results they truly desire, where new and expansive patterns of thinking are nurtured, where collective aspiration is set free, and where people are continually learning to see the whole together.

Though the concept named ORGANISATIONAL LEARNING was introduced in the 1970s by Argyris and Schön, its new form, THE LEARNING ORGANISATION, was coined by Senge who thus gave renewed impetus to the idea in 1990. By fostering inquiry and dialogue, the LEARNING ORGANISATION acknowledged the capacity of its members to take part in its evolution.

It is no surprise that neonyms like EMPOWERMENT and INTRAPRENEURSHIP[58] should have appeared in the same decade: people

58 "Intrapreneurship is the use of entrepreneurial techniques within an enlightened corporation or organisation which allow employees to become Intrapreneurs (or corporate entrepreneurs) within the firm. The employee/intrapreneur can use their creativity and innovative ideas to create for their employer new products, services or new entire divisions for the firm with the

were given more power to express their views and enterprise was encouraged within the firm. With information technology considered as *DISRUPTIVE TECHNOLOGY*, it became necessary to reconsider, redesign or *REENGINEER* business processes and to improve performance measuring. Kaplan's *BALANCED SCORECARD* introduced a change from the traditional measures of performance that only took into consideration the shareholders' point of view: to achieve a balanced assessment of the company, the customers' perspective was factored in alongside the company's perspective; data concerning innovation and improvement were also analysed so as to create value in the future. Elkington's *TRIPLE BOTTOM LINE* concept, associated with the "*3Ps*" that stand for *PROFIT, PEOPLE AND PLANET*, was inspired by Kaplan's ideas and came as a natural evolution in this context. In order to improve their self-assessment as well as their public image, companies were advised to work towards producing three types of bottom line: in addition to the traditional profit and loss account, they were encouraged to assess their social responsibility, producing a *PEOPLE ACCOUNT* and also to show how environmentally responsible they were through *GREEN ACCOUNTING* practices.

As technology became more sophisticated, the idea of *DISCONTINUOUS CHANGE* that came suddenly and threatened to call into question practices that had so far proved efficient prompted a number of new ideas. Sophisticated technology seemed to require greater specialisation, so that companies needed to rethink their strategies and focus on what Prahalad and Hamel called their *CORE COMPETENCIES*, relying on other specialists to perform some of the peripheral tasks. This must be related to Handy's idea of *THE SHAMROCK ORGANISATION*. One of the leaves of the shamrock would represent the core staff of highly-qualified, highly-paid technicians and managers; the second leaf would correspond to contractual specialists; and the third leaf would consist of a flexible workforce made up of part-time or temporary workers. Understandably, Handy's *PORTFOLIO WORKING* could meet the needs of such networked enterprises; the term suggests that workers can offer their services to several companies, instead of having only

full backing of the firm's resources". <http://www.intrapreneurshipinstitute.com/>

one employer, and generalises the idea of freelance work as traditionally understood. Another idea related to the shamrock organisation is that of *INDUSTRIAL CLUSTERS* developed by Porter. It describes the concentration in the same geographical area of businesses, suppliers and related entities that work in the same field with a view to stimulating innovation, business and productivity. One last indication that "people" – whether workers inside the firms or consumers at the other end of the chain – seem to have been the focus of management thinkers' attention is provided by the idea of *MASS CUSTOMISATION*, which translated the wish to reconcile profit and people. In other words, while benefiting from economies of scale when producing a basic model or product, a company was encouraged to show more consideration for individual tastes and offer options that would not be too costly but would give consumers the impression that the model or product was made-to-measure for them only.

Adopting a different perspective, it is possible to link the new concepts of the first decade of the twenty-first century with some of the neonyms of the 1990s. Prahalad's *BOTTOM OF THE PYRAMID* takes people into account again; he focuses on the little people who cannot afford expensive goods but represent a very large consumer base that should not be ignored. Kaplan's *SUSTAINABILITY SCORECARD* owes both to his own *BALANCED SCORECARD* and to Elkington's *TRIPLE BOTTOM LINE*. Bartlett and Ghoshal's *LEFT-BRAIN ORGANISATION* builds upon the need to foster imagination and creativity already expressed by Senge's *LEARNING ORGANISATION*. The Tofflers' neologism, *OBSOLEDGE*, for obsolete knowledge, can be associated with the ideas of *DISRUPTIVE TECHNOLOGY* and *LEARNING ORGANISATION*, launched in the previous decade. Hamel's *RESILIENCE* is to be understood as continuous reconstruction in order to be ready for major disruption; it is connected with emergency planning and ensuring business continuity, and the attacks on the twin Towers in 2001 may have fuelled ideas on the topic. Sull's *ACTIVE INERTIA* was coined precisely to describe corporate tendency to react to disruptive, *DISCONTINUOUS CHANGE* by finding refuge in what had worked best in the past. He felt this attitude was inappropriate and advocated *ACTIVE WAITING* (2005: 4), which requires a different state of mind:

> To survive and thrive in volatile markets, managers can pursue a strategy of *active waiting*, which consists of anticipating, preparing for, and seizing opportunities and dealing with threats as they arise. Like an advancing army, a company proceeding into an unpredictable future can follow a general direction, probe the future for potential opportunities and threats, keep resources in reserve, remain battle ready, and, when the big opportunity or threat arises, strike hard.

Sull's military metaphor is interesting as it points out the obvious common ground between corporate strategy and military strategy, as evidenced by Levinson's *GUERILLA MARKETING*. More is said on this point in Chapter 5 dealing with metaphors.

A broader thematic perspective can show how ideas may lay dormant for a number of years and suddenly lead to breakthroughs when circumstances are favourable. Kahn's *SCENARIO PLANNING* in the 1950s is a case in point. A common thread links his idea, Pascale's *ORGANISATIONAL AGILITY*[59] (1984) and Hamel's *RESILIENCE*[60] (2003). But the 1940s had already paved the way for dealing with change with Levin's *FORCE FIELD ANALYSIS*[61]. Likewise, preoccupations with people's needs and motivation can be traced back to the 1940s, with Maslow's

---

59 "Agility is a concept that incorporates the ideas of flexibility, balance, adaptability and coordination under one umbrella. In a business context, agility typically refers to the ability of an organisation to rapidly adapt to market and environmental changes in productive and cost-effective ways. There are at least three form of agility: operational agility, portfolio agility and strategic agility". <http://www.12manage.com/description_organisational_agility.html>

60 "Organisational resilience is the ability and capacity of a corporation to withstand potential significant economic/systemic risk or systematic discontinuities or business interruption, by adapting or recovering or resisting being affected and resuming its (core) operations to continue to provide an acceptable level of functioning and structure". <http://www.12manage.com/description_organisational_resilience.html>

61 "Force field analysis consists in taking into consideration the interaction of two opposite sets of forces in an organisation: those seeking to promote changes, or driving forces; those attempting to maintain the status quo: the restraining forces. Present organisations are viewed as systems in which the situation was not a static pattern, but a dynamic balance of forces working in opposite directions. In order for any change to occur, the driving forces must exceed the restraining forces, thus shifting the equilibrium". <http://www.12manage.com/methods_lewin_force_field_analysis.html>

HIERARCHY OF NEEDS [62]; it can then be seen to re-emerge in the 1960s with McGregor's *THEORY X AND Y*[63] and Drucker's *KNOWLEDGE WORKERS*, and again in the 1990s with Moss Kanter's *EMPOWERMENT*. Deming and Juran's pioneering work in the 1950s as regards quality offers an opportunity to observe the influence that the experiments they did in Japan were to exert later on the corporate world in the West. Such an influence marked the beginning of a series of ideas coming from Japan: in the 1980s and 1990s, *KAIZEN*[64], *KEIRETSU*[65], *KANBAN*[66] and *KAKUSHIN*[67] entered the terminology of western companies.

Research into these neonyms also provides helpful understanding of the role played by the historical context in shaping new ideas, and the 1940s illustrate this point. It seems that WW2 acted as a cata-

---

62 The hierarchy of needs (1954) originally consisted of 5 layers: the bottom layer described the physiological needs (food, water, shelter, warmth), then came safety needs (security, stability, freedom from fear); then needs for belongingness and love (friends, family, love), for self-esteem (achievements, recognition, mastery, respect) and finally for self-actualisation (the pursuit of inner talent, creativity, fulfilment). More layers were added later. <http://www.12manage.com/methods_maslow_hierarchy_needs.html>

63 According to Theory X, people inherently dislike working and will try to avoid it if they can. Consequently, they have to be coerced or controlled by management. This requires resorting to an authoritarian type of hard management. By contrast, Theory T considers that people consider work as natural. Provided they are motivated, they will do their best. Job satisfaction is then key to engaging them and ensuring their commitment. They seem to accept responsibilities and to even seek them. They are seen as imaginative and creative. Therefore, what is needed is a participative, soft kind of management. <http://www.12manage.com/methods_mcgregor_theory_X_Y.html>

64 *Kaizen* is the idea of continuous improvement in all aspects of the firm, involving everyone.

65 The literal translation of *Keireitsu* is "headless combine". It describes a particular corporate network that can be likened to a spider's web, where several organisations are linked together through stakes they have taken in one another's capital, so that they have developed close relationships. Instead of competing with one another, they work together to their mutual benefit.

66 *Kanban* is closely associated with the just-in-time (JIT) idea. In Japanese, *kanban* means "card", referring to "the card that is sent to reorder a standard quantity of parts as and when they have been used up in the manufacturing processs" (Hindle 2008: 107).

67 *Kakushin* means revolutionary change.

lyst for social sciences in the United States: during this period, it was important to maintain the soldiers' faith and enthusiasm, to prepare strategic operations, and to organise and coordinate the war effort required of ordinary citizens at home. In order to meet those needs, a number of specialists from different horizons were brought together: sociologists, psychologists, mathematicians and engineers. Fruitful ideas emerged from their exchanges and cooperation. After the war, when the GIs returned home and the pace of the war industry slowed down, community problems arose. Kurt Levin, together with another psychologist and an education specialist, created training groups in Bethel (Maine) to help people overcome their problems and deal with one another. The *National Training Laboratories for Group Dynamics* (*NTLs*) turned out to be a successful experiment that endured until the 1960s, later attracting trainees from the corporate world who then became specialists in personal development. This period can explain the introduction of psychological concerns in management theory, such as today's *COACHING*.

Links between economic theory and management theory are of course obvious, as evidenced by the co-emergence in the 1960s of Gary Becker's *HUMAN CAPITAL* concept (1964) and Peter Drucker's *KNOWLEDGE WORKERS* (1969). Interestingly, Drucker, who had a PhD in International and Public Law, was influenced by Schumpeter – a friend of his father's, as were Von Mises and Hayek – and by Keynes, whose Cambridge seminars he attended. Through his writings on management, Drucker is said to have linked the Austrian school of economics and the Austrian school of strategy that produced the theory of the firm. Another parallel between management and economics lies in the fact that, in both disciplines, theories were developed by people who were in turn inspired by mechanical analogies or more biological ones, which has influenced theoretical approaches throughout.

4.3. A synchronic perspective: the recent subprime crisis and the neonyms it produced

Having looked at neonyms as historical landmarks illustrating the evolution of economic or management theory, it is now time to offer a synchronic illustration of how terms can help to feel the pulse of a given period. The recent subprime and financial crises are a perfect opportunity to analyse how a particular context can enhance or revive the terminology of a specific domain, although it is very difficult to state for sure that many new terms appeared during this difficult period. As the corpus[68] that served as a basis for this synchronic analysis confirmed, many of the most frequently used words were not really new to the financial world; they just seemed to surface more often than in ordinary times. More precisely, they sounded new to the general public who suddenly became familiar with them and were given information and definitions to decipher them. Their status is complex and hybrid, depending on the communities and contexts in which they are used (Cabré 2000). They probably underwent a determinologisation process (Meyer & Mackintosh 2000) when travelling from the specialised circles to the public sphere; however, even though their meanings were explained by experts in the media, lay people may not have fully understood the concepts. Given that the general public would never have been led to encounter or use these terms/words were it not for the crisis, they can surely be considered as neologisms in the general language. At the same time, some of these terms that were already in use in very specific circumstances and circles have been appropriated by a larger community of specialists and by the business world. In this respect, they have entered their dis-

68 The corpus was compiled with a view to comparing the terms used in different types of discourse over the period: it included research articles and reports from the *McKinsey Quarterly* and *Strategy+business*, articles from the semi-specialised press such as the *Wall Street Journal* or the *Financial Times*, and magazines used for a larger public such as *The Economist* and *Bloomberg/BusinessWeek*. The 3 sub-corpora were computerised and analysed with the help of the Antconc concordancer, which made it easier to compare them.

course and can be considered as neonyms. In order to understand these new terms, the best way is to introduce them through a brief overview of the problems that shook the United States and the rest of the world and almost led to the collapse of our financial system.

Before describing what led to the 2008 financial turmoil, which was incidentally referred to as an "economic 9/11" for the United States, it is important to go back to 2002 and remember that the economy was already in recession then after the bursting of the technology stock bubble known as the dot.com bubble. When the 9/11 terrorist attacks hit the United States, Federal Reserve Chairman Alan Greenspan and President Bush both feared an even more serious slowdown. In order to stimulate the economy, between October 2002 and June 2003 the Fed implemented a series of interest rate cuts, a policy meant to stimulate consumer spending by making it easier for individuals to borrow money. Ironically enough, though cheaper money did boost demand for credit, it can be said to be partly responsible for the housing bubble and the ensuing tsunami.

At first, the real estate boom enabled many people to realise their dreams of becoming homeowners or to take advantage of the lower rates to refinance their mortgages, remodel their homes, buy new cars or enjoy holidays. Optimism led to more confidence; as the assessed values of people's homes increased, they perceived themselves as richer than they actually were, a phenomenon which is described as *THE WEALTH EFFECT* in economics. As a rule, mortgage underwriters conduct thorough research on potential borrowers' creditworthiness, and consider *THE THREE CS – CREDIT, COLLATERAL, AND CHARACTER* – as standard criteria. However, many banks and non-bank lenders that were eager to take advantage of the housing boom started loosening the rules and targeted customers who would never have qualified for mortgages otherwise. New types of mortgages were created for these poorer borrowers whose credit record was far from perfect. The new borrowers no longer had to produce evidence of their ability to repay their mortgages, which led to the creation of a new category of loans alongside *ALT-A LOANS*[69]: *SUBPRIME LOANS*, *NO-DOCS*

69 An Alt-A loan stands between A-paper loans (or prime loans) and subprime loans, the riskiest type of loans. As it fails to meet some of the established cri-

LOANS, *LOW-DOCS LOANS* or *NINJA LOANS* (for no income, no job or assets) resulted from this particular loose policy. In hindsight, they were also called *DELINQUENT LOANS*, which makes one wonder who the delinquents were – those who could not make their mortgage payments or those who resorted to *PREDATORY LENDING* in the first place. These poorer people were thus offered *ADJUSTABLE-RATE MORTGAGES* (*ARMS*), called *OPTION ARMS*[70] and *HYBRID ARMS*[71] that were attractive at first but quite dangerous, especially when the applicants did not take the trouble to read the small print or ask for explanations. Such instruments had existed since the 1980s, but sounded new to them and were quite complex.

Real estate speculation caused the bubble to inflate, especially as investment banks realised what huge profits they could make from mortgages. Instead of holding onto them until the loans were paid off, they resorted to *CREATIVE FINANCING*: they bought loans from other banks and financial entities and, through *FINANCIAL ENGINEERING*, packaged these loans together, then sliced them up and resold them as securities. Very often, in order to insulate their business from risk, they created *CONDUITS*, also known as *SINGLE PURPOSE ENTITIES* (*SPES*), or *SPECIAL PURPOSE VEHICLES* (*SPVS*). These legal entities enabled a bank, for example, to securitise home loans. As *SECURITISATION* became common practice, a plethora of complex financial instruments or *STRUCTURED INVESTMENT VEHICLES* (*SIVS*) were devised and sold to investors all over the world. The problem is that some of these products were made up of several *TRANCHES*: a super safe higher tier, an intermediate *MEZZANINE* level that was riskier and a lower equity level that was the riskiest tranche. Those who bought such securities were not aware that pieces of *TOXIC LOANS* were hidden in their portfolios. In a

teria for risk-free loans, an Alt-A loan remains a "non-conforming loan", but it is not as risky as a subprime loan.

70 Option ARMs offer several monthly payment options, and interest rate is typically very low for the first three months, but it usually rises to a rate closer to that of other mortgage loans over time. All unpaid interest is added to the amount owed on the mortgage, resulting in a higher balance; this is known as negative amortisation.

71 Hybrid ARMs have a fixed interest rate period and then become adjustable-rate mortgages.

context where home values were supposed to keep on rising, and where homeowners were not predicted to default on their mortgage payments, investors were optimistic. Besides, they could buy insurance policies: *Credit default swaps* (*CDSs*) that were meant to guarantee payment even in the case where the underlying security defaulted. The most common *mortgage-backed securities* (*MBSs*) were *Collateralised Debt Obligations*, known as *CDOs* and *Collateralised Mortgage obligations*, or *CMOs*. They were very popular with hedge funds and sovereign wealth funds and were rated AAA by rating agencies, which blinded investors to the inherent risks. Even America's two largest mortgage companies, Fannie Mae and Freddie Mac, started lowering their standards and buying lesser-quality mortgages, including subprime loans.

As early as November 2002, though, the inflating housing bubble led Alan Greenspan to warn that the "extraordinary housing boom [could] not continue indefinitely". In 2005, he even used the word "froth" to refer to the situation of the housing market in some states, yet he took no particular action to stem the tide as he probably did not think the problem would be contagious. Still, in hindsight, some analysts observed that the loose standards in the mortgage industry, the gap between housing prices and incomes, and a growing number of unsold homes should have been considered as serious signals that the housing market decline was underway. In the third quarter of 2005, prices started dropping and the decline went on quarter after quarter, which prompted mortgage underwriters to react by tightening their standards. As mortgage rates rose, word of a *credit squeeze* or *credit crunch* spread. Borrowers could no longer refinance and were faced with higher monthly payments, while the value of their houses was depreciating. Few options were available to them and if they decided to sell their homes, they would lose money. They could of course try to renegotiate their loans with the lenders but, if they failed to reach a compromise, they would probably be unable to make their monthly payments and defaulting would lead to *foreclosures*. The consequences were dramatic for the homeowners who lost their homes in large numbers: *jingle mail* became common practice, when people who had lost their homes sent their keys to the bank in an envelope, once they had moved out. The situation was also dramatic for the banks that could not re-sell the houses at decent prices and for the investors who finally understood what *TOXIC ASSETS* and *TOXIC WASTE* meant.

June 2007 can be considered as a turning point: two major hedge funds that had invested heavily in subprime mortgages collapsed. Panic spread among investment banks, hedge funds and sovereign wealth funds, especially when rating agencies started downgrading mortgage-backed securities. CDOs suddenly became much less attractive instruments. Within a few months, the housing and credit markets were badly hit and a series of bankruptcies and takeovers affected the banking world. The widespread belief that some institutions were *TOO BIG TO FAIL* was questioned when Bear Stearns collapsed and had to be rescued in early 2008. When the American Government refused to rescue Lehman Brothers in September, notions such as *MORAL HAZARD* and *BAILOUT* were brought to the fore and suddenly became familiar to the general public.

In the next few months, the crisis escalated rapidly into the greatest crisis since the Great Depression and spread to the rest of the world, causing tremendous economic and social damage as millions of people lost their jobs. Governments had to devise rescue and stimulus plans to pull the world out of recession and introduce tight rules to control the financial world and avoid similar problems in the future. The American government came up with the *TROUBLED ASSET RELIEF PLAN* (TARP), which allowed the Treasury to purchase illiquid assets from banks and other financial institutions, using secondary market mechanisms, with a view to helping them stem losses. Banks were also required to undergo *STRESS TESTS* to make sure they had enough capital reserves to be able to resist further declines in the economy.

In addition to the terms highlighted in the preceding paragraphs, four neonyms, all portmanteau words, were coined to describe categories of people that emerged during the crisis. One of them, *NEWPRENEURS,* described the few daring individuals who decided to start businesses in spite of the economic context. The second neonym *BANKSTERS* is quite transparent in its negative connotation: it translates the poor opinion that the general public had of the banking world they held responsible for many problems – whether investment banks or entities dealing in *SHADOW BANKING*. The third neologism *PRECARIAT* referred to the poor working people who, though not jobless, could no longer afford a decent life because their incomes were too low. Finally, recession produced the term *RECESSIONISTA*, coined after 'fashionista', to describe young women on a tight budget who nevertheless managed to dress stylishly by sharing or swapping clothes. It became a new form of *RECESSIONOMICS*.

Strikingly, from the point of view of a researcher in the field of SVE, in spite of the extraordinary circumstances that threatened our financial system, very few of the terms that were used at the time can be considered as really new. Many of them, however, were unknown to the general public and, as such, served as signposts to indicate problems, traps, or abuses to be avoided in the future. They thus performed a useful role in raising the public's awareness to the need for sounder financial education and information.

In some instances, however, new terms appear and revisit a domain or an area of knowledge and draw our attention to a potential questioning of the old assumptions. When dealing with theory, they may signal a shift or even a break from the existing paradigm in a given field. They may introduce or translate a new outlook on reality, a new perspective, a new worldview which will revolutionise a whole sector of research and challenge the status quo. The next section focuses on such cases by examining the new terms expressing new approaches to economics.

4.4. Neonyms as mirrors of a pluralistic stance in economics

As Hicks (1981: 233) remarks very wisely, "There is, there can be, no economic theory which will do for us everything we want all the time". As science progresses and contexts change, former views need to be reconsidered and a healthy process of exploring new avenues of research takes place. It is interesting to note that the same phenomenon occurred in terminology, as described in section 2.1.3: new approaches have been experimented with, that have enriched the field and provided ways of raising new questions and addressing formerly unsolved ones from different angles. Likewise, a pluralistic stance has emerged in economics. In some instances, the new branches have been grafted onto the main body of knowledge, as is the case for *ENVIRONMENTAL ECONOMICS* and *RESOURCE ECONOMICS*; in other instances, more hybrid approaches have been experimented with and can be said to straddle the border of *MAINSTREAM ECONOMICS*, with some sub-divisions belonging to it and others distancing themselves from it (*ECONOPHYSICS* or *BEHAVIOURAL ECONOMICS*); finally, a number of new strands have started questioning traditional assumptions more thoroughly and have clearly diverged from mainstream economics, considering themselves as alternatives (*BUDDHIST ECONOMICS*, *GREEN ECONOMICS*). By simply recording the new terms relating to those new fields (Table 9) it is possible to feel the pulse of the current evolution in economics.

ANTHROPOLOGICAL ECONOMICS	*HUMANISTIC ECONOMICS*
AUSTRIAN ECONOMICS	*INSTITUTIONAL ECONOMICS*
BEHAVIOURAL ECONOMICS	*NEUROECONOMICS*
BIOECONOMICS	*NEW ECONOMICS*
BUDDHIST ECONOMICS	*NEW INSTITUTIONAL ECONOMICS*
ECOLOGICAL ECONOMICS	*REGENERATIVE ECONOMICS*
ECONOPHYSICS	*RESOURCE ECONOMICS*
ENVIRONMENTAL ECONOMICS	*SOCIALIST ECONOMICS*
EVOLUTIONARY ECONOMICS	*SOCIOECONOMICS*
FEMINIST ECONOMICS	*SRAFFIAN ECONOMICS*
GREEN ECONOMICS	*STEADY STATE ECONOMICS*
HOLISTIC ECONOMICS	*THERMOECONOMICS*

Table 9. New strands in economics

ECONOPHYSICS, as the term implies, is a hybrid branch. The term was coined by Eugene Stanley in 1996 to denote more recent applications of physics to economics. Actually, as mentioned in Chapter 3, the influence of physics is not new and, in this respect, the works of Walras and Pareto could well be considered as pioneering research. Likewise, Fisher or Tinbergen, who were trained in physics, could also be considered as belonging to this strand. However, *ECONOPHYSICS* was given a new turn in the mid-1990s when physicists working in the sub-field of statistical mechanics applied their methods to the complex problems of financial markets and other economic problems related to uncertainty or nonlinear dynamics. Traditional economic tools were deemed insufficient to deal with non-equilibrium situations and heterogeneous agents. Complexity has now become a key notion; it is dealt with at greater length in Chapter 7 as an illustration of interface terms resulting from the interconnectedness of disciplines.

If *MAINSTREAM ECONOMICS*, as presented in economics textbooks, conveys the erroneous idea of a homogenous whole, so does the term *HETERODOX ECONOMICS*; it is actually quite vague and misleading. In fact, the different strands outside *MAINSTREAM ECONOMICS* make a very complex web. Though a Confederation for greater pluralism in economics, born in the 1990s, brings together many of the new approaches, it does not draw together all the critics of mainstream economics. Many hybrid or heterodox branches, however, do share a common point: they are interdisciplinary in character, as evidenced by the very terms that describe them: *ANTHROPOLOGICAL ECONOMICS*[72], *BEHAVIOURAL ECONOMICS*[73], *BIOECONOMICS*[74], *NEUROECONOMICS*[75], *SOCIOECONOMICS*[76], *THERMOECONOMICS*[77].

---

72 *ANTHROPOLOGICAL ECONOMICS*, also known as economic anthropology, combines the tools of both economics and anthropology to account for human economic behaviour.

73 *BEHAVIOURAL ECONOMICS* is related to *NEUROECONOMICS*; it takes into account social, cognitive and emotional factors in order to understand economic decisions.

74 *BIOECONOMICS* uses economic models to study the dynamics of living resources; it is interested in resource protection issues and thus related to resource economics. Keeping in mind the issue of sustainability, it tries to determine the threshold of socioeconomic activity beyond which a biological system would no longer be able to regenerate itself.

75 *NEUROECONOMICS* is an interdisciplinary field aiming at explaining human decision making; it focuses mainly on problems that conventional economics cannot explain. It uses methods from neuroscience, *BEHAVIOURAL ECONOMICS*, and psychology, as well as biology, computer science and mathematics.

76 *SOCIOECONOMICS* borrows methods from sociology, history and political science to study the social impact of various sorts of economic change. It ob-

Characteristically, the classification of heterodox approaches offered by the *Journal of Economic Literature* fails to explicitly mention many of the strands that have emerged recently, which underlines how difficult it is to have an accurate picture of the situation. It first mentions SOCIALIST, MARXIAN, SRAFFIAN[78] ECONOMICS, then INSTITUTIONAL[79] and EVOLUTIONARY ECONOMICS, AUSTRIAN ECONOMICS and finally FEMINIST ECONOMICS[80]. A last category, known as "other", remains quite vague. It is worth noting that some of these fields have not always been considered "outsiders" and, for example, the AUSTRIAN SCHOOL, which was influential in the late nineteenth and early twentieth century, originating in the works of Carl Menger, Friedrich von Wiesen and Eugen von Böhm Bawerk, did contribute to MAINSTREAM ECONOMICS. It

---

serves how individuals and groups interact, focusing on social capital, and social "markets". It is also interested in the links between economics, ethics and philosophy. It criticises conventional economics for failing to consider anomalies in economic relationships and is therefore considered as a heterodox branch.

77 THERMOECONOMICS, also referred to as BIOPHYSICAL ECONOMICS, is considered as a school of heterodox economics; the term was coined in the early 1960s by an American engineer, but the approach was later developed by Nicholas Georgescu-Roegen. It applies the laws of thermodynamics to economic theory.

78 According to *Encyclopedia Britannica*, SRAFFIAN ECONOMICS is "an offshoot of general equilibrium theory [that] purports to explain the determination of prices by means of the technological relationships between inputs and outputs without invoking the preferences of consumers that neoclassical economists rely on so heavily".

79 INSTITUTIONAL ECONOMICS is indebted to Veblen, but its name dates back to 1919; it was coined by Walton H. Hamilton in an article published in the *American Economic Review*. INSTITUTIONAL ECONOMICS studies the evolution of institutions, their complex interactions and their impact on markets. It relies on insights from BEHAVIOURAL ECONOMICS.

80 Though its roots date back to the late nineteenth century, FEMINIST ECONOMICS only became official in 1992 with the creation of the International Association for Feminist Economics (IAFFE). It seeks to apply gender-based analysis to economic theory, reproaching mainstream economics with viewing the economy from men's point of view. FEMINIST ECONOMICS offers alternative approaches and values, such as cooperation, caring and provisioning. The ultimate goal is to work towards more humane economic institutions and caring relationships for everyone, whatever their race or gender.

has been considered a heterodox branch only since the middle of the twentieth century and is now firmly based in the United States, mainly at New York University and George Mason University. Likewise, early socialism, like Ricardian socialism, was based on *CLASSICAL ECONOMICS*. *EVOLUTIONARY ECONOMICS*, a term coined by Veblen, was born within the framework of mainstream economics. There are also attempts to integrate some aspects of heterodox approaches into more recent developments in mainstream economics: such is the case with institutionalism under the label *NEW INSTITUTIONAL ECONOMICS*[81]. Still, a number of strands seem to reject the methods of *MAINSTREAM ECONOMICS*, which they refer to as "*ORTHODOX ECONOMICS*".

It is, however, possible to gather some of the new approaches to economics into a broad category because the thinkers that initiated them in the last two decades of the twentieth century shared a common position: they felt that time, space, contexts, purpose and limits had to be taken into account more specifically and that it was high time people started thinking of the future seriously and preparing toward sustainable living and the creation of a new sustainable world. Accordingly, new fields of research emerged, such as *NEW ECONOMICS*[82] (Paul Ekins, Hazel Henderson, Pat Conaty, Manfred Max-Neef, Ernst Schumacher), *STEADY-STATE ECONOMICS*[83] (Herman Daly, John Cobb), *BIOECONOMICS* (Nicholas Georgescu-Roegen), *SOCIOECONOMICS* (Amitai Etzioni), *REGENERATIVE ECONOMICS*[84] (Paul Hawken), *HUMANISTIC ECO-*

---

81 There seems to be room for *NEW INSTITUTIONAL ECONOMICS* in the economic theory of organisations which has broadened its scope to such topics as information or transaction costs.

82 Both the New Economics Institute and the New Economics Foundation work to "improve quality of life by promoting innovative solutions that challenge mainstream thinking on economic, environmental and social issues". They put people and the planet first.

83 The *STEADY-STATE ECONOMICS* model was imagined by Herman Daly, a student of Georgescu-Roegen's; it is associated with the notions of sustainable development, limits-to-growth and zero growth. It borrows from *WELFARE ECONOMICS* and is built on ecological principles. Daly then joined others to contribute to the field of *ECOLOGICAL ECONOMICS*.

84 The idea behind *REGENERATIVE ECONOMICS* is bottom-up instead of top-down development. It is based on the philosophy of working with nature, instead of trying to conquer it.

NOMICS[85], *NEUROECONOMICS*, *ECOLOGICAL ECONOMICS*, and *GREEN ECONOMICS* (Sara Parkin, Molly Scott Cato). All these approaches more or less overlap and vindicate a holistic perspective.

The simplest way to illustrate what differentiates heterodox approaches from conventional, *MAINSTREAM ECONOMICS* may be to focus on three strands that seem to share concerns about ecological and environmental matters: *ENVIRONMENTAL ECONOMICS*, *ECOLOGICAL ECONOMICS* and *GREEN ECONOMICS*. The layperson might understandably be confused and wonder whether *ENVIRONMENTAL*, *ECOLOGICAL* and *GREEN ECONOMICS* are closely related or part of a continuum and it should be made clear that the terms denoting them are misleading and that the three branches have their own identities. While both *ECOLOGICAL ECONOMICS* and *GREEN ECONOMICS* are more critical of conventional economics, *ENVIRONMENTAL ECONOMICS* remains within the realm of mainstream economics. It is considered as a sub-field, "a neoclassical offshoot [that] essentially applies the tools and approaches of the mainstream paradigm to issues of environmental importance" (Goodwin 1995: xxxi), and a chapter on *ENVIRONMENTAL ECONOMICS* is now included in traditional textbooks. In no way, however, does it reverse the neoclassical view of reality, even though it insists on being different from its parent discipline on a number of points (Singh & Shishodia, 2007: 23). For example, it claims to consider the interactions between the environment and economic activities and to deal with public or collective goods for which markets do not exist or are imperfect. It also takes into account the externalities linked with the actions of individuals, groups and organisations and pays attention to time-related decisions, as well as the limited capacity of the environment (Lesser *et al.* 1997). In so doing, though, it draws from all other sub-disciplines of economics – *MICROECONOMICS*, *MACROECONOMICS*, and *WELFARE ECONOMICS* – as well as from natural sciences. In addition, as it is constrained

85 "Contemporary humanistic economics seeks to both describe, analyse and critically assess prevailing socio-economic institutions and policies, and provide normative (value) guidelines on how to improve them in terms of human (not merely "economic") welfare. Basic human needs, human rights, human dignity, human equality, freedom, economic democracy and economic sustainability provide the framework."
<http://www.umaine.edu/economics/old_site/humanisticeconomics/intro.htm>

by the discipline of economics and its requirement of market valuation, it is unable to deal adequately with complex issues such as global warming, ecosystem degradation, intergenerational equity, etc.

Ecological economics, by contrast, "starts from a recognition of the biophysical realities underlying the operations of the economic system" (Krishnan *et al.* 1995: xxxv). It favours long-term sustainability and raises fundamental questions about the goal of economic activity and development. Its priority issues include the preservation of the natural world and the importance of social and intergenerational equity, which leads to considerations on the use of resources and the definition of basic and luxury goods. It is not surprising that ecological economists, who have been trained as ecologists, should take a different stance from environmental economists, who were trained as economists in the first place.

As for *green economics*, it clearly goes one step further away from neoclassical economics, claiming a fundamental questioning of its theoretical bases. It is seen as more radical and political. It privileges caring for people and their concerns rather than focusing on theories or reproducing reality through artificial models using mathematics and formulae. It also insists on the need to show greater respect for Nature and its finite resources, echoing Kenneth Boulding's questions (1958: 21):

> Are we to regard the world of nature simply as a storehouse to be robbed for the immediate benefit of man? ... Does man have any responsibility for the preservation of a decent balance in nature, for the preservation of rare species, or even for the indefinite continuance of his race?

The proponents of *green economics* strongly denounce what Boulding called the "cowboy economy", which they blame for being focused on growth and treating nature carelessly as if resources were infinite and they prefer Boulding's alternative plea for a "spaceman economy" where the Earth is likened to a spaceship. Just like the spaceman in his small capsule, the Earth's inhabitants should think to the future, consume less and spare more. For them, "growth for the sake of growth is the ideology of the cancer cell" (Abbey 1991: 183). *Green economics* explicitly criticises the discipline of economics for being unable to look out of the window and see what is happening in the real world. In this respect, the neonyms it generates deserve closer examination for they could well be considered as signals of dramatic changes in viewpoint.

4.5. Neonyms as signals of potential paradigm shifts: the case of *GREEN ECONOMICS*

GREEN ECONOMICS, as it stands today, has widened its scope and been inspired by many of the figures listed in the previous section, such as Henderson, Schumacher, Dally, Moulden, Georgescu-Roegen and Hawken. It translates a holistic vision of our world: from this angle, the economy is considered as a sub-system, and the broader systems are society, planet Earth and the universe. The proponents of this vision commonly describe their approach as "Economics for People and the Planet" or the economics of the real world, so that their approach should not be understood as focused on the environment only. For them, social transformation and ecological transformation go hand-in-hand.

4.5.1. Key terms for GREEN ECONOMICS vs. key terms for mainstream economics

The key terms presented in Tables 10 and 11 below were extracted from a corpus of 62 research articles selected after reading 95 summaries gathered in a volume by Krishnan *et al* (1995) and three books by Scott Cato (2009), Hawken *et al* (2000) and Nadeau (2003). The three books were chosen because they provided different, complementary perspectives on the topic; the 62 full articles included in the corpus were those available online through university libraries. It was most important to rely on the original sources in order to avoid a bias that could have been introduced by the fact that the 95 summaries were produced by the three editors of the volume: they may well have introduced their own terminology or sought to harmonise terminology across the volume, which would have impacted our research. The Antconc concordancer was then used to analyse the computerised corpus. Only those terms that came with their definitions or were clearly differentiated by the authors from widely-ackowledged mainstream terms were selected. The two tables, organised alphabetically, illustrate two kinds of neonyms. Table 10 offers a list of terms revisited by green economics, while Table 11 illustrates new concepts and the new terms that express them. Though some of the terms in both tables were first coined by ecological economists, they have been adopted by green economists and seem more likely to play a major role towards changing mentalities when included in the fuller picture that is offered by green economics.

GREEN ECONOMICS: terms revisited	MAINSTREAM ECONOMICS
ECONOMICS = the management of our planet's resources	ECONOMICS = the management of business and allocation of resources
COST = natural destruction; worker suffering	COST = opportunity cost
GROWTH = an abundance of natural resources; growth in and of nature; qualitative development	Economic GROWTH = quantitative growth
LAND = common wealth (Cato 2009: 188)	LAND = natural resources as factors of production
SUSTAINABILITY = sustainable development; intergenerational fairness (Pearce 1987: 17)	SUSTAINABILITY = sustainable growth
VALUE = concrete human well-being; sustainability values (Cato 2009:116)	VALUE = exchange value/monetary value
WEALTH = natural capital (Cato 2009:115)	WEALTH = capital wealth

Table 10. Terms revisited by green economics

GREEN ECONOMICS: new concepts	MAINSTREAM ECONOMICS
Carrying capacity = The size of population of species that an ecosystem can support within its natual resource limits and without degrading natural capital for future generations (Cato 2009:216)	
Circular metabolism = re-using and re-circulating resources (Cato 2009: 41)	Linear, progressive economy
Closed-loop economy / closed systems = expresses the need to move towards a system where resources remain in use almost indefinitely. (Cato 2009:	Straight-line thinking leading to a linear process of resource extraction, manufacture, consumption and disposal (a system where there is minimal re-capture of the valuable materials contained in products)
Degrowth / décroissance = the downscaling of production and consumption; the aim is to maximize happiness and well-being through non-consumptive means–sharing work, consuming less, while devoting more time to art, music, family, culture and community. (Cato 2009: 42)	
Ecological footprint = it has no market price; it measures the area of land and water that is required to support indefinitely the natural standard of living of a given human population using prevailing technology (Hawken et al. 1999: 51)	*Shadow price* = it has no market price; it is an imputed valuation of a commodity that lies outside the closed market system (Nadeau 2003: 99)
Emergence; nonlinear dynamics; system dynamics	
Empowerment = enables workers to maintain power over their own work and operate as rounded persons in their work (a cooperative form of industrial organisation) (Cato 2009:63)	
GDH = *Gross domestic happiness* (Cato 2009:119) *GEP* = *Gross Ecosystem Product* (Nadeau 2003 : 143) *GPI* = *Genuine Progress Indicator* *HPI* = *Happy planet index* (Cato 2009:120)	*GDP*

HOLISM = seeing the big picture when making economic decisions, adapting to the environment we find ourselves in, rather than trying to force the environment to adapt to us (Cato 2009:3)	
INTERCONNECTEDNESS = all the aspects of the Planet are related (Lawson 2007:23)	
ISEW = *INDEX OF SUSTAINABLE ECONOMIC WELFARE* : it divides national income accounts into sectors and imposes standards of sustainability, as well as equity, on these sectors. (Nadeau 2003: 142; 199)	
INTERGENERATIONAL EQUITY/FAIRNESS = future generations have equal rights over resource allocation (Pearce 1987: 17)	
INTRAGENERATIONAL EQUITY = fairness between people living on the planet at the same time	
INTERNALISATION OF COSTS	*EXTERNALITIES*
OIKOSNOMIA = focus on managing resources	*CHREMATISTICS* = focus on money and property
QUALITY OF LIFE= in the capitalist ideaology, [...] there is too much emphasis on standard of living [...] and not enougn on quality of life. (Cato 2009: 9)	*STANDARD OF LIVING*= usually meaasured in purely mareial terms
REGENERATION (of individuals, communities, ecosystems)	*ACCUMULATION OF MONEY*
REGENERATIVE CAPACITY = non-renewable resources should not be removed at a rate faster than renewable substitutes can be developed (Cato 2009: 11)	
RIGHT LIVELIHOOD = a means of achieving subsistence without causing offence to one's own values, to other people or to one's environment; the notion of "enoughness" (Cato 2009: 61)	*WORK MAXIMIZING OUTPUT* = always more
SHE ECONOMY = sane, humane and ecological (Cato 2009: 41)	*HE ECONOMY* = hyper expansionist
SELF-RELIANCE, rather than self-sufficiency. It offers a prototype for the localisation of the economy. A self-reliant economy is based on a system of production and consumption of goods that is	

locally-based, and human-focused rather than dominated by the market (Cato 2009: 132)	
STEADY-STATE = non-growth ("sustainable growth" is viewed as an oxymoron)	*GROWTH* (always more) Sustainable growth
STEWARDSHIP OF THE LAND = people belonging to the land	*LAND OWNERSHIP* = land belonging to people
WELL-BEING (Cato 2009:113)	*WELFARE*= material wealth or monetary income
WORK = useful, sustainable and a valid investment of resources; fulfils the requirements of right livelihood as opposed to bad work (repetitive, mindless, soulless work) (Cato 2009: 58)	*EMPLOYMENT* = undertaken within an economic system driven by profit ; exploitative work maximising output
ZERO GROWTH (steady-state)	

Table 11. New concepts in green economics

GREEN ECONOMICS has both intellectual roots and spiritual dimensions. It draws from Greek philosophers, socialists, Quakers and Buddhists, among others, to advocate sharing the earth's resources while respecting the planet. It is committed to the equal treatment of human beings and the other species. Strikingly, the green economists' approach is a plea for going back to the fundamentals, considering the Earth as the household on which we all depend. In this perspective, the term *LAND* refers to our common wealth and our duty as human beings is to take good care of it.

The main difference between *GREEN ECONOMICS* and *MAINSTREAM ECONOMICS* can be illustrated by the opposition between the SHE and the HE economy: SHE stands for "sane, humane and ecological", while HE refers to a "hyper-expansionist" economy. Obviously, it is no easy matter to reconcile these two worldviews. From the HE perspective, markets are closed, self-correcting and self-sustaining most of the time. The part-whole relationships on which the HE and the SHE visions of economics are premised are utterly different: *MAINSTREAM ECONOMICS* considers economic agents and firms as "parts" and the market system as "whole"; for *GREEN ECONOMICS*, the part-whole relationships concern organisms on the one hand and the ecosystem or the biosphere on the other. From the SHE perspective, the earth does not belong to people; people belong to the Earth. Human beings are the stewards of the land and the Planet which is a common treasury, and they have to show respect both for their contemporaries and the generations to come so that all may have equal rights over resource allocation: this is what is referred to as *INTER- AND INTRA-GENERATIONAL FAIRNESS*. Most importantly, the *CARRYING AND REGENERATIVE CAPACITY* of the Earth has to be taken into consideration. It is interesting to realise that growth is revisited in terms of quality rather than quantity; likewise, *VALUE* and *COST* are defined respectively in terms of the good or the damage done to the environment or to people, as clearly reflected in the choice of new indices: *GROSS DOMESTIC HAPPINESS (GDH), GROSS ECOSYSTEM PRODUCT (GEP), HAPPY PLANET INDEX (HPI)* as opposed to GDP or GNP. Adopting a long-term view, human beings have to respect the land and transmit it to the future generations so that they may also enjoy a decent quality of life. Humans are just a link in the natural chain, one species among many others, and the economy should be seen as a subset of the ecosystem, not the other way around (Scott Cato 2009: 5).

For *GREEN ECONOMICS*, sustainable growth is an oxymoron as growth implies always more, which is not compatible with respect for finite resources and the concern for *REGENERATION*. As Boulding insisted (1966: 159): "Anyone who believes that exponential growth can go on forever in a finite world is either a madman or an economist". *NON-GROWTH* or *STEADY-STATE ECONOMIES* are preferred options insofar as they alone can preserve nature. Echoes of some of the notions mentioned in section 4.2 about management neonyms – such as *EMPOWERMENT* or the notion of *ENOUGH*, which refers to *SATISFICING* – highlight green economists' concern for quality of life at work. Work is viewed as contributing to *RIGHT LIVELIHOOD* and should never be repetitive and destructive. Characteristically, the influence of recent approaches such as non-linear thinking and emerging order point at an altogether new way of approaching problems.

4.5.2. Could GREEN ECONOMICS herald a new frontier?

Because a mainstream represents a core of widely accepted knowledge, it imposes a degree of conformity upon views and methods. The mainstream determines the boundaries of the discipline within which debate is acceptable (Krishnan *et al* 1995: xxviii). Outside the mainstream area lies the frontier area. Those who question the premises of the former by pioneering a new analytical framework are likely to be marginalised and ignored, unless they are convincing enough to give rise to a paradigm shift (Kuhn 1962). If the established borders of economics are being questioned, it is precisely because some thinkers consider that the existing paradigm fails to offer the proper approach for critical subjects.

It is difficult to state for sure that *GREEN ECONOMICS* represents a pivotal moment in the history of economic thought, but its call for a reevaluation and redrawing of traditional disciplinary boundaries obviously points at a different worldview. It aims at putting people back at the heart of what economics should be about; the state and the market should be seen as tools or mechanisms to help people achieve what they want, but should not impose their rule on people. Only the future will tell, but the key notions listed in Tables 10 and 11 above are worth paying attention to. Some of them (like the *ECOLOGICAL FOOTPRINT*) have already entered our common language.

The case of *GREEN ECONOMICS* and the number of new terms that structure its worldview seem to signal a shift, a return to the notion of economics as philosophy rather than science; it thus offers a new lens through which to reconsider economics. Heterodox economists do indeed point out that there is something wrong with the ambition of a 'Scientific' economics. According to Read (2007: 308), "Green Economics could avoid the pitfalls of scientism by being rather a political economy, a philosophically sound radical alternative to *ENVIRONMENTAL ECONOMICS*. Such a *GREEN ECONOMICS* is not a science: it is a *praxis*, a project. And any other Economics is in the end a mirage, a collective delusion with potentially utterly catastrophic consequences for the ecosphere". *GREEN ECONOMICS* may be deemed too radical by some, but it causes us to reflect on our place and role and on the meaning and consequences of our actions. The new worldview that is suggested highlights the interdependence and interconnection between the individual and the world. It translates "a new understanding of the relationship between part (individuals) and whole (nature or cosmos) that is consistent with the radical new understanding of part-whole relationships that has emerged in contemporary physics and biology" (Nadeau 2003: 214). It corresponds to a shift from *homo oeconomicus* who was supposed to be rational to *homo reciprocans*. It echoes social preoccupations, insisting on the need for equity, justice, and transdisciplinary as well as transgenerational efforts to solve major problems. The trend will have to be confirmed but this focus on the neonyms of green economics shows the importance of paying attention to and analysing new branches and their new terms in a specific domain.

4.6. Concluding remarks

This chapter has been an opportunity to illustrate the tremendous amount of information neonyms can yield when the researcher inquires beyond their mere definitions. As far as a specific field of knowledge and a discipline are concerned, as is the case with economics and management, new terms undoubtedly reflect the evolution of theoretical thinking. They are particularly meaningful when they are borrowed from other disciplines to enrich a field of knowledge; this point is studied at greater length in Chapter 7. As they do not appear by chance, they can also signal changes in mindsets or herald a turning point in research in the target domain; a diachronic approach is therefore most enriching.

This does not exclude a synchronic approach when the researcher chooses to inquire into a particular event or period of turmoil – as was the case with the housing and financial crises – in order to assess the impact of this extraordinary period on the terminology of the field. A bird's eye-view of the multiplicity of new terms denoting new branches of research in economics today highlights the dynamic character of economic research. Again, as illustrated by the focus on green economics, neonyms can be seen as mirrors of changing social preoccupations. It is therefore most important to track new terms in order to feel the pulse of research communities and assess the mutual influences of science and society at large. Likewise, metaphorical terms are worth analysing for what they reveal about mindsets, viewpoints and their origins. They are the subject of the next chapter.

5. Insights from metaphorical terms

Economic conditions are constantly
changing and each generation looks at its
own problems in its own way.

Alfred Marshall
Principles of Economics (1920: 1)

In spite of the Wüsterian call to avoid terms with any connotation, which may once have led some people to consider the unit "metaphorical term" as an oxymoron, later approaches to terminology (Meyer *et al.* 1997; Temmerman 2000; Humbley 2005) have taken metaphors into account, though from a somewhat different perspective than that which is offered here. In Specialised Varieties of English such as in the field of economics, it is important to pay special attention to metaphorical terms, and not to be content with just any metaphor that we may come across in the semi-specialised economic press, for example. Metaphorical terms make a difference because they denote concepts that are essential for economic theory and therefore reflect the theoretical frame that prompted their adoption. Metaphorical terms may not strike today's economist as metaphorical, simply because overuse may have stripped them of their figurative sense, so that they are considered as lexicalised. The linguist, however, as an "outsider" to the specialised domain will be alerted by the apparent incongruity of these terms: their metaphorical ring cannot and should not escape the careful observer's eyes. Undeniably, these very terms represent a precious source of information when their origins and the context that led to their emergence in the field of economics are investigated.

The reason why the economist may not recognise the metaphorical origin of many economic terms may also stem from the age-old controversy around metaphor, particularly in the field of sciences; if one considers precision as the yardstick that helps to measure a domain's scientific worth, then metaphors are unscientific, as they may introduce ambiguity. Given that economists were concerned with establishing the credibility of their field as a full-fledged science, one might expect them to shun metaphors altogether. Though "few economists recognise the metaphorical saturation of economic theories believed to be literal" (McCloskey 1998: 40), the very presence of terms like *PRICE MECHANISM, MULTIPLIER, ACCELERATOR, VELOCITY, RESILIENCE, PRICE ELASTICITY, LEVERAGE, LIQUID ASSETS,* or *THE CIRCULATION OF MONEY* shows that economics abounds with metaphorical terms. Is this related to the fact that economics is a "soft" science? Or is science compatible with metaphor?

In spite of the controversy metaphor has triggered ever since Aristotle, and particularly among scientists, it seems that metaphor and science are not mutually exclusive. Bicchieri (1988), for example, makes a point of distinguishing poetic from scientific metaphors, insisting that the latter play a cognitive role that is essential to science. Metaphorical terms therefore require careful analysis of the various contexts that generated them. As many such terms are related to the analogies[86] with other sciences mentioned in Chapter 3, further examination into the main metaphorical veins that run through economics is called for. Metaphorical terms cannot be ignored either for the roles they play as vehicles of new ideas and viewpoints, as mediators between scientists and their peers, but also as intermediaries between specialists and non-scientists; sometimes they also act as revolutionaries, calling into question the widely-accepted set of assumptions on which a theory has been built.

---

86 It is important to distinguish between analogy and metaphor. Let it be clear that a metaphor is a verbal construction that can translate an analogy, but by no means is it the only form of expression for an analogy which can be expressed non-metaphorically. Besides, it is not always clear what analogy is at the origin of a metaphor: in some cases, metaphors can be related to apparently conflicting analogies, which makes it all the more important to go beyond the mere verbal expression and trace the metaphor back to the historical context that gave rise to it.

5.1. Metaphor theory, science and economics

5.1.1. Metaphor: a controversial issue

The point of this section is to offer a brief account of the hotly-debated issue of metaphor. Since Aristotle, metaphor has always aroused either veneration or suspicion, and its ambivalence has been pointed out. Aristotle himself considered that logic, rhetoric and poetry were different realms, where language served different functions; accordingly, his positions on metaphor vary from one field to the other and illustrate both the qualities and shortcomings of metaphor. Depending on which of his works one is reading, different conclusions can be drawn, hence the sometimes contradictory interpretations that have been expressed. In the *Poetics*, which is a treatise about tragic and epic verse, metaphor is depicted as the prerogative of a minority of people endowed with a gift for inventiveness. Within the framework of the comparison theory, they have an ability to see resemblances that others cannot detect. Understandably, metaphor is associated with the field of literature and art, where it is particularly relevant as a means for embellishing reality, but its relevance is questioned when it comes to other fields since its potential for distorting the truth is pointed out and its irrational character denounced. By contrast, Aristotle's *Rhetoric* paints a somewhat different portrait of metaphor as a vehicle for understanding what is unknown through the lens of what is already familiar; its cognitive and pedagogical values are thus acknowledged. Obviously, Aristotle's "account of metaphor includes a distinction between the *coinage* of a metaphor and the *usage* of a metaphor" (Mahon 1999: 70). Still, in spite of the usefulness of metaphor underlined by Aristotle in some contexts, critics have warned against its use as a rhetorical device and against its suggestive power, insisting that metaphor may actually be used as a deliberate means to influence, persuade and manipulate people. In addition, critics have pointed out that the choice of a particular metaphor automatically highlights certain aspects while leaving others in the shadows, which means ignoring or hiding part of reality. The risk certainly does exist that the lens through which researchers are going to look into problems will distort what they observe: the biased approach will prevent them from envisaging other angles that might have yielded more appropriate solutions. For an economist, the parallel with forgone opportunities and "opportunity cost" is obvious.

In the seventeenth century, well-known for its rhetorical flourish, philosophers based their arguments against metaphor on Aristotle's functional distinction. In reaction to the exaggeration that was common in the writings of the time, they aimed at a transparent scientific language of observation, free from ambiguity. Locke's attack on rhetoric and its stylistic figures is best illustrated in his famous *Essay Concerning Human Understanding* (1690):

> [...] if we would speak of things as they are, we must allow that all the art of rhetoric, besides order and clearness; all the artificial and figurative application of words eloquence hath invented, are for nothing else but to insinuate wrong ideas, move the passions, and thereby mislead the judgment; and so indeed are perfect cheats: and therefore, however laudable or allowable oratory may render them in harangues and popular addresses, they are certainly, in all discourses that pretend to inform or instruct, wholly to be avoided; and where truth and knowledge are concerned, cannot but be thought a great fault, either of the language or person that makes use of them. (Book 3, Chapter 10, 34)

Other critics argue that metaphors can be dispensed with since the ideas they convey can surely be stated literally; the advocates of the substitution theory have therefore advised against using metaphors. This argument, however, is debatable, as it would often take a long paraphrase to express what a condensed metaphor can synthesise so powerfully. Besides, a literal paraphrase, if and when possible, can only be produced *ex post facto*, i.e. once the metaphor has filled its role of providing new insight. Metaphor can be likened to a ladder which one needs to climb to embrace new horizons (Wittgenstein 1966): only after the new landscape has been seen can one kick the ladder away. Undeniably, metaphor is particularly useful as a facilitator for thinkers and researchers who venture into new, virgin territory; without it, they might not be able to approach problems from a particular angle and to think differently. In this respect, the heuristic role of metaphor is irreplaceable. The advocates of metaphor have emphasised its iconicity and underlined that metaphor does not have a merely emotive or decorative function: it plays an indispensable role as a cognitive tool. Richards (1936) and Black (1962) have developed an interactive model of metaphor whereby the interactions between the "tenor" and "vehicle" or "target domain" and "import domain" give rise to new insights that no literal equivalent could yield. According to the modern cognitive approach (Fauconnier and Turner 1998), beyond the enriching perspective offered by interaction, metaphor can even open up new mental spaces and thereby stimulate new approaches and potential discoveries. Metaphor is also irreplaceable if one considers that it can play a catachrestic role (Black 1962; Boyd 1993) in some instances, filling a lexical or terminological void. Croft and Cruse (2005) regard metaphor as an active, dynamic process of meaning formation. It is essential to realise that natural language, which was first used for referring to objects or basic activities, has relatively limited resources, especially when it comes to supporting abstract thought: metaphor can therefore represent added resources to enrich language, by simply activating secondary meanings. It can thus be viewed as a means by which language develops and thought is enriched:

> Metaphor is a trope through which new vocabulary is created. By means of it, our conceptual grasp of a subject matter (referent) is enhanced by the use of a term with a well established context of use, and thus an existing deep grammar and set of associated commonplaces. A term used metaphorically is a term used in a new context to express a belief for which there is no existing vocabulary. In using a metaphor we are not comparing the subjects of the attribution of the term in the old and the new contexts, i.e. looking for similarities and differences between the old and the new extensions of the term. We are not acquainted with the referent of the term in the new context. But perhaps from theory we know some of the things we want to say about it. We are illuminating the new subject by virtue of the existing intension of the displaced term. In the new context that intension will be modified through the exigencies of the new conditions for its uses. In this way, through metaphor, new vocabulary can be created within the existing structure of language, so securing the intelligibility of the term in its new context of use. (Harré 1986: 77)

The opposing positions expressed by the abundant literature on metaphor can be summarised as follows: on the one hand, metaphor is denounced as an abuse of language that obfuscates the truth, a deceptive ornament that disguises the literal and corrupts thinking (Hobbes [1651]1962); on the other, it is hailed as a "fountain of meaning" (Grey 2000), a dynamic phenomenon essential to creative thought and discovery.

5.1.2. Science and metaphor

It is no surprise that the above-mentioned debate should be reflected in the position of scientists towards metaphor, and Aristotle himself demanded that metaphor be eliminated from the discourse of natural science. Those who consider that science must deal with facts and be rational logically advise against the use of metaphors. Thomas Sprat's *History of the Royal Society*[87], which acted as the United Kingdom's Academy of Sciences, reveals the Society's concerns with its members' discourse in a very telling manner:

> There is one thing more, about which the Society has been most solicitous, the manner of their Discourse [...] They have therefore been most rigorous in putting in execution [...] a constant resolution to reject all the amplifications, digressions, and swellings of style, to return back to the primitive purity and shortness [...] They have exacted from all their members a close, naked, natural way of speaking; positive expressions, clear senses, a native easiness bringing all things as near the mathematical plainness as they can. (1667, part II, section xx)

Yet nineteenth-century scholars and thinkers considered that metaphor "inheres in the man of science as well as in the artist or the poet, and [that] it cannot be suppressed" (Ward 1897: 258). One cannot deny the stimulating, essential role of metaphor in theory construction, its "creative function [...] in the nascent phase of the scientific imagination" (Holton 1984: 96): "[Out of metaphors] many new thoughts have

---

87 The Royal Society's full name was "The Royal Society of London for Improving Natural Knowledge"; its motto "*Nullius in verba*" which can be translated as "Take nobody's word for it" insists that its members were expected to establish facts from experiments.

arisen, and new areas of subject matter have been developed" (Sutton 1994: 64)[88]. It is important to realise that although scientists do not always acknowledge the role played by metaphors when they report the results of their research, metaphors may not have been absent from the process that led to new findings. Clearly, metaphor plays a heuristic role by offering new perspectives to the researcher who can then explore paths that they would not have investigated otherwise. It is worth noting, of course, that not all metaphors are heuristic, and that a heuristic metaphor is only the starting point of an inquiry. Its potential is not revealed at once to the researcher and the connections between one domain and another have to be tested. Schumpeter referred to such probing as "a pre-analytic cognitive act" (1954: 41). Of course, in the process, researchers may correct their initial hunch if they realise that the analogies are inadequate or "negative" and fail to yield productive, fertile metaphors (Hesse 1966: 8).

Even those who contend that metaphor is unscientific admit to the benefits of metaphor in educational settings, in terms of what Kuhn (1993) calls "exegetical metaphors". Though these represent a separate category, they are known to every scientist and researcher whose education in the domain has integrated them: these metaphors are relied on to help generation after generation grasp the theoretical underpinnings of science. In this respect, they play a very important role in shaping minds and elaborating a common ground of foundational knowledge. Accordingly, "it does not seem irrational to state that a scientific field not only reproduces itself through metaphor, but also evolves and is enriched thanks to metaphors, since metaphorical association provides a conceptual seed which may grow into a new discovery or theory" (Resche 2012: 80). Since scientific fields are not immune to influence from other domains, metaphor seems to facilitate cross-fertilisation: thinking of one domain in terms of another helps the scientist and researcher consider problems from a new angle. Metaphor therefore contributes to theoretical dynamics. Lakoff and Johnson (1984: 193) have labelled metaphor "imaginative rationality", an apparent oxymoron pointing out the possibility of reconciling science and metaphor. It should be clear by now that metaphor holds a

88 Quoted by Cortezzi and Jin (1999: 154).

legitimate place in the discourse of specialists and should not be considered only for educational purposes or in the popularisation of science (Henderson 1982, 1994; Klamer 2003).

5.1.3. Economics and metaphor

The case of economics is particularly interesting as far as metaphor is concerned: as underlined in Chapter 3, economists long strove after recognition and did their utmost to establish a niche alongside sciences that were deemed more rational and worthy of respect. Yet, unlike other scientists, economists can neither test their hypotheses in the real world nor conduct their experiments in laboratories. They are compelled to compensate for this handicap by devising models, writing equations and drawing graphs, all of which are illustrations that economic thinking is at root metaphorical (McCloskey 1992: 12). Milton Friedman (1953) himself underlined the importance of "as if" in economic reasoning. The notion of "model" is relevant in the field of metaphor, especially when it comes to metaphors reflecting a specific worldview in a scientific community. As Toulmin (1953: 39) underlines, a good model must be suggestive and exhibit "systematic deployability": a fertile metaphor, able to trigger creative power, is therefore required. However, if science needs metaphors, not all metaphors are indispensable in science. Some metaphors just serve for clarification and their omission would not affect reasoning; they are just used as tools to help a lay audience picture an intricate concept. Such pedagogical metaphors are incidental, but not essential. Heuristic metaphors play a more influential role in the elaboration of science, as already mentioned, while at a deeper, more fundamental level, theory-constitutive metaphors, a term coined by Boyd ([1979] 1993: 486), represent "an irreplaceable part of the linguistic machinery of a scientific theory". Scientists use them to express "theoretical claims for which no adequate literal paraphrase is known".

It is important to make clear, though, that in spite of the hierarchy, so-to-speak, between these different classes of metaphors, used in different settings and for different purposes, the boundaries between these categories are not always hard-and-fast. At the origin of a theory-constitutive metaphor lies a heuristic approach, but a new heuristic metaphor, within the wider frame of a theory-constitutive metaphor, can help the researcher address a problem in a novel way and guide his steps towards new solutions. It can also help him name his discovery and, once things have become clear, the metaphor that opened up new horizons may then be used to get the message across to his colleagues in the scientific community. Finally, it will reach a larger community of students and the general public when the metaphor serves as a basis for explaining the theory. A continuum between theory-constitutive, heuristic, and pedagogical metaphors is thus highly likely. Adam Smith's *INVISIBLE HAND* offers us a perfect example of a metaphor that fills different functions and thus illustrates the continuum. Its heuristic role helped its author imagine the market mechanism; its iconicity lies in its synthetic power which avoids resorting to a long sentence to describe the self-regulating power of the market; it has filled a terminological gap, performing a catachrestic role; it is also an exegetical metaphor that is mentioned in every textbook and has become familiar to every student of economics. Last but not least, it can also be considered as a theory-constitutive metaphor:

> Theory-constitutive scientific metaphors become, when they are successful, the property of the entire scientific community, and variations on them are explored by hundreds of scientific authors without their interactive quality being lost. (Boyd 1993: 487)

The *INVISIBLE HAND* metaphor has given birth to a school of thought and branched out into other metaphors over time, inspiring many researchers and theorists. Though the term itself may be considered as lexicalised, it should not be considered as a "dead metaphor". Actually, rather than use the term coined by Turbayne (1962), it might be more accurate to use the adjective "dormant", for the Invisible Hand metaphor has been revived to inspire new research and give birth to other terms, in various economic contexts, as illustrated in Table 12.

The dead hand	Lindsey, B. 2002.	It is "the dead hand of the old collectivism dream".
The ethereal hand	Donaldson, L. 1990	"The Ethereal Hand: Organisational Economics and Management Theory". (*The Academy of Management Review* 1990)
The grabbing hand	Frye, T. and Schleifer, A. 1998. Schleifer, A. and Vishny, R. 1999.	The grabbing hand view asserts that individuals working in the public sector act in their own self-interest, like any other individual. What is at stake is applied public-choice economics.
The green invisible hand	Emblemsvåg, J. 2003.	Environmental management strategy: an environmental equivalent of money is needed to make the invisible hand "green".
The helping hand	Hopkin, J. and Rodríguez-Pose, A. 2007.	It refers to the role of government in correcting market distortions or failures.
The vanishing hand	Langlois, R.N. 2003	It describes a management revolution towards vertical disintegration, a reverse trend from that described by Chandler.
The visible hand	Chandler, A.D 1990	The visible hand was that of managerial coordination of multiple stages of production, which had replaced Smith's invisible hand of the market.
The handshake (between visible and invisible hands)	Larsson, R. 1993.	It refers to the idea that there are different institutional forms for coordinating economic activity: the invisible hand of the market, the visible hand of hierarchy in the firm, and a combination of those two forms, which results from an interorganisational form of coordination.
The transparent glove	Florini, A. M. 1999.	To promote more financial, environmental and ethical transparency: the "thick glove" of rules, norms, and institutions, including governments seems to be "opaque, obscuring flows of information essential to

		the efficient and equitable functioning of both markets and the national and international institutions that regulate them". (1999 :1)
The invisible fist	Brown, A. 1999. Heinberg, R. 2011.	a) Competition in free market economies: A new era of relentless competition has emerged, turning the "invisible hand" of laissez-faire into an invisible fist. (Brown, A. 1999) b) Limited resources and economic growth: The "invisible hand" of economics became the invisible fist, pounding down world economic growth to match the limitations of crude oil production. (Kenneth Deffeyes, petroleum geologist, quoted in Richard Heinberg's Chapter 3 of *The End of Growth*)
The invisible handshake	Okun, A. 1980.	A term coined by economist Arthur Okun to mean that he argued that social and historical forces – the invisible handshake – often prevent the invisible hand from working.
The invisible foot	Brook, W. and Magee, S. P. 1985.	Government action to benefit particular pressure groups is "the invisible foot".
The green invisible hand / Grafting a green thumb on the invisible hand	Nadeau, R. 2003. Hartley, P. and Porter, M. G. 1990.	The metaphor refers to environmental considerations in management, to environmental economics and to green investing.

Table 12. Offshoots of the Invisible Hand metaphor.

Though some of these metaphors were coined and used by only one researcher, they may have inspired new research: for example, by using the phrase "ethereal hand" to evoke Adam Smith's "Invisible Hand', Donaldson reviews organisational economics as a theoretical framework for studying organisations.

Besides the most often quoted *INVISIBLE HAND* metaphor, the language of economics abounds with metaphorical terms that are worth inquiring into: they can provide much information as to the scientific domains which economics has borrowed from in order to structure itself. *INFLATION, GROWTH, THE ECONOMIC CYCLE, EQUILIBRIUM, FINANCIAL INSTRUMENTS, LIQUIDITY, CAPITAL INFLOWS* and *OUTFLOWS* are but a few examples of terms borrowed from physics or biology. Both veins were present in the original *INVISIBLE HAND* metaphor and they have surfaced at different times or concurrently as economic theory has developed. For purposes of readability and clarity, they will be presented separately, but have been intertwining since Adam Smith.

5.2. Metaphorical terms as windows on theory

Metaphorical terms should retain our attention as the expressions of deeper, broader metaphors underpinning theory and translating a specific conceptual scheme or a "disciplinary matrix" (Kuhn [1962] 1970) that may have prevailed at one time, or been challenged by another at other times. These "root metaphors" (Pepper 1942), or "megametaphors" as they might be called, should be considered in relation to the analogies that were introduced in Chapter 2. Essentially, these metaphors must be seen through the lens of the period when they were introduced in a given field, then adopted and adapted. In other words, though they may have served to enrich other domains as well, they must be considered in the light of how they have been adapted in this given field. In this perspective, Borges was right to qualify his suggestion of universal history as "the history of a handful of metaphors" when he wrote (1964: 192): "It may be that universal history is the history of different intonations given a handful of metaphors". Actually, much depends on how a specific domain interprets and deploys these metaphors, for what reasons, at what time, to what end. Likewise, referring to Pepper's taxonomy of four world hypotheses (1942) with their characteristic metaphors – organicism, mechanism, formism and contextualism – one should concentrate on how economics has interpreted and developed its conceptual scientific frames and models. Scientific megametaphors cannot be dealt with in the same way that Lakoff and Johnson (1980) approach experiential protometaphors which, according to them, shape our thoughts in everyday life. Such systematic analysis would lead the SVE researcher to pass by all the historical influences that have been at play in the making of economics without seeing them and to entirely miss the point. There would be a real risk of hasty conclusions and superficial understanding of theoretical underpinnings, a risk that can be avoided by accepting the invitation of metaphorical terms to investigate the circumstances which led to their being adopted as terms.

5.2.1. The mechanistic mega-metaphor in economics

As mentioned in Chapter 3, Adam Smith is considered as the father of "modern economics". His *INVISIBLE HAND* metaphor can be said, among other interpretations (Resche 2005), to have initiated a mechanistic, clockwork vision of the economy. Later generations of economists in the nineteenth century then tried to imitate physics in order to establish the credibility of economics as a science. Well-known economists like Pareto and Fisher thought of economics as physical mechanics and suggested the concordance tables presented in Chapter 3, in which terms from the source domain were adapted for economics according to the isomorphism that was perceived by the authors. The concept of equilibrium served as a foundation for price theory and did indeed help to establish economics as a science. Francis Y. Edgeworth, who advocated the development of a more mathematically structured economics in the late 1800s, sought to measure utility. His idea of designing a *HEDONIMETER*, an instrument that would give an idea of the metrics of happiness – as mentioned in Chapter 4 (4.2.2) – was rooted in a mechanistic view of economics.

Other machines were imagined by economists to represent economic mechanisms. Quite tellingly, while working on his 1891 Yale doctoral dissertation, Irving Fisher sought to illustrate his theory on price determination. To this purpose, he imagined and built a machine consisting of a wooden tank with what looked like a flotilla of small wooden cisterns connected by a series of levers (Figure 2).

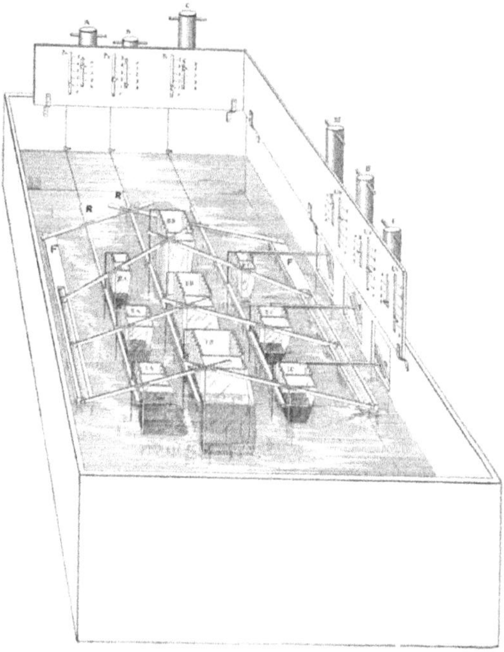

Fig. 2. Fisher's Price Machine
<http://3.bp.blogspot.com/_UKD6iwMrQmQ/SiZ_3lncLpI/AAAAAAAAASo/43Vszi aOy_s/s1600-h/Price-Machine.jpg>

By adjusting those levers, taking into account data on income, supplies, etc., prices could be read off scales on the side of the main tank. A picture of his more sophisticated second prototype can also be seen online[89], with pumps, levers, and pipes. It offers a concrete representation of the metaphor of *THE ECONOMY AS A MACHINE*, a vivid translation of the way theorists were able to represent the economy at the time.

Fisher's machine was an ancestor of the Phillips Machine, another good example of the mechanistic view of economics, which can now be seen at the Science Museum in London. Alban William Phillips, a New Zealand engineer turned economist, is now better remem-

89 <http://homepage.newschool.edu/~het/profiles/image/fishpic2.gif>

bered for the Phillips curve[90] but his machine was designed as a hydraulic model of income flow in the national economy. Actually, the idea first came to Phillips in a paper he wrote in 1949[91] as he was studying in his final year at the London School of Economics. He then devised the diagram reproduced in Figure 3 as a circular model and built his machine, described as a hydro-mechanical analogue computer, which he first demonstrated at the school in November 1949. The Phillips machine also illustrates the continuum between theory-constitutive metaphors, heuristic metaphors and pedagogical metaphors, since it was used until 1992 as a teaching device at LSE first, and then in other universities when improved versions were built. The goal of the machine was to illustrate the impact on total national income of a number of factors including taxes, government spending, imports, exports, saving and investment. When the pumps were switched on, coloured water, representing the movement of money, ran through tanks, pipes, sluices and valves. Then the levels settled, pulleys were set in motion and a pen plotter would trace the results on paper boards. The point was to help understand that economic factors interact: thus, valves and sluices could be used for altering the volume of foreign trade, the tax burden, or the level of investment.

90 A graph showing the trade-off between unemployment and inflation.

91 A more formal and detailed paper, "Mechanical Models in Economic Dynamics", was published in *Economica* in August 1950. A few months later, thanks to his paper and the impressive performance of the machine, Phillips was appointed as Assistant Lecturer in Economics at the LSE.

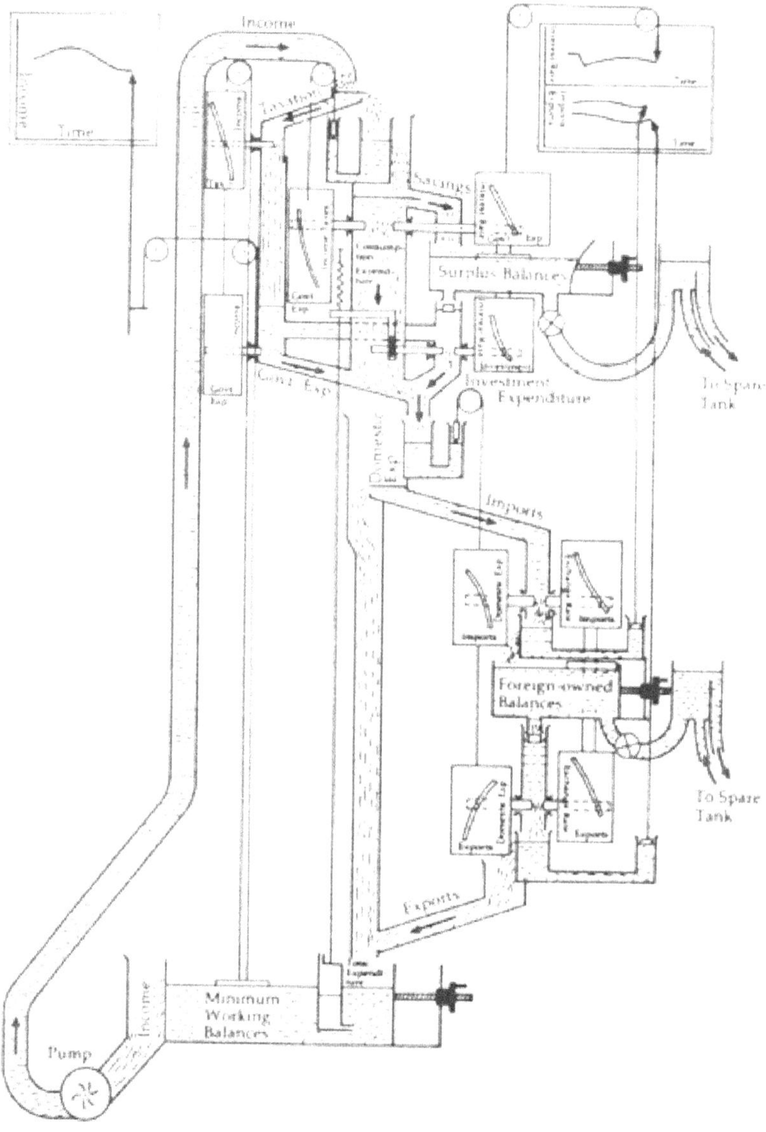

Fig. 3. The Phillips machine

Though the Phillips machine is just a museum piece now, it is interesting to relate its system to metaphorical terms and expressions which are still commonly used today, such as *TO INJECT MONEY INTO THE SYSTEM, A MONETARY INJECTION, TO PUMP MONEY INTO THE SYSTEM, LIQUIDITY TRAPS* or on the contrary, *POOLS OF LIQUIDITY*. Many of the terms with a liquid metaphorical ring – *FLOWS, CAPITAL INFLOWS AND OUTFLOWS, LIQUID ASSETS*, as well as *LEAKAGES* – can thus be linked to the hydraulic representation of the economy embodied by the Phillips machine.

Interestingly, the circular flow diagrams (Figure 4) that are used as a pedagogical metaphor in economic textbooks and are thus familiar to students of economics can be traced back to the Phillips machine. However, as explained in Section 5.2.2 below, circular flow diagrams may also have been influenced by a biological view of the economy: suffice it to state for the moment that they are visual models of the economy, showing how money flows through markets among households and firms (Mankiw 2004: 829).

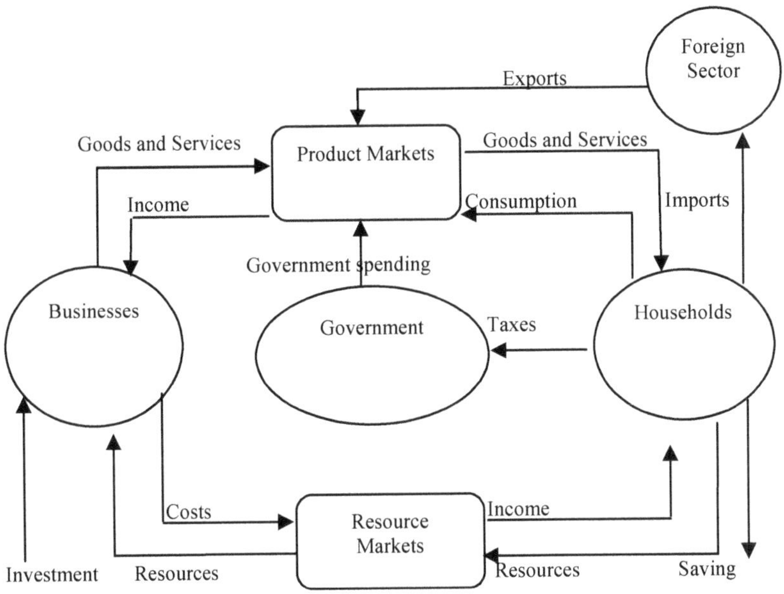

Fig. 4. A full circular flow diagram, with leakages and injections

In Figure 4, leakages are illustrated in terms of savings, taxes and imports, and the money injected comes from investment, government spending and exports. For the economy to achieve equilibrium, total spending must equal total output: all income must be spent by households, businesses and government.

Another instance of the hydraulic physics metaphor can be found in the expression used by commentators of Federal Reserve Chairman Ben Bernanke's monetary policy in response to the recent financial crisis and economic contraction: according to them, his measures translated a consistent "hydraulic Keynesian economic philosophy"[92]. By this, they were referring to his decision to inject money into the system; his loose monetary policy was of course motivated by his fear of liquidity traps, falling demand, unemployment, and inflation. His own comments on monetary policy decisions in his 2010 semiannual speeches are permeated with terms echoing the hydraulic mechanistic metaphor[93]:

> Over the past year, the Federal Reserve has employed a wide array of *tools* to promote economic recovery and preserve price stability. [...] The Federal Reserve's ability *to inject liquidity* into the financial system is critical for preserving financial stability and for supporting depositories' key role in meeting the ongoing credit needs of firms and households. (Semiannual Monetary Policy Report to the Congress, before the Committee on Financial Services, US House of Representatives, Washington, D.C. February 24, 2010)

> First, in response to the periods of intense *illiquidity* and dysfunction in financial markets that characterised the crisis, the Federal Reserve undertook a range of measures and set up emergency programs designed to provide *liquidity* to financial institutions and markets in the form of fully secured, mostly short-term loans. Over time, these programs helped to stem the panic and to restore normal functioning in a number of key financial markets, supporting *the flow of credit* to the economy. [...] Two *tools* for *draining* reserves from the system are being developed and tested and will be ready when needed. (Semiannual Monetary Policy Report to the Congress, before the Committee on Banking, Housing, and Urban Affairs, US Senate, Washington, D.C. July 21, 2010).

---

92 The term "hydraulic Keynesianism" was coined by Alan Coddington (1983).

93 Emphasis added.

Had the Phillips machine still been in use, it would have been possible to reproduce Bernanke's decisions and visualise their potential impact.

Other manifestations of the mechanistic view are translated into such metaphorical terms as MONETARY TRANSMISSION MECHANISM, EQUILIBRIUM, ELASTICITY OF DEMAND, FINANCIAL INSTRUMENTS, LEVERAGE, MARKET FORCES, AUTOMATIC STABILIZERS or FRICTIONAL UNEMPLOYMENT. Their currency can only encourage the observer to inquire into their motivation, and such research inevitably leads to the original theory-constitutive mechanistic metaphor. Once the context that has generated them has been explored, it is possible to observe how surface metaphors can also be related to the original scientific frame. The metaphors used by decision-makers and commentators in the realm of macroeconomics and more precisely as regards economic policy become clearer and more logical; the machine metaphor is often appropriated through the prism of the ECONOMIC ENGINE. It then quite logically branches out into steam engines or motor vehicles, cars, planes, boats, etc. The deployment of the metaphor gives rise to real economic terms like OVERHEATING, as well as expressions derived from the engine and vehicle metaphors. The DRIVER IN THE SEAT may have to REDUCE SPEED by STEPPING ON THE BRAKES to prevent the engine from OVERHEATING and eventually EXPLODING. But if he drives too slowly, the vehicle may "stall", which is not the goal. In cases when the economy is thought of in terms of a plane, the pilot of the plane has to avoid a ROUGH LANDING and a BUMPY RIDE, and ensure a safe, SOFT LANDING. All this requires FINE-TUNING and the "mechanic" must use all the MONETARY or FINANCIAL INSTRUMENTS available to avoid a CRASH.

It might be more difficult to understand the meaning of the GOLDILOCKS ECONOMY metaphor if one is unaware of the underpinning mechanistic view. Obviously, the reader will remember the fairy tale of Goldilocks and the three bears: the little girl found refuge in the house of the bears, tasted the porridge in the three bowls on the table and preferred that which was "neither too hot, nor too cold, but just right". This metaphor refers to the state of the US economy in the mid-to-late 1990s, when the "New Economy", boosted by the new technologies sector, was "just right". The GOLDILOCKS ECONOMY thus refers to an ideal situation, where no policy measures are needed for boosting macroeconomic performance to avoid recession or for helping the economic engine cool down in order to avoid triggering inflation.

It should be clear to the reader by now that mechanical physics has played an important role as a model and a source of inspiration for economics: for the linguist, many basic terms in economics retain the metaphorical flavour that enables them to be traced back to the original theory-constitutive metaphor. However, it is important to realize – as emphasised by Marshall (1898) – that an analogy that may have been valid at one point may no longer be so, especially as the source domain may itself evolve. It is therefore important to consider that the metaphors prompted by analogies are not static, but dynamic processes and to take into consideration the context in which they were envisaged and the influences that were brought to bear on the theories under construction at the time:

> It has been well said that analogies may help one into the saddle, but are encumbrances on a long journey. It is well to know when to introduce them, it is even better to know when to stop them off. Two things may resemble one another in their initial stages; and a comparison of the two may then be helpful: but after a while they diverge; and then the comparison begins to confuse and warp the judgment. There is a fairly close analogy between the earlier stages of economic reasoning and the devices of physical statics. But is there an equally serviceable analogy between the later stages of economic reasoning and the methods of physical dynamics? I think not. I think that in the later stages of economics better analogies are to be got from biology than from physics; and consequently, that economic reasoning should start on methods analogous to those of physical statics, and should gradually become more biological in tone". (Marshall, 1898: 39)

It is of course difficult for scientists to free themselves from patterns that have influenced them and framed research for several generations and suddenly to adopt a different mindset. The history of economic thought shows that though Marshall called for a new source of inspiration that seemed more adequate then, he also realised that people may not be ready yet. As stressed by the Latin subtitle to Marshall's book on *Principles of Economics* (*Natura non facit saltum*) nature does not proceed by leaps, but undergoes a process of slow evolution. This also applies to metaphorical veins: one may seem to gain ground and prevail over another at a given period, and then recede, only to surge again at a later period. It all depends on how open to new findings the scientific community is or how influential the former generation's metaphors still are. Several sources of inspiration may then be at play at a given period.

5.2.2. The natural, organic, biological megametaphor in economics

Long before Marshall mentioned that economic reasoning should "become more biological in tone", the paths of economic thinking and biology had crossed. Medieval medical thinking and the theory of Humours have already been mentioned in section 3.1.1. From that period on, the representation of the economy as a human body seemed quite logical, the ultimate goal being for this body to be in good health. This view of the economy explains why policy-makers are seen as doctors in charge of finding the right "remedies" to "cure" the "ailing economy". Metaphorical terms such as *RECOVERY*, or more surface expressions such as *A HEALTHY ECONOMY* are linked to this root metaphor. In fact, they stem from the deeper biological theory-constitutive metaphor, even though the link may not be explicit. This is what Steen (1999: 82-84) calls "implicit metaphors", simply because "the literal referent is not expressed". Seventeenth-century mercantilists as well as eighteenth-century physiocrats were also attracted by biological metaphors in their conception of the theory of production and exchange. Quesnay's representation of the circulation of riches in the economy as a closed circuit, similar to the circulation of blood in the human body, undoubtedly owes to his being a surgeon before turning to economic matters. The reader may remember another closed-circuit metaphor illustrated by the machines in the former section, and rightly wonder whether the liquid metaphors stem from the mechanistic or the biological metaphorical veins. Actually, odd though it may seem, they stem from both in that the scientific physiology Quesnay was familiar with in his time was a kind of mechanistic physiology, which accounts for the mixing of the body metaphor with a conceptualisation of the body as a hydraulic machine (Mouton, 2012).

More generally speaking, the economy was thought of as an economy of nature. Thus, Smith's *INVISIBLE HAND* could be interpreted as a vision of a clockwork economy, accounting for the mechanistic vision, or as the sign that, behind the clockwork was the clockmaker, who could be God, Providence or Nature. Depending on the interpretation, different visions of the economy could be developed, expressed by different metaphors: on the one hand, static metaphors inspired from physics, with forces coming into play to achieve equilibrium, and, on the other hand, dynamic metaphors supporting the idea of a natural order.

In the next century, many intellectuals were attracted by the notion of evolution that seemed to permeate many spheres of knowledge and ensure progress:

> Whether it be in the development of the Earth, in the development of Life upon its surface, in the development of Society, of Government, of Manufactures, of Commerce, of Language, Literature, Science, Art, this same evolution of the simple into the complex, through successive differentiations, holds throughout. From the earliest traceable cosmical changes down to the latest results of civilisation, we shall find that the transformation of the homogeneous into the heterogeneous is that in which progress essentially consists. (Spencer 1891: 10)

Evolutionary economics was undoubtedly influenced by the nineteenth-century notion of development. It was, of course, based on what knowledge was available at that time in biology, where progress made huge strides. Parallels were drawn between societies or organisations and organisms, including human beings; and the notions of *BIRTH, GROWTH, MATURITY* and *DEATH*, often used for describing the world of business, are of course natural expansions of the theory-constitutive metaphor. The *LIFE CYCLE* notion is to be related to the theory of the firm as explained by Marshall:

> [...] we may read a lesson from the young trees of the forest as they struggle upwards through the benumbing shade of their older rivals. Many succumb on the way, and a few only survive; those few become stronger with every year, they get a larger share of light and air with every increase of their height, and at last in their turn they tower above their neighbors, and seem as though they would grow on forever, and for ever become stronger as they grow. But they

> do not. One tree will last longer in full vigor and attain a greater size than another; but sooner or later age tells on them all. Though the taller ones have a better access to light and air than their rivals, they gradually lose vitality; and one after another they give place to others, which, though of less material strength, have on their side the vigor of youth. And as with the growth of trees, so was it with the growth of businesses as a general rule before the great recent development of vast joint-stock companies, which often stagnate, but do not readily die. Now that rule is far from universal, but it still holds in many industries and trades. Nature still presses on the private business by limiting the length of the life of its original founders, and by limiting even more narrowly that part of their lives in which their faculties retain full vigor. And so, after a while, the guidance of the business falls into the hands of people with less energy and less creative genius, if not with less active interest in its prosperity. If it is turned into a joint-stock company, it may retain the advantages of division of labor, of specialised skill and machinery: it may even increase them by a further increase of its capital; and under favourable conditions it may secure a permanent and prominent place in the work of production. But it is likely to have lost so much of its elasticity and progressive force that the advantages are no longer exclusively on its side in its competition with younger and smaller rivals. ([1920] 1961, Book 4, Chapter XIII/1)

Though the biological metaphors were no longer popular by the late 1920s, they were revived in the 1950s and have since gained ground in the new branches of economics. Whether one considers management or the economy at large, particular markets or economic policy, biological metaphors are commonly used. They entail personification of institutions and markets, as well as deployment of medical metaphors, or natural ones, as illustrated in the few examples below.

In the field of management, metaphorical terms borrowed from biology have changed the vision of firms today: from rigid architectures, they have evolved into *AGILE ORGANISATIONS*, with teams functioning as cells that can grow and shrink according to the needs of the "body". In the early 2000s, Booz & Company introduced the organisational DNA framework, a metaphor based on a parallel between a company's "genetic material" and molecular DNA (Neilson *et al.* 2003: 3, 5):

> We like to use the familiar metaphor of DNA to codify the idiosyncratic characteristics of a company. Just as the double helix of DNA is held together by bonds between base pairs of four nucleotides, we describe the DNA of

> a living organisation as having four building blocks that, combined in myriad ways, define an organisation's distinct traits and behaviors. [...] DNA testing can be as valuable to corporate health as it has become to human health care. An analysis of a company's "genetic material" can isolate the underlying causes of and potential solutions to organisational dysfunctions, and even head off problems before they start.

It has recently been established that, since its introduction about a decade ago, the framework has been used by nearly 200,000 individuals to analyse and improve the health of their organisations:

> The organisational DNA framework is a vehicle for understanding the formal and informal elements that drive and constrain day-to-day behavior in your company. [...] [The four] building blocks [of organisational DNA ...] determine how an organisation executes – what changes it can make and what actions its members can take. The four bases are:
>
> - Decision rights and norms. The rules and practices that govern how actions in an organisation are shaped and focused.
> - Motivators and commitment. The values and principles that drive employee behaviour and engagement.
> - Information flow and mindsets. The patterns of thinking and communication that inform what people do in an organisation.
> - Organisational structure and networks. The links and connections that guide how people work with one another throughout the hierarchy.
>
> When put together, the formal sides of each organisational DNA base make up the official part of the organisation's operating model: decision rights, motivators and incentives, information-carrying channels and metrics, and the structure of reporting relationships (the organisation chart). (Kronenberg 2011)

According to Kronenberg, it is all the more important for companies to be aware of their own *ORGANISATIONAL DNA* as otherwise they risk unintentionally creating their own worst crises. Once they have spotted their flaws, they are better prepared to face problems. Each of the four pillars above can help diagnose weaknesses and remedy them before they reinforce one another and become a source of great problems.

Health depends on how fit and adaptable companies are, and *LEAN MANAGEMENT* has been introduced, as the corporate world realised that being overweight could be a handicap; accordingly, companies have been advised to *GET RID OF THE FAT* and to reduce their workforce. *DOWNSIZING* and *SLIMMING* have entered corporate management language, though excessive workforce reduction has been underlined as noxious: *CORPORATE ANOREXIA* is to be avoided if a firm wishes to take full advantage of recovery and regained activity. Innovation is encouraged and Research and Development departments are supposed to be *INCUBATORS* of new ideas. Likewise, areas where innovative firms are concentrated, such as Silicon Valley, are also referred to as incubators. Individual companies are personified and viewed as human bodies, with heads, organs and members. The metaphor is then broadly deployed: groups are perceived as families, with *PARENT COMPANIES* and *CHILD COMPANIES*. In some sectors of activity or countries, *INFANT INDUSTRIES* sometimes suffer from *TEETHING PROBLEMS* and have to be helped until they have grown in size and strength. *SEED MONEY* is sought by entrepreneurs as a means to kick-start their new companies. The *LIFE CYCLE* of products is now analysed in an effort to reduce pollution to a minimum while recycling as much as possible of the original product: thus, as a result of *LIFE-CYCLE ANALYSIS (LCA),* the *CRADLE-TO-CRADLE* concept has replaced the *CRADLE-TO-GRAVE* one to describe the production process. All these terms derive from the biological approach and are branches of the corresponding root metaphor.

The field of markets is not immune from the influence of biological or medical metaphors either. Stock markets are under constant scrutiny and policy-makers become doctors who regularly feel "the pulse" of the market in order to diagnose potential problems and administer the right remedies: a monetary injection in some cases, measures that will stop the fever in others, *STERILISATION*[94] when neces-

94 *STERILISATION* is "the method by which a central bank prevents balance-of-payments surpluses or deficits from affecting the domestic money supply. If there is a surplus in the balance of payments on current and capital accounts combined, this leads to a rise in the foreign exchange reserves, and an increase in the money supply. If the central bank does not want the money supply to increase, it can prevent this by selling securities so as to sterilize the cash inflow. Similarly, if there is a deficit in the balance of payments on current and capital accounts combined, this leads to a loss of foreign exchange reserves and a shrinkage in the money supply. If the central bank does not want the

sary. Currencies, like markets, are *STRONG* or *WEAK*; markets can be *ANAEMIC* or *DEPRESSED*; they can suffer from *PARALYSIS*, be on the verge of *COLLAPSE*; they can also *RALLY*. Investors may show no *APPETITE*. Markets may need to pause and *GO ON A DIET* in order to avoid *INDIGESTION*: accordingly, corporate or government stock issues have to be carefully timed, if they are to be well *ABSORBED*. In the 2008 financial crisis, a *SUPPORT SYSTEM* or *STIMULUS PLAN* was resorted to in order to *REVITALISE* the economy. Federal Reserve chairman Ben Bernanke himself made sure that there would be enough liquidity in the system and that credit would still be available for creditworthy consumers, stating: "credit is the *LIFEBLOOD* of the economy". *HEMORRHAGE* is commonly used when referring to capital flight. Financial terms like *THE LIFE OF AN OPTION*, letting an option *DIE*, or *MATURITY DATE* are also examples of biological metaphors.

The biological metaphor, as previously mentioned, can also branch out into the Nature metaphor, which itself can be subdivided into two different paths: the natural elements at play and, most importantly, the efforts made to survive in a dangerous world; the latter are expressed in terms of competition and logically deployed though the themes of battle and war. The first path, referring to natural elements, leads to crises being described as *STORMS, TSUNAMIS, MAELSTROMS* that are devastating to the point that nobody can really feel safe, no matter how strong they are. The liquid element is of course often present in metaphors such as ships caught in a storm at sea: hence the frequent use of the metaphor *A RISING TIDE LIFTS ALL BOATS* in times of economic crisis. Captains have to steer clear of obstacles and do their best to find a safe haven. If the ship has a hole, they may also have to prevent it from sinking by bailing water out, hence the economic term *BAILOUT*. Companies gone bankrupt are logically described as *GONE UNDER* or sinking and the term *SUNK COSTS* refers to "costs that cannot be recovered" (Mankiw 2004: 834): in other words, they are lost forever. In another context, that of currency turmoil, investors will find refuge in *SAFE-HAVEN CURRENCIES* that will help them weather the storm, or countries will peg their own currencies to an *ANCHOR CURRENCY*, in an

money supply to fall, it can sterilize the cash outflow by buying securities". (The Oxford Dictionary of Economics) effort to discipline their economy. Such metaphors permeate economic discourse, not only that of analysts and commentators, but also that of economists themselves: "Economists set themselves too easy, too useless a task if *in tempestuous seasons*, they can only tell us when the *storm* is long past, the *ocean will be flat*"[95] (Keynes, quoted by Mankiw 1998: 355). The metaphor of the ship Economy caught in a storm at sea, whose captain must steer clear of the rocks and other obstacles that could cause his ship to sink, has become quite usual, even among laureates of the Sveriges Riksbank Prize in Economic Sciences in Memory of Alfred Nobel:

> The captain [...] has also directed the helmsman to take his hand off the tiller so that, unimpeded by an attempt to steer it, the ship could sail in the direction in which the wind happens to propel it. The waters that we are about to enter are much more treacherous than those we were navigating up until now.[96] (Leontief, quoted by Galbraith 1990: 221)

> This is the season for reviewing the course of the US ship Economy and reconsidering the direction in which its officers are steering it. By general agreement, course corrections are urgently required right now. The captain, his navigators, and the helmsman are getting plenty of advice from the crew and the passengers, and from other vessels in the convoy, too. But the Kibitzers do not agree on the destination. Some want to continue straight ahead on the route to "price level flats", cold and rocky though it may be: they urge the captain to resist the lure of detours and side excursions lest we lose our way. Some are nostalgically preoccupied with reaching once more the comfortable high ground of "long bond island". Others say that if the ship is just steered out of the "red sea" into the "straights and narrows of black ink", all other destinations will be easily within reach. (Tobin[97], quoted by Galbraith 1990: 222)

Strong winds and "turbulence" can also endanger planes. Under such circumstances, the economy's pilot must then do his best to avoid a

---

95 Emphasis added.

96 Professor Wassily W. Leontief, of New York University, was awarded the Sveriges Riksbank Prize in Economic Sciences in Memory of Alfred Nobel in 1981. The quotation is an excerpt from his testimony in front of the Joint Economic Committee which held a hearing on January 19th, 1982.

97 Professor James Tobin, of Yale, was the Nobel Laureate for 1981. He also appeared as a witness before the Joint Economic Committee on January 19th, 1982.

CRASH: with little visibility, he has to have his eyes riveted on the instruments in front of him and instruct his passengers to fasten their seat belts, warning them that they may be in for a *HARD LANDING*.

The second path, battle and war, is particularly relevant when referring to competition, mergers and acquisitions, or takeovers, especially in case of unfriendly takeovers, where the "predator" hunts his "prey", as is the case in nature, and "bloodshed" is expected. The *RAIDER*[98] leads a "battle" and a pitiless war may ensue between the rival camps. Medieval warriors enter the stage, with *WHITE KNIGHTS*[99], *WHITE SQUIRES*[100], *BLACK KNIGHTS*[101], and *GREY KNIGHTS*[102]. There are *SLEEPING BEAUTIES*[103] and *CROWN JEWELS*[104] at stake. All sorts of defense techniques and weapons are used by the target company to protect itself: *SHARK REPELLENTS*[105] include *POISON PILLS*[106], *SUICIDE PILLS*[107], *LOBSTER*

---

98 In the context of a hostile takeover, a raider is an individual or a corporate investor who intends to take control of a target company.

99 When a target company is threatened by a raider, the white knight describes a company that makes a friendly takeover bid.

100 Quite similar to a "white knight", the squire makes a friendly offer; however, instead of purchasing a majority interest, he offers to buy a lesser stake in the target firm.

101 The same as a raider.

102 A grey knight is a third party waiting in the shadows in a corporate takeover with a view to taking advantage of any problems between the first bidder and the target company.

103 An attractive company that has not been approached by an acquiring company yet.

104 The most valuable part of a corporation, in terms of asset value and profitability. Crown jewels can be used by a target company as part of a defence strategy to deter any attack: for example, a specific clause could state that if a hostile takeover occurs, the company will be forced to sell its crown jewels.

105 Measures taken by a company to deter any hostile takeover attempt.

106 A strategy used by a company to make its stock less attractive to the predator. There are two types of disincentives: a "flip-in", which allows existing shareholders to buy more shares at a discount; a "flip-over", which allows stockholders to buy the predator's shares at a discounted price once the merger or takeover has taken place.

107 An extreme version of the poison pill that may lead the target company to make suicidal decisions and go bankrupt rather than be taken over. It is also called the "Jonestown Defense".

TRAPS[108], *SCORCHED EARTH POLICY*[109], *SAND BAGS*[110], *PAC MAN STRATEGY*[111]; the predator's strategy will consist in choosing the time of attack carefully (*A DAWN RAID*[112] or a *SATURDAY NIGHT SPECIAL*[113]), in making *A GODFATHER OFFER*[114], in choosing *A BEAR HUG*[115] or *A SWEETHEART DEAL*[116]. A third party or *YELLOW KNIGHT*[117] can enter the fray and use a *LADY MACBETH STRATEGY*[118]. As in nature, only the fittest is expected to survive.

---

108 Another defensive strategy, consisting in a provision preventing anyone with more than 10% ownership from converting convertible securities into voting stock.

109 In order to make the takeover unattractive to the acquirer, the targeted company liquidates its most valuable assets.

110 A stalling tactic used by management to deter an acquiring company.

111 The targeted company tries to take over the company that has made the hostile bid.

112 A corporate dawn raid is scheduled early in the morning, to take the targeted company by surprise. When the latter tries to react, the investor has already acquired a minority interest in the company. Once the dawn raid has succeeded, the raiding firm is expected to make a takeover bid to acquire the rest of the targeted company.

113 Many takeover bids are announced over the weekend in order to limit publicity.

114 An offer that is difficult to refuse because the acquisition price is extremely generous compared to the prevailing market price. Refusal by the target company's management risks triggering lawsuits or negative reactions on the part of shareholders.

115 A bear hug offer is usually made by an acquiring company to convince the targeted company's reluctant management to sell. The price offered per share stands at a premium over the real market price.

116 The terms of a sweetheart deal are usually so generous for the targeted company that the offer cannot be turned down.

117 A company that once made a takeover bid but finally opts for discussion rather than an aggressive move: it decides to discuss a merger with the target company.

118 A strategy whereby a third party pretends to act as a white knight to gain the target's trust, but then reveals its real self by joining hands with unfriendly bidders. It connotes treason, of course.

5.2.3. Intertwining metaphors

All the examples quoted above illustrate the important idea that theory-constitutive metaphors have not only inspired metaphorical terms that denote economic concepts, but have also made their way into semi-specialised discourse or discourse aimed at popularising economics by means of surface metaphors. This has been made possible because metaphorical terms have played their role as intermediaries and influenced further expansion of either mechanistic, biological, physiological, medical or natural metaphors. Approaching metaphors in economics through metaphorical terms thus yields a more complete picture of the metaphorical networks at play, and avoids erroneous or superficial conclusions that might result from the simplistic observation that metaphors stem from our daily experience and cognitive schemata. For example, the explanation quoted by Temmerman (2000) and provided by Liebert (1995) of the origin of the metaphor *CIRCULATION OF MONEY* seems to overlook the history of economic thinking and the impact of hydraulic physics and fluid dynamics on economic theory, on the one hand, and of biology in terms of body fluids, on the other. It simply considers the cognitive model of a linear waterway with a beginning, a trajectory and an end, while the economic concept is based on a closed-circuit one. This example also tends to illustrate the limits of Lakoff and Johnson's quasi systematic approach to metaphors as experiential when it comes to analysing metaphors in specialised domains. Though current lexical associations resulting from everyday experience may account for the deployment of surface metaphors as found in the pseudo-economic press, they cannot provide any accurate explanation for the inclusion of metaphorical terms in the discourse of specialised domains. Nor can they teach us anything about the historical scientific motivations of these terms. They simply seem to disregard the continuum between theory-constitutive metaphors, pedagogical metaphors and other surface metaphors, leaving aside the rich history of theory-construction and its dynamic character. As poet Etheridge Knight (1987) pointed out, "metaphors are alive. When they come into being, they are informed by the politics and the sociology and the economy of now. That's how language is." It is therefore essential to take into consideration the context in which metaphors were first born, in order to understand their *raison d'être*, and then observe how and why they evolved. Otherwise, there is a real risk of offering an incomplete and somewhat superficial explanation and interpretation of metaphor.

From the two main metaphorical veins described in Sections 5.1.1 and 5.1.2, it appears that determining the origin of some metaphorical terms is not always an easy task. A mixed metaphor, however, is particularly interesting as it is proof of the impact of the social, scientific and historical contexts on worldviews and assumptions. The liquid element in economics is a perfect example. Three influences have been mentioned so far:

- that of hydraulic physics;
- that of biology, by means of body fluids;
- that of nature, and the natural elements, accounting for the depiction of economic turmoil and crises as storms.

If we concentrate on storms at sea and the frequent nautical metaphors, a fourth explanation can be put forward, namely the geographical situation of Britain as an island and the position it enjoyed as ruler of the seas over a long period of time. The term SLUSH FUND in Table 13 is quite revealing in this respect. In his book about the *Battle of Trafalgar*, Adkins (2005: 37) explains the origin of the term: "The term *slush fund* was originally a nautical term: the slush was the fat or grease that was obtained by boiling salted meat, the sale of which could then be used to provide the crew with special luxuries. The money obtained from this sale was placed into the slush fund." The various items in Table 13 have been selected from the field of finance[119] to illustrate the pervasiveness of the liquid element metaphor in this particular sector. As the definitions show, some of the items, marked by an asterisk, are official terms; others are more colloquial expressions, commonly used by both specialists and commentators, and anyone reading the financial press or papers on finance on a regular basis can easily find evidence of this. Some bear the mark of the

---

119 The author has years of experience working with last-year students specialising in banking and finance, which gave her the opportunity to compile a large corpus of papers and articles on the topic.

original metaphorical vein that generated them more clearly than others, but all are derived from the liquid metaphor.

Awash with liquidity	An expression meaning that the market is bubbly.
Bailout*	Financial assistance provided to a bank or savings institution suffering a loss of earnings resulting from loan losses in order for it to avoid bankruptcy. The association with a boat having a hole letting in water is obvious.
Capital drain*	The flow of capital from one country or sector to another. This may result in the drying out of capital in some areas.
Cash flow*	The amount of net cash generated by an investment or a business during a specific period. Among other possibilities, cash flow is now often measured using EBITDA (earnings before interest, taxes, depreciation, and amortisation).
Currency*	A medium of exchange (coins and banknotes).
Dilution*	A decrease in the equity position of a share of stock after new, additional shares are issued.
Float*	The number of shares of a publicly-traded company available to trade.
Managed float*/ Dirty float*	When a government intervenes to change the direction of the value of the country's currency, it is known as a managed float or a dirty float.
Float an issue (flotation)*	(for a firm) To sell a security issue on the primary market in order to raise money to finance expenses.
Float a loan	To borrow money.
Floating currency*	A currency whose value is determined by the supply and demand for it and the amount of reserves held in this currency.
Flood the market	When too many stocks are sold, the market is flooded and risks indigestion.
Fluctuations	The ups and downs in prices.
Frozen assets*	An asset that cannot be sold because, for example, it serves as collateral on a debt that has not yet been paid off.
Laundered money	Dirty money from organised crime or illicit practices has to be laundered in order to become clean again. Once the illicit origins have disappeared, one talks about laundered money.
Liquid assets*	Liquid assets can be easily traded and converted to

	cash, without any negative impact on their price.
Pump money into the system	Government intervention to increase liquidity and boost performance.
Sinking fund*	A means of repaying funds that were borrowed through a bond issue. The issuer makes periodic payments to a trustee who withdraws part of the issue by purchasing the bonds in the open market.
Slush fund*	A term used in accounting to describe an account in which all sorts of transactions can be posted.
Solvency*	The ability for a business to have enough assets to cover its liabilities.
Taking a bath	Wall Street slang for losing a lot of money.
Underwater*	Is said about a stock option for which the option exercise price is higher than the market price of the stock. Is also said of a property with a debt larger than its value (an underwater mortgage).

Table 13. The liquid element metaphor in finance

It is not surprising that metaphors used by the financial press should be influenced by the terms used in the realm of finance. Consciously or not, journalists start from the nodes that metaphorical terms represent and usually deploy the liquid metaphor on the basis of all the common associations that readers will easily understand, even though they may not be aware of the original metaphorical vein that generated the metaphorical terms.

Other instances of intertwined metaphors can be mentioned. Crises are interesting in this respect: they are depicted either in medical terms, natural terms, or in mechanical terms. They may be CHRONIC, ENDEMIC, or considered as CONTAGIOUS, especially as globalised markets are not IMMUNE from CONTAGION or VIRAL DISEASES. As already mentioned, the circumstances of crises are described in terms of natural elements that are difficult to control and must be fought against. It is worth noting that even an apparently transparent origin can hide a more deeply-ingrained metaphor. Let us consider the term TURBULENCE again (White 2004), which can be interpreted as a meteorological reference to strong winds. A more scientific interpretation, however, will take us back to fluid dynamics, engineering and mechanical problems, which shows that the term itself is not exclusively related to the natural metaphor:

> Turbulence is immensely important in many branches of science, from astronomy to meteorology. It's also important in practical engineering problems. Turbulence can destroy a water pipe or an oil pipeline, break up a ship's screw, or cause an airliner to crash. Engineers have devised various methods, ranging from rule-of-thumb to sophisticated statistics, for dealing with practical instances of turbulence. But its true inner nature remains a problem of the highest order. (Stewart 1997: 159)

Depending on the way the metaphor is deployed, policy-makers, as has already been mentioned, will either be doctors, drivers, pilots, captains or mechanics. The problems will be described in terms of fever or overheating and the prescriptions, remedies or solutions they will offer will be more or less aggressive: a diet, a pause, an injection, tightening some screws, or changing the engine altogether. The choice of metaphor may then tell us something about the measures about to be implemented: a loose policy, a belt-tightening policy, aggressive rate hikes, etc. Closely related to crises, *BUBBLES* offer another illustration of a metaphor that contains elements of natural, physical or medical metaphors. First, through the nature metaphor, *BUBBLES* can be associated with air, a natural element. The term *BUBBLE* is also linked with fluid mechanics, and touches on vapour pressure. It is defined as a globule of one substance in another, often gas in a liquid, like air bubbles in water, but also in champagne, or any drink that could cause loss of self-control. When commenting on the difficult task of conducting monetary policy, William McChesney Martin[120] actually said that the role of the Federal Reserve is to "take away the punch bowl just when the party starts getting interesting". By this, he meant that when the economy is too exuberant, the central bank should intervene in due time by raising interest rates. One can also think of water vapour in boiling water, or air mixed into agitated water as below a waterfall. Another common image conjured up by *BUBBLE* is sea foam. A market can be described as *FROTHY*, showing signs of effervescence

120 McChesney Martin chaired America's Federal Reserve Board from 1951 to 1970.

before becoming *BUBBLY*. The metaphor was used by former Federal Reserve chairman Alan Greenspan in 2005[121]:

> Whether home prices on average for the nation as a whole are overvalued relative to underlying determinants is difficult to ascertain, but there do appear to be, at a minimum, signs of *froth* in some local markets where home prices seem to have risen to unsustainable levels. Among other indicators, the significant rise in purchases of homes for investment since 2001 seems to have charged some regional markets with *speculative fervor*.
>
> The *apparent froth* in housing markets appears to have interacted with evolving practices in mortgage markets. The increase in the prevalence of interest-only loans and the introduction of more-exotic forms of adjustable-rate mortgages are developments of particular concern. To be sure, these financing vehicles have their appropriate uses. But some households may be employing these instruments to purchase homes that would otherwise be unaffordable, and consequently their use could be adding to pressures in the housing market. Moreover, these contracts may leave some mortgagors vulnerable to adverse events. It is important that lenders fully appreciate the risk that some households may have trouble meeting monthly payments as interest rates and the macroeconomic climate change. (Semiannual Monetary Policy Report to the Congress before the Committee on Financial Services, US House of Representatives, July 20th, 2005)

In economics, *BUBBLE* refers to speculation and overvaluation of assets like stocks, real estate, precious metals or commodities. The dramatic rise in prices is only due to speculation and is not justified if one considers the underlying value of the assets. Consequently, these inflated prices are bound to collapse suddenly when the bubble bursts or is pricked. Speculation is often depicted as "fervor", "fever", or even "madness": in 1996, Alan Greenspan had warned against speculative fever by using the now famous expression *IRRATIONAL EXUBERANCE*. Historically, the term *BUBBLE* was first used in economics in the eighteenth century in the context of the 1711-1720 British South Sea bubble to refer to the wild speculation over the South Sea Company's shares. In 1720, the company was officially granted a monopoly situation on trade with the parts of the Americas colonised by the Spanish.

---

121 Interestingly, in hindsight, one can realise that the problems that led to the sub prime crisis are described here.

A law was passed prohibiting any other joint-stock company not authorised by Royal Charter. The swings in the share prices of the South Sea Company that same year were impressive: they were worth £128 in January, peaked to £1,050 in July and collapsed to £100 in December, after the bubble had burst. As people considered that the bubble resulted from the law passed by Parliament, they called the law the "Bubble Act". From then on, every major financial crisis linked with speculation of some sort was referred to as a *BUBBLE*[122]. Again in hindsight, the former major crisis due to speculation over tulip bulbs in the 1600s – known as "the Dutch tulip mania" or "tulipomania" – is now quoted as the first instance of a *BUBBLE*: it ended in a panic in February 1637. The *BUBBLE* metaphor conjures up the inflated prices of assets as well as the fragile character of the bubble; after all, foolhardy investors speculate on thin air so that they are vulnerable to a sudden burst that will cause their money to evaporate. Obviously, there is a link between the notion of *BUBBLES* and the idea of "inflated values" or "ballooning prices". Inflation, by extension, is also an exaggeration in prices which must be controlled.

The various properties of the *BUBBLE* metaphor described above have been studied by Van der Yeught (2007), who based his analysis on a mixed corpus of texts written by British and American observers, journalists, economists and financial historians. He identified four main metaphors used by the various authors when dealing with bubbles: flying, weightlessness, gambling and madness. Had he gone one step further, he would have been able to relate these elements to the natural, physical, mechanical or medical root metaphors underpinning economic theory.

A map of the main metaphorical veins that have been reviewed so far is provided in Figure 5 in order to highlight the various branches and to make the mixed origins of some metaphors such as closed-

122 Other notorious bubbles can be quoted here, referred to as craze, crisis or bubbles, and ending in depression or crash: the Florida real estate craze (1926), the Roaring Twenties (ending in the 1929 Great Depression), the market bubble and crash of 1987, the Asian crisis (1989), the dotcom bubble (2000-2002) and the housing bubble and credit crisis (2007-2009).

circuit metaphors, liquid or nautical metaphors, overheating/fever metaphors or crisis/turbulence metaphors more visible.

5.2.4. The importance of contextualisation

Crises and bubbles, like other instances in which metaphorical veins intertwine, draw our attention to the need to consider metaphors in relation to the root metaphors that have generated them and to analyse their sometimes winding itineraries. More generally speaking, metaphorical terms and expressions in specialised domains cannot be dissociated from context. Contextualisation matters and can be understood in different ways: first, discursive and textual contextualisation, then situational and cultural contextualisation, and finally generational and historical contextualisation. Discursive and textual contextualisation enables us to understand co-textual and contextual metaphors. Co-textual metaphors have their explicit referent in the same text or speech, though not in the same sentence or paragraph, while contextual metaphors have their referent outside the text or speech. A good illustration of contextual metaphors is the Goldilocks metaphor explained in Section 5.2.1 which requires familiarity with the general economic context and comes as an echo to other texts or speeches. Though the allusion to the fairy tale and the parallel with the "neither too cold, neither too hot, just right" economy were explicit in the first occurrences of the metaphor, later occurrences just mentioned the *GOLDILOCKS ECONOMY*, assuming that everybody knew the economic metaphor and was able to relate it to the broad mechanical root metaphors, in association with notions such as an overheating engine or a motor having to cool down. It is because of the particular situation of the economy at the time that this metaphor could be understood and adopted as a code.

For metaphors belonging to networks related to theory-constitutive metaphors, generational and historical contextualisation is particularly important as it makes it easier to understand why some metaphors seem to relate to one or other main vein. Circulatory metaphors, again, are a case in point. As already mentioned, in the eighteenth century circulatory metaphors were born of the analogy with the circulation of blood in the human body. By the nineteenth century, however, the analogy was based on mechanical functions, which was probably a consequence of the industrial revolution and the advent of the steam engine: "steam circulated through an engine in the same manner as blood through a human body", so that when bank notes were "circulated", "the precise connotation was open to interpretation" (Alborn 1994: 176). As Alborn points out, the fact that different groups of people resorted to different metaphors is not so surprising if one takes into account the social and political context of the early Victorian period: on the one hand, the centralised economic administration (hence the mechanistic metaphors of state-controlled circulation) and, on the other hand, "laissez-faire naturalism" (which accounts for the natural metaphors of free circulation). Some overlapping was to be expected, especially at the beginning of the nineteenth century, but can only be understood if one is aware of the state of society and the economy at the time. In the 1830s, for example, joint-stock bankers wanted to convince the public that they were better able to ensure quick and regular circulation of currency in industrial England than private bankers. In order to do so, they sought to present their institutions as strong, efficient machines, able to ensure speed and regularity as would a steam engine.

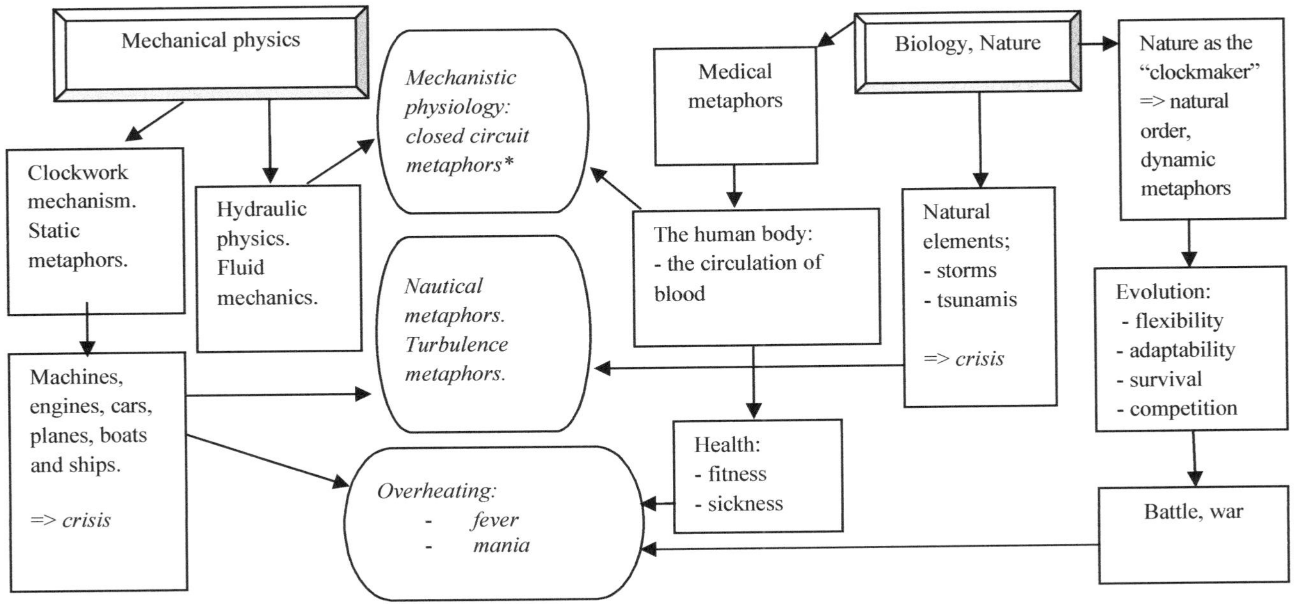

Fig. 5. The main theory-constitutive metaphorical veins in economics
**The metaphors indicated in italics stem from both megametaphors*

Another example of the importance of the historical context when studying metaphors in specialised domains is provided by a focus on the scientific and ideological context; the latter is an explanation of why, during the period from 1914 to 1950, biological metaphors fell out of favour with economists. It is true that, as Hodgson points out, "the relationships between biology and economics has waxed and waned over the centuries", but [...] "what is striking [...] is the temporal variation in the degree of their explicit popularity and use". The reason why biological metaphors became unpopular in social sciences, including economics, for about 40 years during the first half of the twentieth century is to be found in biology itself as well as in the ideological abuse of science. Findings in genetics at the beginning of the twentieth century seem to have been exploited in a negative manner to support racist and sexist inferences as regards human character and behaviour. Some scientists and ideologists took this opportunity to consider that differences in abilities and conduct were rooted in genetic heritage. Such hasty conclusions angered and shocked some liberals in academic circles in America who refrained from using biological metaphors for fear of being pointed at and associated with ideologues. The context of growing racism and fascism in the first four decades of the century was not favourable either. After this long eclipse, biological metaphors returned to the social sciences, prompted by two important events that occurred in the 1940s and in the 1970s. The first event is known as the neo-darwinian synthesis and refers to a synthesis between the theory of natural selection and Mendel's genetics. The second, which was probably less important as far as theory in biology is concerned, had a greater impact on scientists in social sciences: in 1975, an international conference was organised in Paris with a view to stimulating dialogue between biology and politics. These two events prompted the resurgence of evolutionary ideas in economics and new developments (Alchian 1950; Boulding 1950; Friedman 1953; Hayek 1969; Georgescu-Roegen 1971; Becker 1976; Gowdy 1987).

It is clear that the biological metaphors used in the second part of the twentieth century were a different generation of metaphors from those used by Marshall, for example. This reinforces the idea that metaphors evolve with the historical and social context and are dynamic: obviously, a biological conception of the economy is bound to evolve over time and, apart from a few exceptions due to visionary researchers, each generation will deploy a given metaphorical vein on the basis of knowledge available in the scientific community at large. This will feed new insights and yield new metaphorical terms and expressions. A good example is provided by the term *CORPORATE DNA*, which could not have appeared before Crick and Watson discovered the structure of DNA in 1950. Therefore, as Limoges and Menard (1994: 350) remind us, commenting on Marshall's contribution to economics, it is most important to remember this crucial methodological rule:

> In the history of any science, hindsight may prove at times illuminating, but it is not permissible to account for a theoretical construct by later developments of the sciences. This is why we must ignore what we now know about evolution theory as it unfolded after Marshall's time. Marshall's work has to be understood on its own terms, from the viewpoint of what he thought was known, of what he read and commented on.

A last instance of a broader, looser, cultural context must be mentioned here, that of the broad realm of economics. There exist, of course, metaphors that are part of an economist's education though they cannot be traced back to the mechanical or biological, natural, or medical root metaphors. These metaphorical terms or expressions are however part and parcel of the domain's culture and folklore. They are often associated with the thinkers who coined them, but they can also be used as conventional, coded, theoretical, explanatory shortcuts. Some of these metaphors are quoted and explained in Table 14.

Scissors (or crosses) (1961)	Alfred Marshall	When debates raged between supply-oriented or demand-oriented views of prices, Marshall answered by saying that prices were equally dependent on supply and demand, hence the diagrams of demand-and-supply curves. He wrote: "we might as reasonably dispute whether it is the upper or the under blade of a pair of scissors that cuts a piece of paper, as whether value

		is governed by utility or cost of production" (1961: 348). His theory is referred to through the "Marshall's scissors" metaphor. The diagrams are also called Marshallian crosses.
Leaky bucket (1975)	Arthur Okun	Wealth transfers from the relatively rich to the relatively poor are a good idea; but there are inevitable inefficiencies and losses (administrative costs of tax collection and transfer programmes, etc.). "The money must be carried from the rich to the poor in a leaky bucket. Some of it will simply disappear in transit, so the poor will not receive all the money that is taken from the rich." (*Equality and Efficiency, the Big Tradeoff*, 1975: 91)
Beauty contest (1936)	Maynard Keynes	It refers to the reasoning of rational agents in a market. Keynes imagined a newspaper contest where people would be required to choose the most beautiful women from among a number of pictures, knowing that the winner would be the one who had picked the most popular faces. "It is not a case of choosing those [faces] that, to the best of one's judgment, are really the prettiest, nor even those that average opinion genuinely thinks the prettiest. We have reached the third degree where we devote our intelligences to anticipating what average opinion expects the average opinion to be. And there are some, I believe, who practice the fourth, fifth and higher degrees." (Keynes, General Theory of Employment Interest and Money, 1936)
Auctioneer; *Tâtonnement* (French for groping one's way in the dark)	Léon Walras	The auctioneer matches supply and demand in a market of perfect competition, by providing perfect information. General equilibrium, which is achieved when the market clearing

		price has been found for all commodities, can only be reached through a process called *tâtonnement*.
Robinson Crusoe (1881) Box (1881)	Francis Ysidro Edgeworth	The Robinson Crusoe economy illustrates the theory of production and choice in the absence of trade, money and prices. A single individual living on a desert island has to make decisions as regards the amount of time and effort he is going to allocate to different occupations to meet his needs. Edgeworth's box is a tool for analysing trading behaviour, and the interactions of two individuals trading two commodities. It is used for representing how various resources are distributed.
Stove (1909)	Albert Aftalion	It describes overcapitalisation though the metaphor of a stove which is overfed with fuel when a room is cold, without realising that it takes time for the room to heat up. Then the room gets much too hot, the person stops feeding the stove but, after a while, cold sets in again. Lag time should be taken into account.
Tragedy of the Commons (1968)	Garrett Hardin	In the context of a shared limited resource, when individuals think of their self-interest they tend to be careless and overuse the common good, even though they know it is not in anybody's long-term interest since the resource will ultimately be depleted.
Lemons market (1970)	George Akerlof	It illustrates asymmetric information through the example of the market for used cars, or "lemons", reflecting the old adage "let the buyer beware". Since the seller knows more than the buyer, the buyer will take into account potential hidden flaws and offer an average price well below that expected by sellers of "good" second-hand cars:

		consequently the latter will not sell their cars on the used car market. Gradually, the bad will drive out the good and only lemons will remain.
Ricardian vice (1954)	Schumpeter	It refers to abstract model-building and mathematical formulae. It is an allusion to Ricardo's alleged habit of building abstract models based on unrealistic assumptions.

Table 14. Metaphors as part of the common theoretical stock of economists

These metaphors represent the shared knowledge of the specialised community. For the observer, they can also signal an entry point into the position of the authors, their contribution to economic theory, and the period when they were writing. The last example, Ricardian vice, is particularly interesting as it translates Schumpeter's opinion of Ricardo's scientific attitude, underlining the fact that terms can reflect the disagreements that were frequent between schools of thought or approaches, whether within one generation or across centuries. In this respect, metaphorical terms can be regarded as witnesses of the evolution of concepts and theoretical frames over time. They also stimulate new approaches and can therefore be seen as motors of change as well.

5.3. Metaphors as motors and mirrors of change

Precisely because they are embedded in theory, history and time, metaphorical terms can be seen as signposts of change. The change they signal or announce can be gradual and take place over a number of years, witnessing an evolution as the metaphorical term is interpreted and reinterpreted, refined and adapted. Change can also be more categorical, and translate into a metaphorical mutation, in which case the metaphor may herald a paradigm shift in a particular branch of research. For these reasons, metaphorical terms can be considered as mediators or revolutionaries.

5.3.1. The example of HUMAN CAPITAL

Metaphors play the role of mediators at various levels, as has already been mentioned: they are tools for theorists to visualise a new way of approaching their problems; they enable them to explain how they came to adopt the new perspective and share their findings with their peers; they can also help students understand theory; finally, they can even be used with a more general public to illustrate theory differently by relying on whatever the public is more familiar with. The heuristic role of metaphor is worth investigating further, and the case of HUMAN CAPITAL, which has drawn my attention (Resche 2007), will serve as an illustration.

The idea of cultivating one's talent is rooted in a humanistic approach. It lies at the basis of the classical doctrine of the "good life". To some degree, a certain idea of HUMAN CAPITAL can be traced back to ancient times. According to Aristotle, happiness meant self-fulfilment, hence cultivating one's talent. As Edmund Phelps (2007: 15), who was awarded the Sveriges Riksbank Prize in Economic Sciences in Memory of Alfred Nobel in 2006, pointed out, self-accomplishment is a notion that has crossed all ages: from the Renaissance period when Benvenuto Cellini described the joys of creativity and self-accomplishment in his autobiography, through the Baroque and Enlightenment periods celebrating the quest for individual development, to William James Dewey's pragmatic philosophy and John Rawls's self-realisation.

Acknowledgment of the economic value of knowledge and skills is not new either, and can be traced back to the seventeenth century. Historians point out that, as early as 1691, Sir William Petty took into consideration the value of labourers, and thought that estimating the value of what was to become known as HUMAN CAPITAL was a means to underline the power of England; conversely, he felt that when the cost of war was calculated, the cost of men's lives should be factored in. The literature on the historical roots of HUMAN CAPITAL emphasises the consensus among early contributors to the concept that human beings represent an investment that generates a return. Among these theorists were Adam Smith (1776), Jean Baptiste Say (1821), William Roscher (1878) and Henry Sidgwick (1891). Adam Smith's description shows what a pioneer he was in this respect, though he considered workmen's talent as part of fixed capital:

> The second of the three portions into which the general stock of the society divides itself is the fixed capital; of which the characteristic is, that it affords a revenue or profit without circulating or changing masters. It consists chiefly of the four following articles. [...] Fourthly, of the acquired and useful abilities of all the inhabitants or members of the society. The acquisition of such talents, by the maintenance of the acquirer during his education, study, or apprenticeship, always costs a real expense, which is a capital fixed and realised, as it were, in his person. Those talents, as they make a part of his fortune, so do they likewise that of the society to which he belongs. The improved dexterity of a workman may be considered in the same light as a machine or instrument of trade which facilitates and abridges labour, and which, though it costs a certain expense, repays that expense with a profit. (1776, Book 2, Chapter 1)

Other early researchers, however, seem to have been reluctant to regard people as physical commodities. Nevertheless, John Stuart Mill (1848) and other economists recognised the influence of acquired abilities and improved health on productivity, output and wages. Over a century after Adam Smith, Irving Fisher (1897) included human beings in his definition of capital. To support his position, he quoted figures estimating that HUMAN CAPITAL in the United States was worth five times as much as physical capital. He then advocated investment in improving health and spoke in favour of health insurance and the creation of a national department of health. In the 1930s, people in the life insurance business were interested in the notion for determining the premium for an individual's life insurance. However, modern HUMAN CAPITAL theory really started with Jacob Mincer, Theodore Schultz and Gary Becker in the 1960s. At that time, economists were preoccupied with accounting for economic performance and defining the wealth-creating factors that could boost the economic engine.

The story of the circumstances that led Schultz, an agricultural economist, to think of economic problems in new terms is related by McCloskey (1990: 13):

> One day, he interviewed an old and poor farm couple and was struck by how contented they seemed. Why are you so contented, he asked, though very poor? They answered: You're wrong, Professor. We're not poor. We've used

up our farm to educate four children through college, remaking fertile land and well-stocked pens into knowledge of law and Latin. We are rich.

This anecdote provided Schultz with insight into the connection between physical capital and *HUMAN CAPITAL*, more precisely in this case capital produced by investing in knowledge and education. Realising that the farmers' sacrifices had not been in vain since their children would certainly be more productive thanks to their education, he became convinced of the value of educational capital, which can be considered as an offshoot of the concept of *HUMAN CAPITAL*. In a way, the parents had invested in their children's education and in the future. More broadly, talent, wit and learning could be considered as an asset that could produce income. Schultz insisted on the need to consider investment in *HUMAN CAPITAL* when assessing economic performance and studying growth: "This knowledge and skill are in great part the product of investment and, combined with other human investment, predominantly account for the productive superiority of the technically advanced countries" (1961: 3). Of course, when Schultz started thinking along these lines, he was not yet aware of all the possible developments that were to follow. His focus was on accounting for the power and growth of nations, but other developments, notably by Gary Becker, followed. Becker's contribution is most important as underlined by McCloskey (1998: 43):

> [It] illustrates how two sets of ideas, in this case both drawn from inside economics, can mutually illuminate each other by exchanging connotations. In the phrase "human capital", the field in economics treating human skills was at a stroke unified with the field treating investment in machines. Thought in both fields was improved – labour economics by recognising that skills, for all their intangibility, arise from abstention from consumption; capital theory by recognizing that skills, for all their lack of capitalisation, compete with other investments for a claim to abstention.

Becker's originality was to suggest an economic approach to human behaviour and to analyse the motivations behind the decisions to invest in education, whether at government level, or at the level of the individual. The model he developed took into consideration the costs and benefits of extra years of education. To the direct costs of paying for books, board and tuition were to be added indirect costs: after all, deciding to go into higher education means giving up the income a job could provide. These costs were to be measured against the expected benefits linked with college or university education: higher wages, a more pleasant job, hence a better standard of living. In the concluding comments to his book *Human Capital,* Becker (1964: 251) announced future developments: "I would venture the judgment that human capital is going to be an important part of the thinking about development, income distribution, labor turnover, and many other problems for a long time to come." Actually, he was right: many issues have been revisited by the *HUMAN CAPITAL* theory, including the problems of migration and human capital flight (also known as "brain drain"), and the questions of immigration policy to attract human capital, of investments in health and safety including safety regulations, of economic development, competition, education policy and investment in general. Some modern analysts (Laroche *et al* 1998: 88) have even broadened the concept of human capital to include innate as well as acquired skills: "We define human capital as the aggregation of the innate abilities and the knowledge and skills that individuals acquire and develop throughout their lifetime."

It is worth noting that Becker's book on human capital (1964) and Bourdieu's work on social capital (1964) were published the same year and were complementary. Though they did not share the same political opinions – one being a neo-liberal and the other a neo-Marxist – they were both interested in studying the effect of education on people's lives and chances of success, on wage differentials and inequalities. The major difference was that where Bourdieu's analysis of social capital underlines the determining impact of a person's past, in terms of their family background and culture, on their present behaviour and chances of success, *HUMAN CAPITAL* theory emphasises the need to look ahead and anticipate when making decisions as regards present behaviour. Interestingly, Becker's later presentation of the notion of *HUMAN CAPITAL* in an online encyclopedia[123] (2007) also took into consideration family influence: "No discussion of human capital

123 *The Concise Encyclopedia of Economics* <http://www.econlib.org/library/enc/HumanCapital.html>

can omit the influence of families on the knowledge, skills, values, and habits of their children". In addition, when interviewed by Manville (2001: 4) about his view of social capital and the inclusion of social capital in *HUMAN CAPITAL*, he answered:

> I certainly think social capital is important; I've worked on that myself and just came out with a book called *Social Economics*. Yes, social capital is a form of human capital. When I spoke about corporate culture before I was really talking about social or corporate capital – how people are connected with a company. Social capital as a concept has become very popular in recent years; but it is very difficult to quantify, and emotional capital would be even more so. But they do seem important because they do affect the productivity of individual workers and certainly of companies overall.

The *HUMAN CAPITAL* metaphor is interesting when one considers its long itinerary through economic theory: it has enabled different generations of researchers and theorists to refine on it until they were able to deploy it fully. The surprising association of the two components of the term suggests that what applies to material capital can be transferred to immaterial assets: as one accumulates capital, one can accumulate knowledge; in both cases, this requires investing time and effort, and giving up immediate pleasure in the hope of future gain; in order to avoid depreciation, the owner of *HUMAN CAPITAL* has a duty to make his capital fructify. Time is an important factor; it can cause machines, as well as skills, to become obsolete. The heuristic function of the metaphorical term has generated inroads into two fields: it has quietly brought about a major shift in economic theory, and it has stimulated new research in management theory and affected the corporate world.

As far as economic theory is concerned, the *HUMAN CAPITAL* metaphor is to be considered against the background of the three factors of production that are commonly identified as land, labour and capital. Traditionally, though no mention of the human element was explicit, people were considered to belong to the second category. Simply, they were referred to through a process of metonymy, i.e. their work (or their hands). The introduction of the term *HUMAN CAPITAL* calls into question the traditional view as the new term becomes a hyponym of capital: people now seem to be identified with the third category (Table 15):

The traditional factors of production	LAND	LABOUR	CAPITAL
The impact of the human capital element	LAND	⇨	CAPITAL Human capital

Table 15. Shifting concepts

By causing the human element to change categories, the *HUMAN CAPITAL* metaphor triggers questions and reactions. From a theoretical perspective in terminology, it illustrates the idea that concepts are not related to one another in a static manner, so that when new concepts are introduced they may cause the system's organisation to evolve. This underlines the dynamic character of a domain's or sub-domains's conceptual organisation (Kageura 1997: 120). From a theoretical perspective in economics, understandably, the idea that people can be considered as capital, along with machines, can provoke negative reactions and feed the debate about the proletariat/capital-owners divide. An extreme interpretation could lead one to suggest a modern form of slavery. However, two positive arguments can be put forward: one is that, for the first time, the human element is explicitly named, which can be interpreted as a sign of respect – people are no longer reduced to the work they do (labour) but are seen as whole beings. The other argument is that, instead of considering workers as the property of others, the metaphor changes each individual into an owner or a capitalist: the owner of his or her own capital. The second interpretation requires some explanation, based on the elements pointed out by the theorists in the field. If, as Schultz understood from the farmers who invested in their children's education, or as Becker stated, education and training can yield positive results in terms of material well-being and also intellectual satisfaction, anyone who invests time, money and effort in their own education becomes the owner of the capital they have invested in. More importantly, unlike machines which can be kept and used by different workers, human capital is not separable from its owner:

> Expenditures on education, training, medical care, […] produce human, not physical or financial capital, because you cannot separate a person from his or

> her knowledge, skills, health, or values the way it is possible to move financial and physical assets while the owner stays put. (Becker 1993: 16)

Therefore, workers with increased human capital are "richer" and also freer in a way: the more they have capitalised on their education and training, the stronger they are. If their capital is deemed precious and rare, they are likely to be treated with more consideration as their employer will seek to retain them.

Naturally, the latter aspect has had repercussions in the corporate world, especially among HR officers. The term "human resources" is still used, but should certainly be replaced by "human capital", if only to reflect the change in the way the men and women who are employed in the corporate world should be considered: again, one can interpret the metaphor as a shift from a mechanistic to an organic view of workers. They can no longer be regarded as resources in the sense of exploitable resources, and this is all the more obvious as ever-dwindling natural resources are being treated with greater care now that their finite character has been acknowledged: it is common to refer to them as *NATURAL CAPITAL* too. When jobs on the assembly line were repetitive and did not require particular skills, any worker whose work was not satisfactory could be replaced by any other worker, just as a flawed part in a machine could be replaced by a new part. Once automatons started replacing people, the latter were given tasks that required more skills and had to be trained and retrained. Gradually, as the service sector grew, and processes became more sophisticated, knowledgeable workers were in greater demand. It was only natural to change the terminology from human resources to *HUMAN CAPITAL*. In addition, now that the line from labour to capital has been crossed, another line could be crossed on the balance sheet: from liabilities, workers should be considered as assets. This was officially acknowledged by the US Government Accounting Office (GAO 1999: 102):

> An organization's employees are its *human capital*, a term more useful than "human resources", because it allows us to consider employees as assets rather than as resources that are to be consumed. [...] Human Capital views people as a valuable asset rather than merely as a cost. Assets are those things that bring long term value to an organization. When viewed this way, it is easy

> to think of people and/or what they accomplish as adding long term value to an organization. […]
>
> One would not equate people with more classic assets such as facilities, property or financial capital. However, this concept makes it easier to see the need to "invest" in and "develop" people as an asset, much as we invest in other types of assets. It is easier to understand why it is important to invest resources to obtain and keep the right people in the right jobs, and to develop them through appropriate training and recognition. […] The most important point to remember is the "human" part of *human capital*. People respond as whole individuals; organizations need to consider the whole individual in managing their *human capital*.

Obviously, taking into consideration the individual as a whole human being called for giving up any recourse to metonymy as in "hands", "labour", or even "workforce". Training, re-training and also retaining workers has become a challenge for the corporate world. In this respect, Becker's distinction between general and specific training (1964) should be heeded, as well as Gibbons and Waldman's subdivision between task-specific and company-specific types of human capital (2005:203). General training provides people with skills and knowledge that are portable, which means that, wherever the worker goes, he or she will be able to use the same skills to enhance productivity, and will also be able to adapt their general skills to new situations. Such flexibility can be an asset and a drawback for the firm. Workers who are offered a more attractive job by a rival firm may not hesitate to leave and will take their human capital with them. Task-specific training refers to competences acquired through professional training to perform certain tasks or work with particular machines: they are still transferable to other jobs and firms. Company-specific human capital is more directly linked with a particular firm and its culture, and it might well be a better idea for firms to invest in such training: if workers are provided with skills that can only be used for a specific job within a firm, they are less likely to be able to use the same skills elsewhere, so that the firm will not have invested in them in vain. Characteristically, as a consequence, the tools used for managing human capital have also been rephrased from "workforce planning tools" to "human-capital-management software" (Agrawal *et al*

2003: 79). Apart from this technical detail, companies have also integrated their changing relations with their employees in their policies, and their mission and vision statements highlight their new philosophy, centred on respect for diversity and recognition of the worth of the men and women working for them and contributing to their success.

As is the case with any science and any theory-constitutive, dynamic metaphor, HUMAN CAPITAL theory continues to evolve. Interestingly, in the field of management, echoes of the human capital metaphor have translated into new approaches: the terms *KNOWLEDGE WORKERS* (1969), *EMPOWERMENT* (1990), *LEARNING ORGANISATION* (1990) and *OBSOLEDGE* (2006), which have already been mentioned as neonyms in Chapter 4 (Table 8) are germane to the *HUMAN CAPITAL* concept. Apart from social and educational capital, a number of new terms have also been inspired by the *HUMAN CAPITAL* metaphor, which introduced the idea of immaterial capital or intangible assets, as shown in Table 16:

Cultural capital	Knowledge, skills, education, and advantages that cause a person to enjoy a higher status in society. For Bourdieu, children are provided with cultural capital by their parents who transmit the attitudes and knowledge needed to succeed in the current educational system.
Emotional capital	In the business world emotional capital refers to the way outsiders (customers and external stakeholders) and insiders (employees) perceive the company, which can affect the company's worth.
Environmental capital	In the context of sustainable economics, protection of the human and natural environment has to be taken into account if business is to endure.
Knowledge capital	Intellectual property, patents, processes. (Weatherly 2003)
Intellectual capital	Intellectual capital tends to be synonymous with structural capital. (Forman 2004)
Organisational capital	The company's external relationships: distribution networks, brand image, partners and customers, licences. (Weatherly 2003)
Social capital	Group membership, relationships, networks of influence and support. For Bourdieu (1983: 249), social capital was "the aggregate of the actual or potential resources which are linked to possession of a durable

	network of more or less institutionalised relationships of mutual acquaintance and recognition".
Structural capital	See intellectual capital. That part of intangible capital that persists if employees leave. (Forman 2004)
Symbolic capital	A term coined by Bourdieu: it refers to an individual's status, prestige, recognition, etc.

Table 16. Offshoots of the human capital metaphor.

All the terms mentioned above are now familiar to anyone interested in management theory: they are widely used or referred to in articles published in Mananagement Reviews and Journals as well as books[124].

For all that has been underlined as regards the consideration that increased knowledge should bring people in the working world, it would be unrealistic to paint too rosy a picture of the reality. Investing in one's own education is one thing, being a visionary able to detect the sectors that will offer the best future opportunities is another. In times of technological revolutions, people may not be prepared to take on new responsibilities and meet the new demand. Schumpeter's CREATIVE DESTRUCTION concept, which causes some jobs to disappear and others to emerge, may well bring some disillusionment. Though an idealistic view might conjure up images of empowered workers taking their future into their own hands and deciding what to learn, becoming "entrepreneurs" and managers of their own human capital (Gorz 2005), the risk remains that their self-production will not lead to self-fulfilment. More generally speaking, the HUMAN CAPITAL theory continues to fuel debate as new questions are being raised. Since the theory postulates that spending on training and education is a worthwhile investment expected to bring returns, one may wonder whether the present school system is able to fulfill its role and prepare students to take up the challenges of the working world. Investing in one's children's education or in one's own education as a young adult is actually a bet on the future, in the hope that the sacrifices are worth it. The current data on the number of over-skilled, underemployed or unem-

124 All the management terms dealt with in this book have been collected by the author over the past 15 years. Teaching fifth-year students enrolled in an International Trade and Management course requires keeping up with the evolution of research and knowledge in the field.

ployed people may cast doubt on the ability of education and training to ensure upward social and professional mobility. Government policies are surely influenced by the expected benefits from a better-educated, more competitive population: quantitatively, decisions to make school compulsory until a later age, to increase the number of grants, to increase the share of the national budget devoted to education and research, to set up continuous training programmes, or make internships compulsory for students all stem from the realisation that education, productivity and competitiveness are somehow linked. Qualitatively, the risk could be to rid the curricula of all the cultural, humanistic content and only teach what will bring return on investment, which could result in a commoditisation of education.

Whatever opinion one may have on the matter, HUMAN CAPITAL has triggered research and generated a rich literature that brings evidence of the numerous applications the metaphor offers. Observing how the term has introduced changes in education, in government policies, in personal choices and in the corporate world makes it possible to trace the itinerary of the concept over a period of sixty years. It illustrates the insight that can be gained from focusing on one single metaphorical term and studying how it has brought theories and ideas to evolve, mirroring societal changes in the process. Thanks to the HUMAN CAPITAL metaphor, people have ceased to be considered as machines and are now considered as whole human beings. Likewise, the reemergence of the organic metaphor has prompted a new approach to the theory of the firm in economics, and to management theory, which has in turn affected practices.

5.3.1. The case of CHAOS and COMPLEXITY metaphors: BIONOMICS and CHAORDIC MANAGEMENT

On the surface, BIONOMICS could be considered as a logical offshoot of the biological, organic, metaphorical vein that was introduced in Subsection 5.2.2 in this chapter. It describes the world "in terms of adaptation, intelligence, selection, and ecological niches"[125]. However, as

125 <http://www.feedmag.com/96.10borsook/96.10borsook.html>

Rothschild explains (1990: 4), the new perspective is no common evolution, but a fundamental questioning of a number of assumptions:

> Like ecosystems, economies are spectacularly complex and endlessly adaptable. Consequently, it is bionomics – which studies economic relations among organisms and their environment – that offers the best vantage point for a total rethinking of the received economic wisdom. [...] The traditional notion of government's economic role – pushing the buttons and twisting the dials of society's economic machinery – is replaced by a vision of government as the astute cultivator of society's economic ecosystem, patiently nurturing the natural processes of growth.

The ideas of ecosystems and of complexity are most important here, and they are naturally linked with those of self-organisation and chaos. Undoubtedly, they are connected with a modern evolutionary approach to economics, which also finds its illustration in the neonym *ECONOSPHERE*. Though the term could be interpreted as the abbreviation of economic sphere, the context in which it is used leaves no doubt as to the analogy with the biosphere defined as the "region of the earth that encompasses all living organisms: plants, animals and bacteria"[126]. The *ECONOSPHERE* encompasses all living organisms or autonomous agents such as organisations, markets, companies and individuals.

The new approach suggested by the bionomic metaphor is undoubtedly revolutionary, as becomes clear on the Bionomic Institute website[127]:

> Where mainstream economics is based on concepts borrowed from classical Newtonian physics, bionomics is derived from the teachings of modern evolutionary biology. Where orthodox thinking describes the economy as a static, predictable engine, bionomics sees the economy as a self-organizing, "chaotic" information ecosystem. Where the traditional view sees organizations as production machines, bionomics sees organizations as intelligent social organisms. Where conventional business strategy focuses on physical capital, bionomics holds that organizational learning is the ultimate source of all profit and growth.

---

126 <http://cnx.org/content/m16693/latest/>. UCCP (University of California College Prep)

127 <http:// www.bionomics.org>

In his very last book, Hayek (1988) mentioned how isolated he had felt in his own pioneering research when he showed interest in self-organising systems, insisting that "[...] the analysis of self-ordering processes must be the chief task of any science of the market order" (1988: 146). He could see how things had changed since then, to such a point that he could no longer keep up with the literature on such issues as "autopoiesis, cybernetics, homeostasis, spontaneous order, self-organisation, synergetics, systems theories, and so on" (1988: 9).

The technical terms in this list require some explanation and, for purposes of clarity, they are reorganised to start with the more general ones: *CYBERNETICS* and *SYNERGETICS*. As a broad interdisciplinary subject, *CYBERNETICS* can be defined in various ways: to simplify, it is the science of interactive systems, concerned with complexity and circularity and, when applied to management, the science of effective organisation or the art of steermanship. *SYNERGETICS* is also an interdisciplinary field of research first explored by Hermann Haken in 1969. The literal meaning of the term is "working together" and this field of research is interested in how new qualities, processes or functions spontaneously emerge in systems composed of many individual parts. *AUTOPOIESIS* literally means "self-production"; it refers to the way a biological cell, a living organism, a corporation or even a society as a whole can generate its own organisation. *HOMEOSTASIS* describes the ability of a system to regulate itself and thus maintain a stable, constant condition.

The concepts defined above point at emerging order, self-regulation, self-organisation in interactive complex systems and require considering the new approach that lies behind them, i.e. non linearity and non-linear thinking. Our western culture has not prepared us for non-linear thinking; on the contrary, we have been trained to think in a rational manner, and to analyse processes, facts and events in terms of cause-effect relationships on a linear basis. Yet, as pointed out by MIT Professor Jay Forrester, whose training as an engineer explains his interest in industrial dynamics and his borrowing from thermodynamics and cybermetics, causes and effects do not follow a linear route, but tend to influence and feed one another; consequently, we should think in terms of circularity or feedback loops. Linear thinking can only yield linear solutions to problems whereas other choices can be envisaged thanks to non-linear thinking. Senge (1990) insists that it is then possible to identify at what level it is necessary to intervene either to strengthen the positive effect of the feedback loops or to counter any negative impact.

Non-linear thinking is required, for example, for conceiving of companies as open, dynamic, adaptable and complex ecosystems. Through this lens, individuals can be seen as molecules and groups or teams as cells – as illustrated by the term *CELLULAR MANUFACTURING*; likewise, various categories of people within the company can be likened to species and the company's social environment to its ecology. Companies are complex systems in several ways: firstly, they involve a great many people who constantly interact internally. Secondly, they depend on a number of outside partners and stakeholders without whom they would not be able to survive. Thirdly, they also interact with the rest of society and often on a global scale, which adds to the number of networks they belong to. Complexity, which also implies a number of challenges such as unpredictability, having to deal with multiple parameters and interdependence, therefore calls for a holistic approach. Companies consist of separate parts that can function as separate entities but, just as in a biological organism, each of these parts is vital for the system to function as a healthy whole. They are thus mutually dependent, though diverse, and share a common goal. The system as a whole is the more adaptable and the stronger for its diversity. As a result of advances in information technology, all these agents are now involved in an increasing number of complex internal and external networks, which can be both beneficial and dangerous. It is no doubt necessary to foster relationships that can give rise to new, fruitful ideas, but the impact of such relationships is sometimes unpredictable; consequently, the challenge for managers consists in finding the right balance between control and disorder, efficiency and experimentation, standardisation and diversity, stability and innovation.

The need to reconcile seemingly opposed ends has given birth to a new concept: *CHAORD*, a portmanteau term coined by Dee Hock[128]

128 Dee Hock was the founder and former CEO of the Visa credit card association.

(1995:5), to express a state that is neither chaos nor order, but a combination of the two:

> By Chaord, I mean any self-organizing, adaptive, non-linear, complex system, whether physical, biological, or social, the behavior of which exhibits characteristics of both order and chaos or, loosely translated to business terminology, cooperation and competition.

The term may understandably be disquieting, especially if one considers chaos as "complete disorder and confusion" according to its dictionary definition[129]. However, chaos or lack of regularity should not be understood as danger or abnormality, and nature provides interesting examples that can help us to consider that, in some instances, as Orwell would have put it, "chaos <u>is</u> order":

> Chaos is not disorder; it is a higher form of order. Chaos covers everything that seems to be disorderly but in fact adheres to underlying patterns. The weather is a perfect example. A diseased heart beats with extreme regularity. It is the healthy heart that beats chaotically. Brain waves of the mentally healthy are chaotic, while those of an epileptic during seizure are regular. [...] Chaos will prove to economists that erratic oscillations are normal and healthy for the economy. (Rothschild 1995: Chapter 23)

When applied to organisations and companies, chaos should be understood as "order (a pattern) within disorder (random behaviour)" (Stacey 1993: 228). In this context, chaos conjures up the idea of emerging order, common examples of which are ant colonies or beehives, where apparent disorder hides utmost efficiency. For companies to remain successful and competitive, chaos should be preferred to equilibrium as the latter risks encouraging being content with the status quo. In an ever-changing world, a static attitude implies vulnerability: how can a company be ready to take up challenges when it has not even suspected they were likely to emerge? Surely, it cannot count on former recipes to be efficient to solve new problems. Thus, the idea was launched that a company should not be afraid to find itself "at the edge of chaos":

129 *The Collins English Dictionary*, 2011.

> If you tell most executives that they need to move their company to the edge of chaos, they will immediately think of a place – a precarious spot. The image is one of taking your canoe to the edge of a waterfall. In fact, the edge of chaos is a condition, not a location. For an executive, that means operating your company in such a way that it experiences the maximum and most productive levels of mutation. (An interview of Richard Pascale by Webber 2001, online)

Once the definition of the concept has become clear, companies should even consider the new posture as an opportunity to "thrive on chaos" (Peters 1988). In order to help companies reinvent themselves, Pascale invited them to sharpen their senses:

> […] When the world around you changes, maintaining your equilibrium is a threat to your future existence. That's when you need a new kind of agility that enables you to reinvent yourself. Very simply, prolonged equilibrium dulls an organism's senses and saps its ability to arouse itself appropriately in the face of danger. Survival favors heightened adrenaline levels, wariness, and experimentation. (An interview by Webber 2001, online)

It is therefore vital to create a working environment that will promote "a continuous learning process for creating meaning and value through service with and for others" (Hench 1999, online). In this respect, Hench states, management no longer consists in planning, leading, organising and controlling, but rather in experimenting, serving, stimulating people's ability to self-organise and facilitating knowledge accumulation. *THE LEARNING ENTERPRISE* can describe this state of mind and obviously the *HUMAN CAPITAL* concept is useful in such an approach. From this perspective, managing means accompanying, coordinating, and acting "with" or "for" and not "on" something or someone. "Essentially, an organisation must be flexible enough to adapt, creative enough to innovate, and responsive enough to learn" (Crossan *et al.*1996). Managers must foster an environment where teams can be flexible enough to grow or shrink depending on the importance of their projects and dissolve when need be. They must support experimentation and risk-taking, which implies tolerating failure, and encouraging trial-and-error processes. They must also be able to create a state of tension that will trigger dynamic imagination, while making sure that their teams can handle the stress generated by constant change. Converting conflict into cooperation requires giving everyone a sense of shared purpose and values so that healthy debate can take place and spontaneous order can eventually emerge. This new conception of inventive and dynamic companies has been referred to as *IMAGINISATION* (Morgan 1986) since it requires thinking along new lines. Precisely, as an extension of the living organism, companies have been viewed as human beings with brains; the brain metaphor has in turn been deployed to lay emphasis on the fact that companies have too often relied on their left brain, with its ability to reason, analyse and process information, disregarding the right intuitive brain, and its potential for innovative, non-linear thinking.

What is worth noting is the pervasive character of the new approach in management and business reviews, as translated in the widespread use of such adjectives as *ADAPTIVE, INTERACTIVE, EMERGENT, CONNECTED, AGILE, FLEXIBLE* and *PROACTIVE* or nouns such as *NETWORK, DYNAMICS* and *COOPETITION*. Phrases like *FLATTENING HIERARCHIES, INTERDEPENDENT ENTERPRISES, COLLABORATIVE RELATIONSHIPS, A DYNAMIC WEB OF RELATIONSHIPS* or *BORDERLESS ECONOMY* are also representative of the inroads the new way of thinking has made into the realm of management and the corporate world. The fact that complexity science is also called upon to gain a better understanding of markets such as Nasdaq and simulate various situations thanks to software programs based on genetic algorithms is another sign of the potential fecundity of the *CHAORD* metaphor. The world of finance and money markets is often referred to as a jungle and the jungle metaphor, provided one gets better acquainted with what the real natural jungle is about, is related to the chaordic metaphor. Very often we tend to associate the idea of a "jungle" with the dictionary definitions. The Merriam-Webster definition online defines a jungle as "a confused or disordered mass of objects" (a jumble), "something that baffles and frustrates by its tangled or complex character" (a maze), or "a place of ruthless struggle for survival". Obviously, these definitions conjure up ideas of danger, confusion, and pitiless fight. However, seen from the perspective of nature, a jungle is characterised by its richness and diversity; it is an organic, complex, interactive, self-contained system that requires no interference from human beings to spread and thrive. It is a chaordic ecosystem. When applied to money and finance, the metaphor simply stresses the organic interconnectedness and interdependency of markets and people; if species in the jungle depend on one another, so do human beings for the circulation of money and riches. In no way can money markets be "fixed" like an engine for they result from a great number of individual decisions and actions that are interdependent.

The point of analysing this metaphor was to illustrate the revolutionary aspect of metaphor when it is unsettling enough to call into question the prevailing frame of thinking which can imprison imagination and bring about a form of sclerosis, erecting a barrier to any change in viewpoints. Foster and Kaplan (2001: 44-45) warn us against such cultural lock-in in companies:

> Why does cultural lock-in occur? The heart of the problem is the formation of hidden sets of rules, or mental models, that once formed are extremely difficult to change. [...] Mental models are invisible in the corporation. They are neither explicit nor examined, but they are pervasive... But once constructed, mental models become self-reinforcing, self-sustaining, and self-limiting. And when mental models are out of sync with reality, they cause management to make forecasting errors and poor decisions.

The revolutionary character of metaphor can thus be used to awaken people's minds to new perspectives, preparing the way for a new paradigm:

> [...] the scientist who embraces a new paradigm is like the man wearing inverting lenses. [...] It is rather as if the professional community has been suddenly transported to another planet where familiar objects are seen in a different light and are joined by unfamiliar ones as well. (Kuhn 1962: 122)

Actually, as is the case with a new paradigm, metaphors can free people's minds. As dynamic processes, they act as pioneers and engines of change. In the present case, the new perspective offered is an accurate illustration of the difference between *ACTIVE INERTIA* – i.e. the propensity of managers faced with critical and unsettling change to apply the same practices that have succeeded in the past – and *ACTIVE WAITING*, which requires rethinking their approach in order to be ready to deal with uncertainty (Hindle 2008: 7). In the past decade, starting with the terrorist attacks of September 11th, 2001, unexpected catastrophes and severe disruptions have underlined the need to get ready for the unimaginable. Not only do earthquakes, floods, tsunamis, as well as social and political upheavals affect the countries where they occur, but their negative effects may also ripple around our interconnected world. Such major disruptive events have been called "black swans"[130] by Taleb (2007: xxii), who defines a black swan as:

> an event with the following three attributes. First, it is an outlier, as it lies outside the realm of regular expectations, because nothing in the past can convincingly point to its possibility. Second, it carries an extreme impact. Third, in spite of its outlier status, human nature makes us concoct explanations for its occurrence *after* the fact, making it explainable and predictable.

Obviously, the likelihood of black swans disrupting operations, production, sales, and stakeholders cannot be ignored by companies. Enterprise risk management (ERM) departments are in charge of imagining where the next potential business disruptions may lie. Only then can they begin to map their most likely effects, devise mitigation and contingency plans to ensure business continuity. This can only be achieved by thinking along non-traditional, non-linear lines. In this respect, the CHAORDIC ORGANISATION metaphor has introduced a mutation in the more general biological vein that has inspired economics.

---

130 In the introductory paragraph to his Prologue, Taleb (2007: xxi) explains what he means by a black swan: "Before the discovery of Australia, people in the old world were convinced that all swans were white, an unassailable belief as it seemed completely confirmed by empirical evidence. The sighting of the first black swan might have been an interesting surprise for a few ornithologists (and others extremely concerned with the coloring of birds), but that is not where the significance of the story lies. It illustrates a severe limitation to our learning from observations or experience and the fragility of our knowledge. One single observation can invalidate a general statement derived from millennia of confirmatory sightings of millions of white swans. All you need is one single (and, I am told, quite ugly) black bird."

5.4. Concluding remarks

By now, it should be clear to the reader that theory-constitutive metaphors offer the observer a much richer vantage point than surface metaphors used for popularising science; even though the latter may be related to deeper root metaphors, the link may not be so clear to the lay observer to begin with. For a linguist, focusing on metaphorical terms and inquiring into their origins, tracing them back to their authors, their historical and cultural context provides a clearer map of a discipline's evolution. Metaphor's role as a mediator and sometimes a revolutionary is particularly revealing in times of transition (Sandbothe 2000: 81):

> In times of transition, metaphors boom. And it is little wonder. For the metaphor, i.e. the transfer from one semantic realm to another is the linguistic instrument which allows us to grasp a transition as transition in words. The metaphor is an expression which in itself changes, i.e. represents historical transition as a process of semantic transmission. In times of transition, in which concepts start to move along with the phenomena, hardly any linguistic instruments are more exact and appropriate.

In this respect, the existence of a body in charge of monitoring emerging metaphorical terms in a given field would enable scholars to detect potential turning points or paradigm shifts. On a broader scale, it would offer the opportunity to highlight convergences or divergences between various disciplines and areas of knowledge. Metaphors could then be relied upon to feel the pulse of society at a certain period of time.

As has been shown, metaphors testify to the ideas and views borrowed from other disciplines, whose influence has been brought to bear on economic theories and practices. Depending on the time, a metaphorical vein has been either in the foreground or in the background. Seventeenth-century physics no longer applies and twentieth-century quantum physics must now be taken into account. Likewise, nineteenth-century biology must be put in perspective and the teachings of twentieth-century ecology cannot be ignored. For example, the mechanistic vein which suggested that as machines break they can be repaired is no longer satisfactory, whether it applies to management, with workers seen as "fungible parts", or to the economy at large. Machine metaphors, based on linear thinking, and suggesting that problems could be fixed easily, are no longer appropriate for our modern economy and an alternative must be envisaged. Wagner (2003) suggests the "garden" metaphor, which will induce people to think of solutions in terms of "cultivation", while the machine metaphor conjures up ideas of "repairs":

> Consider alternatives, like "gardens." We tend gardens. We don't fix them. Conversely, merely tending imperfect machines will leave them broken. A tended garden is self-correcting, but requires time and patience. Gardens are calm; machines are not. Same issues, different metaphors, different attitudes. Both models imply technical skill. One requires force and resistance; the other rewards serenity and tenderness. [...] Newtonian organisations are "downsized" and "streamlined." Gardens are "weeded" and plants are "pruned." Newtonian organisations fear "non-productivity" and reward instant results; gardens "lie fallow," anticipating "fertility" and "generativity" in nature's time.

It would of course be too categorical a position to conclude that anyone who now mentions economic forces, for example, or resorts to the expression "fine-tuning the economy" is to be considered as having a mechanistic view of the economy; however, when people have a choice between inanimate and animate metaphors, it might be worth analysing their discourse to determine their positions:

> What is significant about the use of inanimate metaphors for the conceptualisation of market movements as compared with the use of animate metaphors for the conceptualisation of the economy and economic organisations is that the economist seeks to create a very different social perception of his role. [...] By describing market movements in terms of inanimate, almost random, movements, the economist is freeing himself from the expectation of having to come up with the right answers. If market behavior is seen as something uncontrollable – like the weather – the economist cannot be blamed for making inaccurate predictions, for getting it wrong. (Charteris-Black 2000: 160-161)

The rhetorical use of metaphor should not be overlooked, which requires considering metaphorical terms and any other type of term against the background of discourse and in their situational context, i.e. *in situ*. Chapters 4 and 5 have shown that neonyms and metaphorical terms are embedded in their historical, cultural and social contexts. Other types of terms that draw the linguist's attention for their atypical character cannot be considered as isolated elements and extracted from their discursive context. The next chapter is devoted to those terms and the questions they raise. The answers to those questions can bring new insight into the mutual influence of terms and their discursive environment.

6. Insights from indeterminate terms with relation to discourse

> Indeterminacy in contexts of strategic interaction […] is an issue that is constantly swept under the rug because it is often disruptive to pristine social theory. But the theory is fake: the indeterminacy is real.
>
> Russel Hardin
> *Indeterminacy and Society* (2005)

> How wonderful that we have met with a paradox. Now we have some hope of making progress.
>
> Niels Bohr, quoted in R. Moore,
> *Niels Bohr, the Man and the Scientist*
> (1967: 140)

Keeping in mind the efforts of economists to have their field recognised as a respectable science (Chapter 3), it might seem incongruous to mention the inclusion of loose, equivocal, ambiguous, euphemistic or oxymoronic terms in economics. Inevitably, they raise the question of the compatibility of indeterminacy, vagueness and uncertainty with science in general and with economics in particular. They also beg the question of the viability of indeterminate terms and require investigating further into what can justify their *raison d'être*. The aim of this chapter is to present different types of terms that can be considered as "anomalous" with reference to the ideal of stable, transparent, univocal terms. Section 1 first offers an overview of the concept of indeterminacy and its manifestations and then considers the issue against the background of a broader analysis of the evolution of sciences. Section 2 presents the case of economics, and the positions of some economists on precise terms, concepts and definitions, before going on to deal with puzzles, paradoxes, oxymora and misnomers. Section 3 discusses the specificity of economic discourse and style, underlining the inherent uncertain and risky character of economic analysis, which helps to understand the existence of loose terms. A number of euphemistic terms are used as illustrations. Again, the information on economics discourse provided in this chapter was collected thanks to the questions raised by the "atypical" terms encountered in the broad field of economics.

6.1. Indeterminacy and its compatibility with science

6.1.1. Is indeterminacy the most appropriate term?

When dealing with such issues as vagueness, fuzziness or imprecision, the first challenge is to find a single appropriate term to include all the instances of ambiguous, misleading, inappropriate, inaccurate, fuzzy or vague terms that can be found in economics. The decision to opt for "indeterminacy" was motivated by the multifaceted nature of the term and its broad acception. In scientific contexts, indeterminacy can apply to concepts of uncertainty, and in more general linguistic contexts it refers to questions of loose meaning, concept or definition as well as to the difficulty of interpreting texts. Anything that is not determinate is difficult to quantify or to test, to predict or to prove, which explains why scientists usually try to avoid indeterminacy, except for researchers in modern quantum mechanics or chaos theory.

Although indeterminacy and vagueness are sometimes used interchangeably, it seems that indeterminacy remains a broader category as cases of indeterminacy without vagueness may be found. Consequently, vagueness can be said to be an example of indeterminacy. This is confirmed by Andersen (2002: 137), who considers vagueness and ambiguity as types of indeterminacy and therefore presents them in positions of hyponyms[131]. As this is not a philosophical treatise, it is not necessary to go into the details of supervaluationist semantics

131 He further subdivides ambiguity into polysemy and homonymy.

proposed as a way of accommodating truth-value gaps or the Sorites Paradox, but the reader who is interested in such issues can refer to the extensive literature by philosophers of language who have studied these phenomena[132]. Suffice it to say that vagueness applies to borderline cases where a proposition neither applies clearly nor fails to apply. For example, if one says "X is rich", one remains vague as to how much money is needed in the bank to qualify for the "rich" category. As vagueness might be associated with unspecificity, it may be helpful to agree on these concepts. A term is said to be unspecific if it applies to a variety of cases, while it is ambiguous if it has more than one meaning: in the latter case, it is polysemous. For example, "loose terms" is ambiguous out of context depending on whether one is dealing with terminology that is not precise, or investment – as in "Banks move to renegotiate loose terms on buyouts". "Bank" can refer to a river or a banking institution. However, as such terms are also context-dependent the ambiguity should be easy to remove. "Loose terms" can also be considered as unspecific, since it does not state clearly what type of "looseness" is concerned. Finally, a vague term need not be ambiguous if it has only one vague meaning.

Apart from the differences between the various terms referred to above, it is also important to distinguish between unintentionally and intentionally misleading terms. Some terms are misleading because the concept they denote has evolved over time, in which case the link between meaning and form has been so stretched that one may be confused. The reason can also be fluctuating concepts that have not yet been stabilised. Some terms are puzzling because of their paradoxical character, as is the case with oxymoronic terms. Other terms can be referred to as misnomers when they are inadequate or unsuitable, though there is no intention on the part of their author to deceive people. In other instances, weasel words are intentionally evasive or misleading, resulting in equivocation or obfuscation. Euphemisms, for example, can be either intentional as a code reserved for those who can decipher them, or simply a fashion or a natural way of expression.

---

132 Van Fraasen (1966), Fine (1975), Williamson (1994), Schiffer (2000), Wright (2006).

When studying such terms as euphemisms and oxymora, it is essential to distinguish between objective and subjective appraisal of these terms. Since “beauty is in the eye of the beholder”, or so they say, the euphemistic or oxymoronic character of some terms may be underlined by an individual out of irony and not because the terms were intrinsically euphemistic or oxymoronic. This reinforces the idea that terms should be studied in their textual and discursive environment, if only to avoid misinterpretations. Though “indeterminate terms” does read like an oxymoron, there seem to be instances of indeterminacy in all sciences. The question of the commensurability of indeterminacy and science therefore needs to be investigated further.

6.1.2. Indeterminacy vs. clarity in science

Philosophers of science have expressed two conflicting opinions on the importance of clarity in science. Tenants of the “traditional” view hold that precision and conceptual clarity are essential for differentiating between science and faith; in addition, precise and clear concepts limit the risk for scientists to commit errors of logic and draw false conclusions whereas shifting boundaries might lead to an uncontrollable expansion of concepts. Frege ([1903] 1952: §56), for example, called for concepts with sharp boundaries: “a concept that is not sharply defined is wrongly termed a concept”. This view was shared by Weber ([1904] 1949: 107): “the construction of sharp and unambiguous concepts relevant to the concrete individual viewpoint which directs our interest at any given time affords the possibility of clearly realising the limits of their validity.” It then seems that, by being too accommodating, vague concepts can only be an obstacle to scientific progress. From this perspective, conceptual clarity is a precondition for science to be able to carry out empirical tests, to verify or refute hypotheses, and to validate results.

Other philosophers contend that conceptual vagueness may offer an interesting alternative, and can even be an asset. Feyerabend (1975) claims that vagueness can fuel creativity while obsession with conceptual rigour and precise language can be detrimental to creative thinking. Wittgenstein argues that concepts that have blurred boundaries are more adaptable and that, instead of reducing concepts to a single definition, it might be more advisable to think in terms of "family resemblance"; more particularly, it might be more fruitful when a concept is used across disciplines. His series of questions, implicitly answered by the last two, clearly translates his position ([1953] 2009: 71): "But is a blurred concept a concept at all? Is an indistinct photograph a picture of a person at all? Is it even always an advantage to replace an indistinct picture by a sharp one? Isn't the indistinct one often exactly what we need?"

In the debate on clarity, precision or indeterminacy in science, both positions have advantages and drawbacks. Whether one deals with scientific concepts or communication, indeterminacy cannot be categorised as a positive or negative phenomenon so easily. As Antia (2007: xvi), referring to Beaugrande (1997) points out, "indeterminacy can manifest negatively as vagueness but also positively as openness, 'hospitality' or ability to accommodate concurrent possibilities. Determinacy, on the other hand, can manifest negatively as bias that ignores certain kinds of data and positively as clarity or perspicuity." The debate should also be seen against the background of the history of philosophical, scientific and intellectual positions. The eighteenth century, which experienced the first industrial revolution, marked a break with religion as a traditional source of authority: the Age of Enlightenment resolutely opted for rational thought and science. Following on, the nineteenth century ushered in a mechanical, mathematical, empirical and rational view of the world which influenced the way science was considered: it was the way to get at truth, to understand the world and to predict it. The era of positivism and the "mechanistic theory" reinforced the idea that concepts could and should be clearcut. The 1950s, however, marked a shift to post-positivism, which was not merely an adjustment, but a rejection of the central tenets of positivism. Based on the notion that measurements and observation are fallible, theories revisable, and that scientists are unavoidably biased by their cultural experiences and worldviews, it promoted triangulation across a number of sources to avoid errors. In so doing, it highlighted the relative validity of concepts. The current period is sometimes referred to as post-normal (Funtowicz and Ravetz 1993, 2003) to insist on the idea that we are living in a complex, chaotic world, which calls for adaptability, imagination and humility, thereby reinforcing the idea that no concept is valid forever, as research takes place in a highly uncertain environment. Undeniably, the twenty-first century is much more uncertain than the eighteenth century, even though Benjamin Franklin already stated then that "in this world nothing is certain but death and taxes". Interestingly, and quite logically, the evolution in the approaches to terminology parallels that of people's awareness of the relative validity of scientific concepts in the course of the twentieth century. In this respect, as pointed out by Arthur (1999: 1), one should consider the twentieth century as marking the end of certainty in science:

> The story of the sciences in the twentieth century is one of a steady loss of certainty. Much of what was real and machine-like and objective and determinate at the start of the century, by mid-century was a phantom, unpredictable, subjective and indeterminate. What had *defined* science at the start of the century – its power to predict, its clear subject/object distinction – no longer defined it at the end. In the century just past, science after science lost its innocence. Science after science grew up.

6.2. Indeterminacy and economics

What is true for other sciences is also true for economics. Its credibility as a science and the worldview that prevailed when it tried to impose itself alongside other well-established sciences such as physics required discipline and clarity in the elaboration of the theory. Admitting uncertainty might have meant recognising the field's ineligibility for the status of a science. In today's fast-paced and increasingly uncertain world, the situation has changed. For all that, it does not mean that economists should not make an effort to discipline themselves and agree on concepts and terms as far as possible. This section offers a review of economists' preoccupations with indeterminacy and clarity, reinforcing the remarks in Chapter 4 about economists as wordsmiths. It also points out the inevitable uncertainty theorists and practitioners have to deal with. In the light of the number of theoretical paradoxes and puzzles left unanswered, oxymora do not seem so incongruous. The illustrations provided in this section suggest that oxymoronic terms may coincide with periods of disturbing change that call former theoretical assumptions into question or introduce challenging innovations for practitioners. In order to understand this section and the next, it is essential to keep in mind that economic theory finds its practical applications in political decisions and economic policy as well as in management decisions. It is thus important for theorists as well as practitioners and decision-makers to factor in uncertainty in the way they communicate their analyses and decisions; unavoidably, the high stakes involved affect the type of discourse that they can afford to use, and caution, at both lexical and syntactic levels, is the rule. At the same time, it would be a mistake to consider that these people can be cautious in most of their discourse and straightforward in the concepts they refer to by means of set, transparent terms; the two go together. Undeniably, there may be some discrepancy between the theoretical requirements for clarity and exactness, and the practical, pragmatic needs for convincing, credible pronouncements whose impact on the targeted audiences may be decisive for the evolution of a country's or the world's economy. Still, if one wishes to understand how terms adapt to the overall content to serve the purpose of efficient communication, one should not analyse them in isolation from discourse, but *in situ, in vivo* as advocated by a number of researchers in terminology who have adopted a communication-oriented, discourse-centred approach.

6.2.1. Economists' preoccupations with indeterminacy and clarity

For a long time, researchers and theorists in economics were faced with the challenge of imposing their field as a discipline and as a serious, reliable science, hence the preoccupation with clarity and agreement on definitions and terms, which was expressed regularly. Though laxity cannot be tolerated, positions seem to have evolved from intolerance of loosely-defined terms to more open-mindedness as regards justifiable change in terms and concepts. Back in 1826, Nassau W. Senior, who held the first chair of political economy at Oxford University, provided basic information for an Appendix to a revised edition of a book by Archbishop Richard Whately. The title of the appendix clearly announced his concerns: "On Certain Terms which are Peculiarly Liable to be Used Ambiguously in Political Economy". An interesting statement read: "There would be as little difference of opinion among Political Economists as among Mathematicians if they had possessed a vocabulary of general terms as precisely defined as the mathematical". Senior also regretted the lack of precise definitions when some ordinary terms were used in a specific sense or new ones coined, and the inconsistent use of some terms, which could only confuse the reader:

> The English Work which has attracted the most attention during the present century, Mr. Ricardo's *Principles of Political Economy,* is deformed by a use of words so unexplained, and yet so remote from ordinary usage, and from that of other writers on the same subject, and frequently so inconsistent, as to perplex every reader, and not infrequently to have misled the eminent writer himself. We do not complain of all his innovations in language: such innovations are, for scientific purposes, frequently indispensable, and we shall be forced to make many ourselves. What we do complain of is, that his innovations, such, for instance, as the substitution of the word *Value* for *Cost,* are frequently unnecessary, and are almost always made without any warning to his readers; and that the same words, such, for example, as the adjectives *high* and *low,* when applied to wages, are used by him sometimes in their popular sense, as expressing an amount, and sometimes in a technical sense of his own, as expressing a proportion. ([1850]1854: §1.10)

One year later, Malthus echoed this view in the preface to his *Definitions in Political Economy*, considering that the differences of opinions among political economists were due to "the different meanings in which the same terms [had] been used by different writers":

> It has sometimes been said of political economy, that it approaches to the strict science of mathematics. But I fear it must be acknowledged, particularly since the great deviations which have lately taken place from the definitions and doctrines of Adam Smith, that it approaches more nearly to the sciences of morals and politics.

> It does not seem yet to be agreed what ought to be considered as the best definition of wealth, of capital, of productive labour, or of value; – what is meant by real wages; – what is meant by labour; – what is meant by profits; – in what sense the term 'demand' is to be understood, etc. (It may seem strange to the reader, but it is nevertheless true, that the meanings of all these terms, which had been settled long ago, and in my opinion with a great approach towards correctness, by Adam Smith, have of late been called in question, and altered).
>
> As a remedy for such differences, it has been suggested, that a new and more perfect nomenclature should be introduced. [...] yet in such sciences as morals, politics, and political economy, where the terms are comparatively few, and of constant application in the daily concerns of life, it is impossible to suppose that an entirely new nomenclature would be submitted to; and if it were, it would not render the same service to these sciences, in promoting their advancement, as the nomenclatures of Linnæus, Lavoisier, and Cuvier, to the sciences to which they were respectively applied. (1827 *Chapter 1: Rules for the definition and application of terms in political economy*)

He then suggested four rules that should help solve the problems: 1) recommending clear and stable definitions and 2) advocating the need, when in doubt, to refer to the definitions provided by the founders of terms. He insisted that (3) terms and definitions should be changed only when necessary and that, in most cases, (4) "the same terms should always be applied in the same sense". Otherwise, and unless the context made things clear, any particular use should be clearly specified. Some parallels with Wüster's positions are quite striking.

In the early twentieth century, Moore (1906: 211) also stated the need to use terms more carefully, choosing the example of the term "competition" and wondering about the confusion created by the number of modifiers used to qualify it: "How far has the analysis of this term proceeded towards definiteness and precision? [...] In what respect is the idea of competition changed when the modifiers 'perfect', 'unlimited', 'indefinite', 'free', 'pure', are added?" His paper on the topic of *Paradoxes of competition* opens on a long, interesting statement on the historical development of terms:

> Economic terms seem to pass in their historical development through a series of stages which without pretension to rigidness, may be described as follows: first, no definition is given but it is assumed that everyone has a sufficiently

clear idea of the subject to make a formal definition unnecessary; second, a definition is attempted and a number of exceptional forms are noted; third, with the further increase of data, the relative importance of the various forms changes, confusion in discussion is introduced, logomachy takes the place of constructive investigation; fourth, a complete classification of the forms embraced under the original term is made, and problems are investigated with reference to these classes. The bewildering vagueness of economic theory is largely due to the fact that the terms used are in all of these stages of development.

Inconsistency in the use of some terms may not only give rise to misunderstandings, but also trigger major controversies. Such was the case with Keynes's use of the terms "savings" and "investment" as defined in the *General Theory* (1936) "in direct contradiction to the definitions he had used six years earlier in his *Treatise on Money*" (Coats 1990: 73). The question of whether the variation in definitions was just a matter of denomination or, more significantly, a matter of substance and theory, was obviously seriously debated in the economic journals of the time.

Fisher's concern with the proliferation of neonyms around the question of utility has already been mentioned (Chapter 4, Sub-section 4.2.1). In the 1960s, Machlup also expressed his interest in and concern with the use of economic terms in a series of papers where he examined such "terminological ambiguities and conceptual obscurities" as "marginal product" (1937), "forced or induced saving" (1943), "balance of payments" (1950), "equilibrium and disequilibrium" (1958), or "statics and dynamics" (1959). He described the latter pair as "kaleidoscopic words" and highlighted the confusion that can result from the use of such ill-defined, ambiguous terms. His goal was to contribute to "the terminological cleaning-up job that becomes necessary from time to time" ([1963] 1991: 3). He was however more open to change than some of his predecessors, provided the change was motivated:

To complain about the continuous change of concepts and terms, and about the conversion of ideas and names, is to misunderstand the nature of growth in a body of knowledge – at least in the social sciences. [...] To be sure, willful innovations sometimes suggest change merely for the sake of change. If concepts and terms shift like women's fashions, the change may confuse discus-

> sion and become a nuisance. But otherwise, we must accept it as a fact that new problems and new treatments of old problems may require changes in concepts and in terms. [...] Better understanding of the concepts usually results in better understanding of the phenomena whose explanation they are to serve. (1943: 26)

This more pragmatic position had already been expressed by Fraser (1937: viii); although he clearly disapproved of unnecessary individualistic usage of terms and warned against the resulting confusions, he also explained variations in meaning as the signs of a dynamic field of research, able to adapt to new circumstances and phenomena:

> If economists as a whole were to adopt a corpus of technical terms, each one with an unalterable meaning and content, there would be a real danger of their being left behind by the march of events. A static terminology is not well suited to the study of dynamic phenomena.

The presence of indeterminate terms in economics can also be explained by its very nature: apart from "black swans", which describe major disruptive events characterised by unpredictability, a lot of situations deal with strategic interaction and choice-making, and in such situations, indeterminacy is pervasive. Economics, it must be remembered, relies on human beings, not on orderly mechanical parts. As human beings have emotions and weaknesses, their reactions are not always predictable. Under such circumstances, one can only guess what other agents will do, but there is no real certainty. While aleatory uncertainty is irreducible, epistemic uncertainty is reducible in principle, since access to information is easy. Yet, the sheer bulk of information may well be an obstacle; besides, many domains may find that projections far into the future are virtually impossible, due to the complex or chaotic nature of the elements likely to bear on people, events and phenomena (Lempert *et al.* 2004). The difficulty of accurately predicting events in the long-term led Keynes (1923, Ch.3) to declare: "The long run is a misleading guide to current affairs. In the long run, we are all dead. Economists set themselves too easy, too useless a task if in tempestuous seasons they can only tell us that when the storm is past the ocean is flat again." Degrees of uncertainty must, of course, be taken into consideration. In addition, a conceptual distinction should be made between risk and uncertainty as regards decision-making (Knight 1921): when making decisions under risk, the decision-maker can rely on mathematics to determine with certainty the probabilities of the consequences of this or that choice, which is not possible for decision-making under uncertainty. In the field of macroeconomics, for example, whenever theory is inconsistent with observed data, one refers to the phenomenon as a puzzle. It seems that uncertainty, indeterminacy, risk and asymmetric information or asymmetric perceptions of the same information are inherent in economics, which, again, is not an exact science. Another element contributing to the lack of certainty and predictability in the economy is technological progress, which causes the economy to undergo constant changes. These changes in turn cause economists to realise that no theory can be considered as proven forever since reality may contradict analyses that had gone unchallenged for years.

6.2.2. Paradoxes, puzzles, oxymora and misnomers

The theoretical paradoxes and puzzles, which are officially acknowledged in economics, as shown in Table 17, bear witness to the intrinsically uncertain character of the domain.

paradox	puzzle
ALLAIS PARADOX	BACKUS-KEHOE-KYDLAND PUZZLE
ARROW'S PARADOX (ARROW'S IMPOSSIBILITY THEOREM, ARROW INFORMATION PARADOX)	BACKUS-SMITH PUZZLE
BERTRAND PARADOX	DIVIDEND PUZZLE
BRAESS'S PARADOX	EQUITY HOME BIAS PUZZLE
CONDORCET'S PARADOX = VOTING PARADOX	EQUITY PREMIUM PUZZLE
DEMOGRAPHIC-ECONOMIC PARADOX	FELDSTEIN-HORIOKA PUZZLE
DIAMOND-WATER PARADOX (OR PARADOX OF VALUE)	HOME BIAS IN TRADE PUZZLE
DOLLAR AUCTION PARADOX	REAL EXCHANGE RATE PUZZLES
DOWNS–THOMSON PARADOX	SHIMER PUZZLE
EASTERLIN PARADOX	WAR'S INEFFICIENCY PUZZLE
EDGEWORTH PARADOX	

ELLSBERG PARADOX	
EUROPEAN PARADOX	
GIBSON'S PARADOX	
GIFFEN PARADOX	
ICARUS PARADOX	
JEVONS PARADOX	
LEONTIEF PARADOX	
LUCAS PARADOX	
MANDEVILLE'S PARADOX	
METZLER PARADOX	
PARADOX OF THRIFT	
PARADOX OF TOIL	
PARADOX OF VALUE	
PLEASURE PARADOX (= THE PARADOX OF HEDONISM)	
PRODUCTIVITY PARADOX (ALSO KNOWN AS SOLOW COMPUTER PARADOX)	
SCITOVSKY PARADOX	
SERVICE RECOVERY PARADOX	
ST. PETERSBURG PARADOX	
THE TRIFFIN DILEMMA (OR THE TRIFFIN PARADOX)	

Table 17. Terms referring to theoretical paradoxes in economics[133]

When one considers the list of enigmas left unanswered in the course of economic theory-building, it is not so surprising to find a number of oxymora among economic and management terms. It is of course impossible to draw up an exhaustive list of such terms but a few examples[134] will help illustrate the phenomenon, once the definition of oxymoron and the types of oxymora taken into consideration here have been made clear.

The definition of oxymoron by the Merriam-Webster dictionary is "a combination of contradictory or incongruous words (as *cruel kindness*); broadly: something (as a concept) that is made up of contradictory or incongruous elements; a word or expression that combines two contradictory elements". Oxymora destabilise precisely

133 These terms were extracted from *An Eponymous Dictionary of Economics* (Segura & Braun 2004).

134 All the examples mentioned in this section have been collected from economics and management textbooks.

because of their paradoxical nature. They are used in literature as well as in everyday conversation, where their frequency tends to make people blind or deaf to their inner contradiction and incongruity: for example, "virtual reality" will not shock many users as being an oxymoron. Without claiming to offer a taxonomy of oxymora, it is important to establish a distinction between inadvertent, intentional and opinionated oxymora. Examples of inadvertent oxymora can be found in everyday use as in the expression "found missing" or in the oft-quoted example of "an original copy". Deliberately coined oxymora are often meant to draw people's attention to a paradox. Opinionated oxymora will be left aside here as they contain no objective contradiction; in this respect, they are not oxymora *per se* but the speaker perceives them as such and calls them so just out of irony or for ideological purposes. An example in the field of management could be "business ethics": though there is no contradiction between ethics and business, some people might want to insist on the fact that "the business of business being business" (Friedman 1970), it is not compatible with behaving in an ethical way.

The first example of an economic oxymoron, CREATIVE DESTRUCTION, a term associated with Schumpeter, is particularly characteristic of a deliberate desire to signal a period marked by an unsettling transition accompanying radical innovation. New entrepreneurs enter the market and destroy the value of older companies. Technological progress is at the root of such rapid transformation: a textbook example is the record, which was replaced by the cassette tape, which was itself replaced by the compact disc until MP3 players appeared. As a consequence of technological progress, sharp demand for new specialised skills causes old jobs to disappear and people to be out of work… until they update their skills and can be hired for the newly-created jobs. This is an optimistic interpretation of an often much darker reality, for there is no guarantee that the people with obsolete skills will be able to acquire the new skills that could give them a chance to find new jobs. In the short term, there is a price to pay and CREATIVE DESTRUCTION does indeed result in layoffs. In the longer term, it creates new opportunities for more rewarding jobs in more creative companies; society as a whole is said to benefit as the overall quality of life improves and the next generations are better off. Thus the two elements in the oxymoron translate the negative and positive aspects of the phenomenon. But the order of the words has a more positive impact than if it had been inverted and presented as "*destructive creation[135]". It is always a good idea to start with the positive aspect.

The second example, *RATIONAL EXPECTATIONS*, illustrates a term that was probably not intended as an oxymoron, though expectations and reasoning belong to different realms. As a rule, even though one may reasonably know that the future will not be rosy one may nevertheless hope and expect it to be so. Expectations are usually positive. The term deserves our attention because its oxymoronic character underlines an important shift that has taken place in economic theory. For a long time, *homo oeconomicus* was a fictitious person governed by self-interest and premised to be rational, and it was taken for granted that all economic agents would make the best choices on the basis of the information available to them. However, *homo oeconomicus* is only rational in models and theorists have gradually come to realise that economic agents are human beings and, as such, may make decisions in a stochastic manner: behavioural economists and researchers in neuroeconomics and socioeconomics have factored in emotional and cognitive biases, which call into question the very concept of rational expectations and choices.

The third example refers to the way economists describe graphs, resorting to terms such as *FLAT CURVE* or *ZERO SLOPE*, which obviously raise a few questions. How can you speak of a *STRAIGHT-LINE DEMAND CURVE* or a *HORIZONTAL DEMAND CURVE* as do Samuelson and Nordhaus (2005: 72-73)? In the context of yield curves, the yields of similar-quality bonds against their maturities are plotted on a graph, ranging from shortest to longest. Thus, investors can compare the yields offered by short-term, medium-term and long-term bonds. There are three main types of yield curves that correspond to three different shapes: an upward-sloping yield curve (a positive or "normal" curve), a downward-sloping yield curve (a negative or "inverted" curve) and a *FLAT YIELD CURVE* when there is little or no difference between short- and long-term yield. Not only is *FLAT CURVE* an oxymoron,

135 The asterisk in front of the expression signals that it does not exist and cannot be considered as a term.

but it is also indeterminate in its dual definition: "little" or "no" difference does not refer to the same reality, and the confusion is fed by the existence of "humped curve" as an alternative term for "flat curve". This is translated on a graph through a quasi-horizontal or horizontal line, or a *ZERO SLOPE*. In general, in economics, the concept of slope is used to measure the rate at which changes are taking place. Thus, economists can measure how demand changes when price changes or how consumption is affected when income changes. When referring to a dome-shaped curve, the slope is always positive in the rising region, negative in the falling region and exactly zero at the peak or maximum of the curve.

In the realm of management, a series of oxymora resulting from recent research in management theory also deserves attention; two of them have already been mentioned as neonyms in Chapter 4: *FLAT HIERARCHY* and *ACTIVE INERTIA*. In both cases, the elements seem mutually exclusive. For the layperson, hierarchy usually conjures up the idea of a pyramidal structure which can be translated into a chart showing the various layers of power and decision on a vertical axis, and the various functions, or divisions on a horizontal axis. What then is a *FLAT HIERARCHY*? It is simply an organisation with fewer layers, where the chain of command is much shorter, which can lead to improved communication and foster strong team spirit. As for *ACTIVE INERTIA*, it is also puzzling as a term. It translates the idea of inefficient measures and obsolete solutions; it does not refer to a lack of action as in inertia, but it points out vain, inappropriate action. Another pair of oxymora is *MASS CUSTOMISATION* or *A MASS MARKET OF ONE*. These synonymous terms belong to the field of marketing strategies and the association of ideas they suggest is rather startling, since large numbers of people seem irreconcilable with individualisation. However, after the era of marketing to the masses, motivated by economies of scale, this new strategy involves conceiving a basic model that is flexible enough to be adapted to consumers' individual tastes at a later stage of production, while retaining the low unit costs of mass production. These oxymora were probably originally coined on purpose to sell the idea of a marketing strategy likely to attract customers from competitors.

The case of *KNOWLEDGE MANAGEMENT* is more difficult to deal with as an oxymoron, but it nevertheless exhibits an odd combination of words: knowledge belongs to the field of cognition which is individual, while management involves overall organisation. As mentioned in Chapters 4 and 5, knowledge workers are the owners of their human capital. However, they also represent added value for a company and so it is easy to understand that no company can afford to ignore this type of asset, which needs to be managed carefully and appropriately; new positions as CKOs (Chief Knowledge Officers) have even been created to identify human capital and to stimulate knowledge gathering and sharing. Thus, *KNOWLEDGE MANAGEMENT* does make sense and requires turning personal knowledge into corporate knowledge. The apparent paradox disappears once the meaning has been verified.

The next set of examples introduces the transition between oxymora and misnomers. The general context is the theoretical debate on growth against the background of concerns for the future of our planet. Four terms contain an internal contradiction, namely *ZERO GROWTH, NON GROWTH, NEGATIVE GROWTH* and *DE-GROWTH*[136]. They are often used in reaction to *SUSTAINABLE GROWTH*, so the debate is quite confusing. Opponents to *SUSTAINABLE GROWTH* or even *SUSTAINABLE DEVELOPMENT* claim that these terms themselves are oxymora, unless development is associated with no growth, which again underlines the paradox. *SUSTAINABLE GROWTH* or *SUSTAINABLE DEVELOPMENT* are currently used by a wide range of people – politicians, corporate managers, environmentalists, various lobbyists – and they are given different definitions depending on who uses them and for what purpose. It is true that no one would dare venture the idea of "unsustainable development". Accordingly, one may wonder what use the terms actually are. When analysing their components, depending on whether one is optimistic, realistic or pessimistic, one will obviously end up with different interpretations. Some people will conclude that it is the sort of development or growth that will take the finite resources of the planet into account and guarantee a decent quality of life for future generations; others will con-

136 The idea of de-growth, *décroissance* in French, can be traced back to Romanian economist Nicholas Georgescu-Roegen (1971) who pointed out that the very fact of exploiting the Earth's finite resources has a negative impact as it causes the total store of energy available to diminish.

sider that sustainability and development cannot be reconciled and that the real meaning of the terms is "endless increase". The proponents of *ZERO GROWTH, NON-GROWTH, NEGATIVE GROWTH* and *DE-GROWTH* envisage a new approach, though they may not fully agree on how to achieve their goals. The terms *ZERO GROWTH* or *NON-GROWTH* raise the question of whether one can speak of growth if nothing changes; *STEADY-STATE ECONOMICS* is also used as a synonym, though it may be denounced as a misnomer, for even the present state may not be satisfactory for those who consider we have already gone too far in endangering the future of the planet. As for *NEGATIVE GROWTH* and *DE-GROWTH*, they make one wonder if growth is compatible with the idea of shrinking or regressing, so that when one considers their meaning, one realises that these oxymora are misnomers. They are, however, not synonyms. According to Latouche[137] (2011), one of the leading voices of the *DÉCROISSANCE* movement, "a de-growth society project is radically different from negative growth". He describes the former as "an austere therapy that is voluntarily undertaken to improve one's well-being when we are under the threat of obesity through overconsumption" (2008, online). For him, the drastic measures to reduce consumption and return to a more simple life are more advisable than *NEGATIVE GROWTH* which he likens to the forced diet that "can lead to death through famine". "As for non-growth or zero-growth", he adds: "It has

137 <http://www.goodplanet.info/eng/Contenu/Points-de-vues/Degrowth-whether-you-like-it-or-not/%28theme%29/2386>
Serge Latouche is emeritus professor of economics at the University Paris-Sud 11 (Orsay). According to him, "Growth for the sake of growth" can only lead to a loss of well-being. De-growth requires reconsidering the activities that have a negative impact on the environment and do not yield any satisfaction. This can be achieved by putting an end to the increasing number of people and goods needlessly travelling across the globe and by reorganizing local economies; the advertising industry should be done away with as it incites people to desire and consume always more. The artificial, accelerated obsolescence of goods and machines should also be fought against as its sole aim is to feed the economic mega-engine. To the 6-R program – reassess, restructure, redistribute, reduce, reuse, recycle – suggested at the NGO Forum in Rio in 1992, a few more Rs could be added: reeducate, redefine, remodel, rethink and relocate. Quality should prevail over quantity, cooperation over competition, and altruism over selfishness.

been said time and time again. There is nothing worse than a growth society without growth." What is interesting in this hot debate about wasteful consumption, unrestrained resource depletion and growing populations is the emergence of a number of indeterminate terms – oxymora or misnomers. It tends to suggest that a period of disagreement on diagnoses and cures is likely to generate terms that can sometimes be considered as empty shells, but nevertheless signal that change is at stake; such debate and the underpinning questioning require close monitoring.

Another case worth mentioning in the borderline category between oxymora and misnomers is *AN L-SHAPED RECOVERY*. Although there is no explicit contradiction in the terms "L-shaped" and "recovery", when one considers the positive notion of recovery and the letter L supposed to refer to the curve representing the evolution of the economy on a graph, one may rightly wonder about the appropriateness of the term. By definition, "recovery" means improvement whereas the L-shape describes a sharp downward movement followed by a long flat period, which in no way suggests any improvement. The notion of recovering seems to have been stretched to mean "not getting worse", which points at the implicit oxymoronic character of "L-shaped recovery": it is definitely a misnomer.

Misnomers, as the name implies, are incorrect and therefore misleading as they suggest an interpretation which does not correspond to the real meaning of the term. One possible reason is for an older name to be retained while the notion has evolved. A typical example of this kind of problem is *HEDGE FUND*. The layperson may reasonably consider that investment in a hedge fund is safe, since "hedging" in finance means protecting oneself against risk. Actually, this was the original meaning and purpose of hedge funds. However, the notion has evolved and many hedge funds are now highly risky investments promising high returns, the returns being commensurate with the risks at stake. A similar disconnect between the original motivation for the terms and the evolution of the underpinning concept can be illustrated by the terms *EUROMARKET, EUROCURRENCY* and *EUROBONDS*, which have nothing to do with the euro in spite of their prefix. In fact, a *EUROCURRENCY* refers to stateless money and is defined as follows (Scott 2003):

> Funds deposited in a bank when those funds are denominated in a currency differing from the bank's own domestic currency. Eurocurrency applies to any currency and to banks in any country. Thus, if a Japanese company deposits yen in a Canadian bank, the yen will be considered Eurocurrency.

Likewise, a *EURODOLLAR* is a US dollar deposit outside the United States and, according to Farlex Financial Dictionary (2009), *EUROBONDS* are:

> issued or traded in a country using a currency other than the one in which they are denominated. This means that the bond uses a certain currency, but operates outside the jurisdiction of the central bank that issues that currency. Eurobonds are issued by multinational corporations; for example, a British company may issue a Eurobond in Germany, denominating it in US dollars.

The "euro" element in these terms stems from the fact that originally the deposits were made with European banks. Obviously, the euromarket has been extended to the rest of the world, but the terms have not been adapted accordingly, hence the potential confusion.

Other misnomers, which belong to the category of euphemisms, are left for further analysis later in this chapter. The examples that have been quoted in this section point at a number of situations which are signalled by oxymora or misnomers: periods of disagreement on hotly-debated issues, periods of innovation, periods of unsettling change that puzzles theorists, periods of disruptive change for practitioners and managers. All these situations involve some kind of uncertainty and naturally give birth to indeterminate terms. A number of other indeterminate terms, which can be described by the broad umbrella term euphemisms, can be accounted for by the challenges involved in communicating in the field of economics, whether between specialists or when addressing a larger public of economic agents. The next section focuses on the specificity of economic discourse and provides examples of how terms are subdued in order to suit the requirements of cautious communication.

6.3. The specificity of economic discourse

The specificity of economic discourse – in itself a generic term including different types of discourse – is the uncertainty of economics; this requires particular caution on the part of anyone who ventures to make a forecast, analyse a situation, express an opinion, announce findings or communicate decisions. Academics, experts, advisers and decision-makers are different, too, but they share a common denominator, the need to hedge pronouncements.

As Klamer insists in the last chapter of his book *Conversations with Economists* (1984: 234):

> [e]conomists do not only construct models and conduct empirical tests, they also argue on what a good model should look like. Moreover, they philosophize, appeal to common sense, and talk about other economists and their work. Economics involves the art of persuasion. In the absence of uniform standards and clear-cut empirical tests, economists have to rely on judgments, and they argue to render their judgments persuasive. This process leaves room for non-rational elements, such as personal commitment and style and social discipline.

A number of elements require our attention here. First, as is stated in the discussion on economics as a science at the end of Chapter 3, economic theory is based on models that make up for the impossibility of conducting real-life experiments. In this respect, it inevitably contains a fictional element; "economic theory is a convenient fiction, an 'as if', against which to measure the habitual, irrational, logical, egoistic, self-interested, bigoted, altruistic actions of individuals, firms, or governments – but it is not a model of reality" (Bell 1981: 70). As the validity of such models can always be questioned, there is a real need to account for their construction, and since they result from simplification, idealisation and abstraction, it is most important for their authors to hedge against potential criticism, which they do by resorting to such phrases as "*ceteris paribus*" / "all other things being equal", for example. The British economist Sir John Richard Hicks (1981: 232), who was awarded the Sveriges Riksbank Prize in Economic Sciences in Memory of Alfred Nobel with Kenneth Arrow in 1972, considered economics as a discipline rather than a science, simply because economic phenomena are neither permanent nor recurrent; on the contrary, they keep changing and some of them can even be unique. History has shown that no model, however sophisticated it may be, can guarantee flawless predictions. Analyses and projections are often contradicted by facts, as was the case in 1982 and 2009, when recessions had not been announced in the USA, and during the 2008 financial crisis when, week after week, forecasts turned out to be wrong.

The second important point in Klamer's remarks refers to the controversies that arise between the tenants of different schools of economics, whether about methodology or results. Economics as it is presented in textbooks may wrongly give the impression that theory construction has followed a smooth path and that most of the knowledge that is presented results from a consensus among economists. Disagreements and rivalries do exist, however, and economists, be they advisers or researchers, have to defend their point of view, bolster their arguments, and convince their peers if they wish to establish their reputation and authority. As McCloskey ([1985] 1998: xx) underlines, "the scientist doesn't speak into the void, or to herself. She speaks to a community of voices. She desires to be heeded, praised, published, imitated, honored, and loved. These are the desires. The devices of language are the means." This is true for all scientists, but particularly so for economists since they deal with a field whose material is the activities and reactions of human beings. They cannot afford to sound presumptuous and overtly discredit other researchers who have investigated the same field and reached different conclusions; they cannot ignore them either, which would be an insult or a sign that they have not read the relevant literature; as a result, they must remain polite in their criticism and politically correct, while justifying their position and establishing a research "niche". In order to present new results and conclusions that might contradict former papers by other economists, for example, they will resort to such expressions as "given the data available to this date", which is also a means to protect their own findings from future criticism.

Lastly, because even the best theory will fail if no one can be persuaded that it is valid, style is most important, and respect for the prevailing conventions of the community matter. Language and theory-construction cannot be dissociated:

> An awareness of language matters to a discipline because claim to knowledge can be made only by using language.[...] Language cannot be understood independently of the social context in which it is used, and written text provides one type of evidence concerning the way in which meanings are negotiated and knowledge is socially constructed. (Backhouse *et al.* [1993] 2007: 1)

Although many economists "pride themselves on their ability to speak like scientists, without colour, passion, or values, preferably in the language of mathematics" (Heilbroner 1990: 38), it can be said that "rhetoric – the art of persuasion – is the rock on which the mighty edifice of economics stands". And before persuading a larger audience of economic agents, economists have to persuade each other: "good science is good conversation" (McCloskey [1985] 1998: 162). The three pillars of rhetoric – logos, ethos and pathos – can serve the purpose of good communication. Logic is obviously required and achieved by means of sound argumentation, flawless methodology, reliance on facts, statistics and mathematics but it must be underlined explicitly; ethos refers to the position of authority of the author or speaker, who must prove worthy of scientific attention; pathos relies on appealing to others to share one's point of view, on being committed enough to win over one's audience to one's ideas.

Even though, historically, the smaller community of "pure" economists felt they belonged to a separate sphere and were uneasy about the practising economists who sold their services to the public or private sectors (Goodwin 1988), the distinction has now been blurred since a number of well-known economists have moved from one sphere to the other, in some cases leaving academe to work for the government, private business or think tanks before going back to their original occupations. The current Chairman of the Federal Reserve, Ben Bernanke, was formerly a tenured professor of economics at Princeton University. Another example is Arthur Okun, who started out as Professor of Economics at Yale University; he then served as the chairman of the Council of Economic Advisers under President Kennedy before becoming a fellow at the Brookings Institution in

Washington, D.C. Joseph Stiglitz, a university professor who currently teaches at the Columbia Business School and was awarded the Sveriges Riksbank Prize in Economic Sciences in Memory of Alfred Nobel in 2001, held various positions on the national and international stage: he was Chairman of the Economic Policy Committee of the OECD from 1993 to 1995 and Chairman of the Council of Economic Advisers from 1995 to 1997, before spending three years at the World Bank as Senior Vice-President and Chief Economist (1997–2000). He was then appointed Chairman of the Commission of Experts on Reforms of the International Monetary and Financial System by the President of the General Assembly of the United Nations; more recently (2008-2009) he chaired the International Commission on the Measurement of Economic Performance and Social Progress. He has also been acting as consultant for a great many institutions and organisations.

Economic discourse, therefore, should not be restricted to the discourse of theorists, academics and researchers. Economics is both a discipline, the realm of scientists seeking the "truth", and a profession, with practitioners, counsellors, managers and decision-makers. Depending on the circumstances, economists are thus impelled to address a multiplicity of audiences, a tentative list of which is provided by Coats (1990: 70). As academics, they deal with undergraduates and graduates, as well as "noneconomist academics, for example deans, promotion committees or research grant committees"; they also address fellow economist academics and other academics. As professional economists, they deal with nonacademic economists involved in business, banking, government, or international agencies; in addition, they also communicate with larger "nonacademic audiences including 'experts' in other fields, government and international agency bureaucrats, business persons, politicians, journalists", and, of course, members of the lay public.

In all cases, persuasion is an essential component of their discourse (Goodwin 1990: 209):

> persuasion of economic colleagues of the merits in contributions to the discipline (represented in journal articles, papers presented to conferences, and claims for tenure); persuasion of skeptical students and college administrators

> of the value of studying the subject; persuasion of patrons, such as foundations and governments agencies, that funds should be directed to it; persuasion of legislators, the media, and a broad lay public that the subject's "answers" to popular questions are worth attending; persuasion of clients that advice based on economic analysis is sound; and persuasion of judges and other arbiters that a client's case is sound while an opponent's is weak.

Technical progress is also dependent on rhetorical means: without persuasion, even a good idea remains an idea and fails to materialise. Inventors and entrepreneurs, for example, must find capital and inspire confidence. If they fail to convince investors, they will never be given the slightest chance to test their ideas. The stakes are also very high for the experts and decision-makers themselves, be they policy-makers or corporate managers: they all know that good policy is good conversation and that their discourse is going to be scrutinised and analysed, commented upon and explained to a larger, unsophisticated public, so that they cannot afford to commit the slightest mistake. Experts who are interviewed by or write for the media are fully aware that their assessment of a situation risks being questioned or proved wrong the next day or month. Policy-makers must carefully announce and justify their measures if they want to have the best chances of succeeding in their strategies. The Chairman of the Federal Reserve is well aware of the risks involved and of the power of words and good communication, which accounts for his use of the well-known Fedspeak, characterised by its "fuzzy transparency" (Resche 2004*b*): finding the right balance between saying too much and not saying enough is an art. Considering, for example, the time lag which separates decisions such as decreases or increases in interest rates and their actual impact on the economy, it is sometimes more efficient to talk the general public into reacting as one wishes them to than to opt for more aggressive measures that will only bear fruit months later. Careful selection of the appropriate terms and phrases will help achieve the desired effect. Similarly, managers in the corporate world have to face the judgment of all the stakeholders (employees, investors, customers, partners, suppliers, local communities, government, NGOs, etc.) if they make the wrong decisions or fail to communicate their decisions well. CEOs cannot afford to merely pay lip service to principles that are now so important in the eyes of society, whether in terms of workers' rights and safety, respect for the communities in which their factories are implanted or respect for the environment[138]. At a lower level, middle-managers know that teamwork also depends on persuasive speech and shared values.

Cautious statements and hedged discourse thus characterise all types of economic discourse, whether academic, pedagogical, managerial or political in the broad sense of the term. As data are constantly being reviewed in the light of new information, figures are used with utmost care: approximate quantifiers help to qualify statements. Economists, policy-makers and managers are neither magicians nor fortune tellers with crystal balls, but more like doctors trying to diagnose problems and to suggest and apply the best possible remedies. They must refrain from sounding aggressive, critical of rivals, or overly categorical. They must also make sure they have taken into consideration all the aspects of a problem and neglected no one. They must do their best to avoid being misunderstood, especially by the ordinary citizen in the context of communicating economic or monetary policy decisions, in which case the consequences could be disastrous for the general equilibrium of the country's economy.

The above was intended to highlight the common characteristics of various types of economic discourse, which confirm the fact that communication is never strictly informational. All the types of discourse mentioned here are produced in specific circumstances, and have to comply with conventions and norms. All those who write or speak in such circumstances are in positions of authority and must capitalise on their credibility. They all have a lot to lose from failing to assess the risks accurately and not playing by the rules. They are also accountable in one way or another for their statements: researchers and theorists have to justify their findings, experts their analyses and policy-makers and managers their decisions. In order to protect themselves from Face-Threatening Acts (FTAs), they use the whole range of "hedges" (Hyland 1994) or "shields" (Pindi & Bloor 1987) available under such circumstances. Quirk *et al.* (1972: 452-458) men-

138 All these elements fall under the umbrella term "corporate social responsibility" (CSR).

tion adverbs and phrases which they call "downtoners", and they distinguish four categories: compromisers (rather, sort of, kind of), diminishers (partly, slightly, to some extent), minimisers (possibly, hardly, in the least) and approximators (almost, practically, virtually). In addition, such discourse abounds in modal verbs, non-factive verbs, modifiers, vague quantifiers, signals of hypotheticality, and conditionals. An example of hedged discourse is offered below; it is an excerpt from Federal Chairman Ben Bernanke's speech on the US economic outlook at the International Monetary Conference in Atlanta (Georgia) dated June 2011[139]:

> US economic growth *so far this year looks* to have been *somewhat slower* than expected. Aggregate output increased at only 1.8 percent at an annual rate *in the first quarter*, and supply chain disruptions associated with the earthquake and tsunami in Japan are hampering economic activity *this quarter. A number of* indicators also *suggest some loss of momentum* in the labor market *in recent weeks*. We are, of course, monitoring these developments. That said, with the effects of the Japanese disaster on manufacturing output *likely to dissipate in coming months*, and with *some moderation* in gasoline prices *in prospect*, growth *seems likely to pick up somewhat* in the second half of the year. Overall, the economic recovery *appears to be continuing at a moderate pace*, albeit at a rate that is both uneven across sectors and frustratingly slow from the perspective of millions of unemployed and underemployed workers. (June 7th, 2011)

Characteristically, the very uncertain period requires even more caution than is usual: the not-so-good news cannot be hidden, of course, but is surrounded with a veil of vagueness as indicated by the words or expressions marked in italics. Indications of time are carefully chosen to suggest that if economic growth and output increase have been disappointingly slow in the "first quarter" and "so far this year", activity may pick up in the following quarters. The unemployment figures also concern the "recent weeks", but may improve in the coming months. The verbs also serve as hedges (look, seem, suggest, appear). The phrases that have been underlined here highlight the argumentative stance: economic activity has been affected by external factors that are temporary. US citizens can trust the monetary policy authori-

139 Emphases added.

ties for being alert to the situation, ready to act whenever necessary. Economic recovery is carefully mentioned, so as to be reassuring, and empathy with the unemployed or underemployed is expressed. The desired effect is to maintain credibility and confidence by acknowledging and sharing the population's frustration at not being able to feel any concrete impact of the announced recovery. This excerpt shows how important it is to weigh every single piece of information released and to be most humble and cautious in one's pronouncements as regards the evolution of the situation. As terms are unavoidable elements in specialised discourse, and are not isolated in watertight compartments, they are themselves submitted to the law of qualified, smooth discourse. This is why it is essential to analyse them while keeping in mind the reasons for constrained discourse in real situations of communication.

6.4. Economic euphemisms

Euphemistic terms in economics seem to be a necessity and they can be considered in the framework of a broader phenomenon described by *The Economist* through the neonym "euphenomics". Before examining various examples of euphemistic terms, it would be helpful to start with a number of definitions of euphemism and to build up a sort of mind map in order to have a better idea of the ideas associated with and the functions of this linguistic device. It will then be possible to determine how far they apply to euphemistic terms in the context of economic discourse.

Leech (1981: 45) defines the use of euphemism as "the practice of referring to something offensive or delicate in terms that make it sound more pleasant". Johnstone (2008: 59) underlines "the use of a supposedly less objectionable variant for a word with negative connotations". For Allen and Burridge (1991: 11), "euphemism is used as an alternative to a dispreferred expression, in order to avoid possible loss of face: either one's own face or, through giving offence, that of the audience, or of some third party". Sounding too aggressive, failing to respect the conventions of a discursive genre or of a given group or culture, being polemical, contradicting oneself, having a poor command of facts and figures, arousing fear, disbelief, disappointment or mistrust will automatically have a negative effect on the addressee and in return damage the addresser's reputation. Crespo Fernández (2005: 79) insists that euphemism is not just a matter of lexical choice or "linguistic makeup", but a real choice made by the speaker in a given discursive situation. Euphemism, however, must be differentiated from understatement. Though both processes aim at toning down a statement, their pragmatic aim differs. When using a euphemism, an author or speaker wishes to mitigate their statement and to convey less in order for people to understand less; when resorting to an understatement, they wish to convey less in order for people to understand more.

A network of connected ideas can be derived from the definitions provided above. First of all, the wish to soften or tone down a statement may imply resorting to circumlocution, metaphor or metonymy, which means leaving some aspects in the shadows and hiding part of the reality. Substitution of a less offensive, softer term for one that is deemed improper results in approximation and some guesswork is required for the addressee to understand the real message. If they are able to decipher the real message, they will realise and probably appreciate the precautions taken by the author or speaker, their consideration for others and respect for the norms and conventions. If, however, the addressee is not able to understand what is implicit, he or she will naively take what they read or hear literally and will be deceived. This is what happened when the subprime crisis erupted and people were left with *NEGATIVE EQUITY* which actually meant that their homes were worth less than they had paid for them. *DOWNVALUATION* was also conveniently used to account for the discrepancy between the sale price that had been agreed upon and the subsequent valuation by the mortgage lender's surveyor. Euphemism can thus be seen as a veil, which can be used positively or negatively. Naturally, a veil can be used as a sign of decency, prudishness, reserve, out of respect for others and oneself, in order to avoid shocking others and to protect oneself. But a veil can also be used to hide what one does not want to reveal, to disguise or distort reality under illusory appearances, to lie and to manipulate others. Euphemism, then, is both a "shield" and a "weapon" (Allan and Burridge 1991). Since euphemism can be understood as such or completely overlooked, it seems obvious that words or terms are not intrinsically euphemistic but become so because of the context in which they are used. It is also important to keep in mind that the reception of euphemism may differ from one person to the next: the same message may well be understood as euphemistic by one and not so by the other. Interpretation is always somewhat subjective. For Farb (1973: 91), "Any word is an innocent collection of sounds until a community surrounds it with connotations and then decrees that it cannot be used in certain speech situations. It is the symbolic value the specific culture attaches to the words and expressions." Fairclough (1992) highlights the functional purpose of euphemism in social discourse, and Allen and Burridge (1991: 4) state that "[E]uphemism and dysphemism are principally determined by the choice of expression within a given context: both the world spoken of, and the world spoken in." In the field of economics, or the world spoken of, there is little certainty, as has been discussed, and the world spoken in, i.e. that of most economic agents, expects appropriate measures, answers, advice and efficient solutions. Obviously, bridging the gap between those two worlds is a most challenging task which leaves little room for error and requires utmost care.

The current uncertain economic environment offers an opportunity to assess the impact of certain news items on the ordinary citizen and the world of investors. More precisely, the business cycle is a good illustration of how and why euphemistic terms are used in economics, even though some of these euphemisms also qualify as misnomers and can be dangerously misleading. The very term *BUSINESS CYCLE*[140] has been questioned by Milton Friedman who claimed it was

140 In the mid-twentieth century, a number of economists studied business cycles according to their periodicity: Joseph Kitchin proposed the Kitchin inventory cycle of 3-5 years; Clément Juglar identified the Juglar fixed investment cycle of 7-11 years (it is also considered as the typical business cycle); Simon Kuznets suggested the Kuznets infrastructural investment cycle of 15-25 years and Nikolai Kondratiev is known for the Kondratiev wave or long technological cycle of 45-60 years.

a misnomer because there is no real cyclical nature in what recent economic theory now refers to as *BUSINESS FLUCTUATIONS*. *BUSINESS CYCLE* is still used, however, by economists out of habit and the 1946 definition (Burns & Mitchell) still applies:

> Business cycles are a type of fluctuation found in the aggregate economic activity of nations that organize their work mainly in business enterprises: a cycle consists of expansions occurring at about the same time in many economic activities, followed by similarly general recessions, contractions, and revivals which merge into the expansion phase of the next cycle; in duration, business cycles vary from more than one year to ten or twelve years; they are not divisible into shorter cycles of similar characteristics with amplitudes approximating their own.

The first instance of recourse to euphemism in this sub-field dates back to 1936, when *RECESSION* started replacing *DEPRESSION* after the trauma caused by the Great Depression. Since then *DEPRESSION*, which has retained its negative connotation, has been consistently avoided. Nevertheless, the textbook definitions for *RECESSION* and *DEPRESSION* mention a difference in intensity between the two terms (Samuelson 2005: 736,749):

> Depression: a prolonged period characterised by high unemployment, low output and investment, depressed business confidence, falling prices, and widespread business failures. A milder form of business downturn is a recession, which has many of the features of a depression to a lesser extent.

> Recession: a period of significant decline in total output, income and employment, usually lasting from 6 months to a year and marked by widespread contractions in many sectors of the economy.

Interestingly, the definitions are a good example of the evasive character of economic discourse when it comes to dealing with quantities and duration: in the definition for *DEPRESSION*, we have no real idea of how "prolonged" the period, how "high" unemployment and how "low" output must be for *DEPRESSION* to be diagnosed. The same holds for how "milder" a downturn must be to decide that the situation corresponds to a *RECESSION* rather than a *DEPRESSION*. In addition, *RECESSION* is defined as lasting from six months to a year, while, for a long time, it was defined as two consecutive quarters of economic contraction. The vagueness related to time can be explained by the fact that in the 1990s the economic cycle seemed to have stretched, with each stage of the cycle lasting longer than usual. At the time, some observers explained the phenomenon by referring to "the new economy" while others suggested that the business cycle might be dead. This called into question the classical yardsticks and showed the former definition to be inadequate. Today's official definition, which serves as a reference, can be found on the NBER's[141] website. It is characteristic of the cautious discourse of economics and the NBER is clearly trying not to be disproved by facts:

> The NBER does not define a recession in terms of two consecutive quarters of decline in real GDP. Rather, a recession is a significant decline in economic activity spread across the economy, lasting more than a few months, normally visible in real GDP, real income, employment, industrial production, and wholesale-retail sales.

As it is extremely difficult to decide for sure when a period of recession started and ended, the NBER's Business Cycle Dating Committee is most cautious when announcing the end of a recession. Under such circumstances, mentioning a *DOUBLE-DIP RECESSION*[142] may be premature until any official announcement of the end of a given recession has been made. Consequently, any talk of a *DOUBLE-DIP RECESSION* can be considered as a dangerous misnomer: what is more, because it can frighten the general public into thinking that the economy will move back into a longer and perhaps more serious recession, it may make recovery even more difficult[143]. The time lag between the actual beginning and end of a recession and their official announcements is due to the need to wait for figures to be revised twice before declaring any official dates. The Committee insists that "There is no fixed timing

141 NBER: National Bureau of Economic Research.

142 A double-dip recession implies that, after a short-lived recovery following a recession, the economy falls back into recession.

143 However, seen from a different angle as a more technical term, it can serve as a euphemism for a less pleasant description of an anaemic recovery or a "non-recovery".

rule. The committee waits long enough so that the existence of a peak or trough is not in doubt and until it can assign an accurate peak or trough date." The official announcement for the trough date of June 2009 was made with utmost caution 15 months after that date, on September 20th, 2010:

> At its meeting, the committee determined that a trough in business activity occurred in the US economy in June 2009. The trough marks the end of the recession that began in December 2007 and the beginning of an expansion. The recession lasted 18 months, which makes it the longest of any recession since World War II. Previously the longest postwar recessions were those of 1973-75 and 1981-82, both of which lasted 16 months.
>
> In determining that a trough occurred in June 2009, the committee did not conclude that economic conditions since that month have been favorable or that the economy has returned to operating at normal capacity. Rather, the committee determined only that the recession ended and a recovery began in that month. [...] The trough marks the end of the declining phase and the start of the rising phase of the business cycle. Economic activity is typically below normal in the early stages of an expansion, and it sometimes remains so well into the expansion.
>
> The committee decided that any future downturn of the economy would be a new recession and not a continuation of the recession that began in December 2007. The basis for this decision was the length and strength of the recovery to date.

Earlier determinations took between 6 and 21 months, which illustrates the extreme difficulty of identifying troughs and peaks. Incidentally, it is worth noting that the very terms *TROUGH* and *PEAK*, though they are not misnomers, remain misleading for the layperson: peak is often interpreted as having a positive connotation, though it announces bad news, as the economy is bound to decline once it has reached a peak. Likewise, *TROUGH* is wrongly given a negative connotation.

A specific analysis of the comments on the 2001 recession in the semi-specialised press (Resche 2004*a*) highlighted the potentially traumatic effect of the ominous term recession itself, which was often replaced by the *R-WORD*, as if the mere fact of writing the full term could bring bad luck on the economy. Here again, the psychological dimension needs to be taken into account. If the general public hears about recession too clearly and too often, it is likely to start panicking and to overreact: consumption will decline along with confidence and this will precipitate recession before any measures taken to avoid the worst can have the slightest chance of becoming effective. Significantly, now that *DEPRESSION* is out of use, *RECESSION* and *DOWNTURN* tend to become increasingly interchangeable, even in textbook definitions: "A recession is a downturn in economic activity" (Lipsey & Chrystal 1999: 337). As a result, in order to fill the void left by *DEPRESSION* and to refer to different degrees of *RECESSIONS* or *SLOWDOWNS*, a series of adjectives is now commonly used to qualify the terms. This new trend only adds to the confusion, since it is very difficult to compare a *SHARP DOWNTURN* and a *MILD RECESSION*, or to distinguish between a *MEANINGFUL SLOWDOWN* and a *SUPERFICIAL DOWNTURN*. Besides, as is often the case, "terms typically do not remain euphemistic for long either. The negative perception people have of whatever the euphemistic word refers to ends up contaminating the word itself" (Burridge 1996: 43). Accordingly, *DOWNTURN* is likely to be replaced by *SLOWDOWN*; however, both terms retain a negative connotation inherent in "down". They are likely to be replaced in turn by *DECELERATION* or the oxymoron *DOWNGROWTH*. This phenomenon is referred to as the "euphemism treadmill" (Pinker 2007) and is comparable to Gresham's law in economics, according to which "bad money drives good money out of circulation"[144]. Here approximation and euphemisms drive out the "appropriate" terms and the process of erosion seems inevitable; once a euphemism no longer performs its role and loses its euphemistic power, it tends to be replaced by a new one.

The effect of a euphemism can be quite damaging if one considers that, as a misnomer, it can lead experts to wrongly diagnose the severity of a problem and commentators to downplay its consequences when writing for the general public. For example, probably in order to avoid using the traumatic term 'depression', the financial crisis resulting from the subprime crisis was referred to as *THE GREAT RECESSION*.

144 If coins containing metal of different value have the same value as legal tender, the coins composed of the cheaper metal will be used for payment, while those made of more expensive metal will be hoarded or exported and thus tend to disappear from circulation. (Encyclopedia Britannica online)

Though the term may have been consciously chosen as a euphemism, one may wonder whether experts and analysts were all able to assess the situation correctly or whether the euphemism induced some to underestimate the seriousness of the problems. This might have led them to consider that the situation should be dealt with as if it were an ordinary recession, only more severe: they might have made wrong forecasts and consequently resorted to the wrong policy tools, such as more generous bailouts and a more accommodative fiscal policy. Besides, such misperception may have a ripple effect on the general public that fails to anticipate a more serious economic situation. Reinhart and Rogoff (2009) contend that a more accurate term should have been used: *THE SECOND GREAT CONTRACTION*[145]. Admittedly, it would have been a less reassuring euphemism than recession, but it would certainly have been more appropriate for a situation when not only did output and employment contract, as in an ordinary recession, but also debt and credit. Contraction also applies to a situation when deleveraging will take years to complete. The authors highlight the difference between a *RECESSION* and a *CONTRACTION* as regards the resumption of growth. Typically, in a conventional *RECESSION*, the situation returns to normality quite rapidly: not only is the lost ground regained but it takes just a year or so for the economy to resume its rising long-term trend. By contrast, in a deep financial crisis it takes the economy over four years to reach its pre-crisis peak. Though the use of the euphemism *GREAT RECESSION* was probably motivated by a desire to mitigate the impact on the public and avoid panic, it seems that the unintended effect was on analysts and even some policy-makers who, according to Reinhart and Rogoff, were then imprisoned in the wrong framework and failed to look for the right signals to assess the situation.

An illustration of rewording by means of euphemisms can also be found in the realm of the Stock Market where it is most important not to trigger any panic among investors. When the market declines, one tends to speak of a *MARKET CORRECTION* or a *TECHNICAL ADJUSTMENT*. These conventional choices suggest that the previous rise was artificial and that the situation is merely returning to a more normal state. Admittedly, a healthy market will correct itself from time to time. So,

145 The first Great Contraction was the Great Depression.

CORRECTION seems to indicate that the situation was predictable and is therefore nothing to be alarmed at. Nevertheless, a CORRECTION refers to a price decline of at least 10% in a stock, bond, commodity or index; though temporary, it ends an uptrend in the market or assets and is never pleasant news. *EASING* is also a reassuring option. Three other euphemisms related to the Stock Market are worth mentioning for their misleading character: *DISTRESSED SECURITIES, DEAD CAT BOUNCE* and *BAGEL LAND*. Though it is obvious that *DISTRESSED SECURITIES* have declined in a dramatic way, pointing at a company's severe problems – either near bankruptcy or bankruptcy – it may be less clear to the outsider that *DISTRESSED SECURITIES* often become attractive to investors who are looking for a bargain and are willing to accept a risk. These investors gamble on the company's situation not being as bad as the market believes it to be: if they are right, the company will survive and if it is liquidated, they hope it will yield enough money to cover their initial investment. Therefore, the term *DISTRESSED SECURITIES* hides a promising opportunity behind its negative connotation and could be considered as an understatement. A *DEAD CAT BOUNCE* is also a misleading, coded term as it refers to a temporary recovery that occurs after a prolonged decline or bear market, before the market continues to fall. Though the situation is far from good, the term sounds positive because of the last element that is likely to be associated with "bounce back", which can conjure up the idea of a market rally. Yet, this positive connotation is blurred by the "dead cat" element: how can a dead cat bounce? The term is thus unclear and, in this case, the real meaning is hidden behind a metaphor. The last example, *BAGEL LAND*, is based on a metonymy that serves as a euphemism since the real meaning remains an enigma until one understands what it refers to. When a stock or any other security is said to "arrive in bagel land", it simply approaches $0 in price. In this case, there is little hope that the company will solve its problems. The stock has simply fallen out of favour. The term, which is motivated by the resemblance between $0 and the hole in the middle of a bagel, is used to describe a nearly worthless security[146].

146 It should be differentiated from penny stocks that are traded over the counter at a relatively low price. Penny stocks are highly speculative and very risky

With relation to the Stock Market, euphemisms are also commonly used by analysts whose job it is to assess the value of the shares of a number of companies and to give their opinion on their likely evolution over a given period of time. In addition to providing habitual investors with information, the result of their investigations may send strong signals to those interested in mergers and acquisitions. Given the impact that their pronouncements may have on the companies' future and on investors, they cannot afford to make a mistake, nor should they be too straightforward, with the result that they have developed a euphemistic code. Statistics reveal that the S-word (for sell) is seldom used, which is understandable as analysts tend to focus on shares of companies that are fairly reliable and worth their attention, time and energy. Although recommendations have been made by Goldman Sachs to opt for a reduced number of possible terms such as *BUY, NEUTRAL* and *SELL*, these terms are clear only on the surface. Since, for obvious reasons, *SELL* is seldom used, *NEUTRAL* actually often means *SELL*. Many other analysts resort to a much wider range of expressions, many of which are euphemistic. Depending on the reference scale that is adopted, a term like *HOLD* may not necessarily mean that the investors should keep their shares: it may well mean *SELL*. As for *BUY*, it should not be understood as a systematic invitation to buy, especially if there is a *STRONG BUY* option. For instance, when an opinion on a company's shares is lowered from *STRONG BUY* to *BUY* or from *BUY* to *HOLD*, the shares have obviously been downgraded, and the analysts may actually be suggesting *SELL*. In order to understand the real meaning of such pronouncements, it is vital to be aware of the full range of options available to the analysts and to have a larger picture of the evolution of the company's health by comparing the present assessment with the advice issued in the previous months. Other possible euphemistic ways analysts suggest *SELL* include referring to the shares as *UNDERWEIGHT*, or declaring that the shares *UNDERPERFORM* or *MARKET PERFORM*. They can also advise the investors to *REDUCE* the number of such shares in their portfolios. Of course, investors will react differently when reading such advice, depending on whether they have

because of their lack of liquidity, small capitalisation and limited disclosure.

long-term, medium-term or short-term strategies, how old they are and how diversified their portfolios are.

The corporate world is also familiar with euphemistic terms meant to match the overall cautious, political, diplomatic discourse that characterises its communication style. One particular field where euphemisms abound is that of layoffs, a good illustration of the idea of "overwording" put forward by Fairclough (1992: 193) to refer to the existence of many different euphemisms for the same idea. The question is of course very painful and risky, so that the term "layoffs" seems to have become taboo. Emphasis is often laid on another aspect of the phenomenon, such as the uselessness of having too many people to perform the same tasks: *REDUNDANCIES* will naturally be a preferred term. The need to have a more agile, flexible company can also be stressed in order to focus people's attention on the importance of remaining competitive. In order to do so, the best idea is *LEAN MANAGEMENT*, which can be achieved by introducing reorganisational changes. These are expressed through a plethora of euphemistic verbs, as shown in Table 18:

rationalise	reengineer
realign	reposition
reconfigure	resize
redeploy	restructure

Table 18. Euphemistic verbs referring to organizational changes

Although, initially, *RESTRUCTURING* and *REENGINEERING* were not meant as synonyms for automatically cutting jobs, they were often interpreted as such, and some companies announced a *REENGINEERING PLAN* (American Express) or a *COST-IMPROVEMENT PLAN* (Fidelity) which were convenient euphemisms, alongside *STREAMLINING* or, in other words, *TRIMMING*, *SLIMMING* or *DOWNSIZING*. It is also worth noting that, though all these euphemisms for layoffs are meant to clothe an unpleasant truth in relatively innocuous language, some euphemisms themselves need to bc sugar-coated. Such is the case with euphemisms containing a potentially negative element like "down". Consequently, instead of *DOWNSIZING*, companies now tend to prefer *RIGHTSIZING*, insisting on the appropriate strategic size that must be achieved for the company to be in good health. A particularly misleading euphemism for laying off is *SMARTSIZING*, since it seems to suggest it is the best option for the company's future, hence for saving jobs and boosting competitiveness, while it actually means getting rid of the least efficient and productive employees. Only those who understand the coded language will fully grasp the meaning of the euphemistic term: HR and human capital considerations are the criteria here. Another euphemism for reducing the number of employees is *DELAYERING*, which, though it may apply to a number of strata in the structure of the company, very often implies reducing the ranks of middle managers. It is also referred to as *DISINTERMEDIATING*. A company announcing a *ZERO-LAYOFF POLICY* is also resorting to a euphemism. Despite claims that no employees will be laid off for economic reasons, it does not exclude termination as a result of poor performance or other breaches of the employment contract. Though employees feel more secure, especially in times of economic crisis, they may not realise that in order to make up for the costs of not laying anybody off, the company may be forced to take other cost-cutting measures that may affect them, such as limiting the number of hours worked, reducing perks, or not replacing those who retire or are on sick leave.

A few terms already mentioned as neonyms in Chapter 4 are also euphemistic. One is *EMPOWERMENT*, which diverts people's attention by insisting on the increased power or say they are given, but may also come as a consequence of delayering. If middle management disappears, the layers above and below will automatically have to take on the responsibilities of the middle managers, which will increase their workload too. In addition, the race to remain competitive may lead companies to outsource some of their activities abroad with a view to cutting costs. When announcing that they have decided to *OFFSHORE* part of their production, they avoid mentioning the inevitable layoffs. Now that offshoring has lost its euphemistic power, it tends to be replaced by *BESTSHORING*, or *RIGHTSHORING*, which focus attention on the best or right choices for the company, leaving the negative consequences in the shadows. The decisions are, of course, justified by the

CHALLENGING TIMES the company is going through – which sounds less serious than " a crisis" – and the efforts required to avoid FILING FOR CHAPTER 11 PROTECTION, the term for an American legal device that is more technical and less frightening than bankruptcy.

Accounting is not spared by the euphemistic trend and whether innocent or not, mention of fraud is generally avoided and replaced by FINANCIAL IRREGULARITIES. Instead of being accused of lying, cheating and stealing, companies guilty of fraud will be said to have MISSTATED their earnings, OVERSTATED their profits or used IMPROPER ACCOUNTING METHODS. Since the Enron scandal, followed by Tyco's, Worldcom's and others', attempts at "massaging the figures" or "cooking the books" are referred to as CREATIVE ACCOUNTING, EARNINGS MANAGEMENT, FINANCIAL INNOVATION, AGGRESSIVE ACCOUNTING or COSMETIC ACCOUNTING. A clever cartoon at the time depicted a two-entry book with "accounts receivable" in one column and "accounts deceivable" in the other. When accused of shredding compromising documents to hide information from the authorities, Enron claimed it was only involved in DOCUMENT MANAGEMENT. Auditors responsible for checking and validating the accounts and tracking irregularities are now involved in FORENSIC ACCOUNTING, which avoids mentioning the F-word (fraud). Officially, however, the Webster's dictionary defines "forensic" as "belonging to, used in, or suitable to courts of law or to public speaking or debate". Based on this definition, one might consider that "forensic accounting" refers to any accounting work done in anticipation of litigation, so that it can cover many areas other than fraud, such as bankruptcy, valuation or expert witnessing. However, "forensic accounting" very often focuses on accounting fraud. CREATIVE ACCOUNTING as a term resurfaced lately when Greece was mentioned again for having cheated on the reality of its economic health to make believe it had met the Maastricht criteria in order to be accepted as a member of the euro club[147].

147 Even though its failure to meet the criteria may have been mentioned at the time, everyone seems to have turned a blind eye to this piece of information, as what seemed to matter was to increase the number of members in the eurozone.

Finally, it is also important to realise that indeterminacy does not only materialise in the guise of misnomers, oxymora or euphemisms. It may paradoxically stem from a profusion of theoretical definitions whose initial aim was to circumscribe a phenomenon that is hard to grasp, analyse and communicate upon. Though the terms may not be inherently euphemistic, the resulting confusion for the lay public may be felt as a desire to downplay the figures and hide them behind a veil of secrecy. The example of unemployment will help to illustrate this point. Most textbook chapters on unemployment distinguish between various types of unemployment including *CYCLICAL UNEMPLOYMENT*[148], *FRICTIONAL UNEMPLOYMENT*[149], *STRUCTURAL UNEMPLOYMENT*[150] and *NATURAL RATE OF UNEMPLOYMENT*[151]. They also often mention *SEASONAL UNEMPLOYMENT*[152], *HARDCORE UNEMPLOYMENT*[153], and *HIDDEN UNEMPLOYMENT*[154]. In addition, a distinction between *VOLUNTARY* and

---

148 "Cyclical unemployment results from a low level of aggregate demand in the context of sticky wages and prices." (Samuelson & Nordhaus 2005: 739)

149 "Temporary unemployment caused by changes in individual markets. It takes time, for example, for new workers to search among different job possibilities, even experienced workers often spend a minimum period of unemployed time moving from one job to another." (Samuelson & Nordhaus 2005: 739)

150 "Unemployment resulting because the regional or occupational pattern of job vacancies does not match the pattern of worker availability. There may be jobs available, but unemployed workers may not have the required skill, or the jobs may be in different regions from where the unemployed workers live." (Samuelson & Nordhaus 2005: 751)

151 The natural rate of unemployment is "the normal rate of unemployment around which the unemployment rate fluctuates" (Mankiw 2004: 603). It refers to a labour market in equilibrium, without any pressure in terms of either rising or falling inflation. Another technical term is the Non-Accelerating Inflation Rate of Unemployment (NAIRU), though it is not always easy to determine what the actual figure for the NAIRU should be.

152 Unemployment figures are seasonally adjusted to allow for seasonal unemployment or unemployment expected at a given time of the year: for example, amusement parks can experience seasonal unemployment during the winter months.

153 Unemployment among people who have been without work for a long time and who are the least likely to want or find jobs. < http://lexicon.ft.com/>

154 "Hidden unemployment" is also referred to as "covered unemployment". As the term implies, it escapes official unemployment statistics, due to the way they are collected. In many countries, only those who are actively looking for

INVOLUNTARY UNEMPLOYMENT is commonly offered, with the former referring to a person's decision not to accept a low-paid job, for example, while the latter can result from an unfavourable economic environment when some companies decide to restructure or react to an economic crisis. The US Bureau of Labor Statistics[155] (BLS) offers no fewer than 6 possible measures of what is termed euphemistically *LABOR UNDERUTILISATION* (Table 19).

U-1	Persons unemployed 15 weeks or longer, as a percent of the civilian labor force
U-2	Job losers and persons who completed temporary jobs, as a percent of the civilian labor force
U-3	Total unemployed, as a percent of the civilian labor force (official unemployment rate)
U-4	Total unemployed plus discouraged workers, as a percent of the civilian labor force plus discouraged workers
U-5	Total unemployed, plus discouraged workers, plus all other persons marginally attached to the labor force, as a percent of the civilian labor force plus all persons marginally attached to the labor force
U-6	Total unemployed, plus all persons marginally attached to the labor force, plus total employed part time for economic reasons, as a percent of the civilian labor force plus all persons marginally attached to the labor force
NOTE:	Persons marginally attached to the labor force are those who currently are neither working nor looking for work but indicate that they want and are available for a job and have looked for work sometime in the past 12 months. Discouraged workers, a subset of the marginally attached, have given a job-market related reason for not currently looking for work. Persons employed part time for economic reasons are those who want and are available for full-time work but have had to settle for a part-time schedule.

Table 19 BLS definitions of alternative measures of "labor underutilisation"

work are counted as unemployed. Those who have given up looking for work (and who may be on government-sponsored retraining programmes) are not officially counted in the statistics. The workers who have opted for early retirement to avoid being laid off but would certainly prefer to be working are not counted as unemployed. Nor are those who have accepted part time or seasonal jobs though they would rather have full time jobs. In addition, the students of working age who are enrolled in full-time education are usually not taken into account in government statistics. As a result, unemployment rates are often underestimated in official statistics.

155 <http://www.bls.gov/news.release/empsit.t15.htm>

Obviously, depending on the definition that is used, the unemployment figures will differ and it will be difficult for the layperson to have an accurate idea of the real situation.

Before concluding this chapter, it is worth mentioning that terminometrics offers a means to measure the frequency with which some euphemisms are used at a given period of time and to detect changes in the terms used for referring to a problem. For example, in the context of an earlier analysis (Resche 2004 *a*) based on a corpus of texts extracted from *The Economist* dealing with the economic outlook, it was possible to detect a noticeable increase in the use of *RECESSION*; there were two possible interpretations, depending on whether one considers that the journalists were influenced by the general atmosphere of concern prevailing at the time, echoing the mounting pressure, or whether their articles influenced the readers into reacting to the announcement of the impending recession. Whatever the interpretation, with hindsight it is possible to verify that the peak that had been statistically measured corresponded to the month that was later determined by the NBER as the starting point of the recession. This would tend to indicate that the frequency of use of key terms, even though they are euphemisms, can be considered as an accurate barometer of the economic situation, especially in terms of public perception. Such an approach also enables the researcher to feel the pulse of social change by focusing on shifts from transparent terms to more euphemistic ones, or changes from an "outdated", inefficient euphemism to a new one.

6.5. Concluding remarks

This chapter has underlined the benefits that can be derived from investigating terms that do not coincide with the traditional view of a terminological system that, as Sager (1981: 212) reminds us, echoing one item in the ISO R 704 checklist, "should ideally be constructed in such a way that it is transparent in its reflection of the knowledge structure, so that inferences about the reference of an unknown term are possible on the basis of its form alone". It is to be noted that such transparency is an ideal to aim at for terminologists who find themselves in a situation when they have to coin a new term or make recommendations on term formation. In no way, however, would today's terminologists, influenced by more recent contributions to their field, ignore the study of terms that are not transparent or well-formed by ideal standards. Actually, a significant portion of their work is descriptive. Thus the anomalous character of oxymora, misnomers, euphemisms and vague terms resulting from various competing definitions deserves our attention since every one of these terms can be considered as a clue. The examples quoted have shown that in the social sciences in particular, the psychological and social aspects play an important role and that communication between peers or between experts and practitioners and the general public requires utmost care. Obviously, when dealing with lay audiences, economists play the role of interpreters of their science and, "linguistically speaking, [their] rhetoric [is one] of translation, of intercultural communication" (Galbraith 1990: 221); this requires carefully selecting the information they release and the terms they use. The original terms are therefore revisited and adapted to be in harmony with the textual or discursive environment; terminological correctness is in itself a source of information. From this perspective, terms are precious indicators of new conventions, standards and preoccupations and the questions they raise force us to look for the reasons why they fluctuate. They become a means to better track the relative instability of scientific knowledge, to understand the discursive conventions of a given milieu, the stakes in a specific scientific or technical domain, and to observe the changes dictated by the necessary interactions between the various categories of specialists and a more general public. Paying attention to how frequently such terms are used and to any sudden changes in their frequency may also alert us to imminent problems being downplayed or may simply mirror new preoccupations.

7. Insights from interface terms

We are not students of some subject matter, but students of problems. And problems may cut right across the borders of any subject matter or discipline.

Karl Popper
Conjectures and Refutations: The Growth of Scientific Knowledge
(1963: 88)

It would be interesting to inquire how many times essential advances in science have first been made possible by the fact that the boundaries of special disciplines were *not* respected… Trespassing is one of the most successful techniques in science.

Wolfgang Köhler
Dynamics in Psychology
(1940: 115-116)

The last type of terms which require our attention, for what they can reveal about new directions in and new approaches to a specific science, discipline, or field of specialised knowledge are "interface terms". "Interface terms" is undoubtedly an oxymoron if one is still influenced by the traditional principles of terminology with clearly-delineated domains where terms are defined precisely depending on the domain and sub-domain to which they belong. Progress in science, technology and knowledge, however, has brought about a two-fold phenomenon: increased specialisation on the one hand, and a blurring of traditional borders on the other. The latter can be explained by the need to rely on the expertise of a wider range of researchers from various horizons in order to deal with ever more intricate problems. Consequently, a more flexible approach to terminology has emerged in order to take into consideration the concepts resulting from the confrontation of ideas from a number of formerly separate fields of investigation and scientific disciplines. Today's terminology research is inherently corpus-based, and the aim and scope of any terminological project determine the corpus. Thus interface terms cannot be ignored.

What is meant here by interface terms must be differentiated from interface terminology as commonly understood, when referring to user-friendly, consumer-friendly terminology in the field of software, for example, or to patient-friendly terminology in medicine. In this chapter, "interface terms" are to be understood as terms signalling or translating the evolution of disciplines such as economics, where a great variety of new branches have appeared, with the result that a number of problems which were not traditionally considered as pertaining to economics are now being addressed by economists and logically cause the terminology of economics to be enriched. Thus, economics imports concepts from other sciences and may or may not revisit them in the process; the new terms that appear result from the application to economic problems of novel approaches inspired by cooperative research with experts from other fields. Obviously, such exchanges also cause economic concepts and terms to ignore disciplinary boundaries. These increased inter-disciplinary exchanges undoubtedly enrich both the importing and exporting fields and the resulting interface terms deserve our attention as they can serve to assess the vitality and scope of a given discipline. Such a phenomenon should be seen as the manifestation of a "trade in concepts" and "commerce of ideas" taking place between disciplines.

The current trend illustrates the evolution of disciplines and research in general. In the traditional process of theory-building, it seems that the prime goal for sciences is to gain recognition and credibility as independent fields of research with their own conceptual framework and the corresponding terminology; once they have established themselves as autonomous disciplines, with a history, a set of methodological rules, assumptions and conventions, and a community of researchers having contributed a sizeable body of knowledge, they may feel that their territory is no longer in danger of being colonised by other disciplines. Only after reaching maturity can they consider opening their disciplinary borders. In today's globalised world, monodisciplines seem anachronistic. It is no longer possible for disciplines to remain isolated, simply because new challenges have arisen and intricate questions cannot be given simple solutions: they require collaboration between experts from various fields. The trend towards pluralism in economics illustrated in Chapter 4 both results from and illustrates the need for multi-, inter- or transdisciplinary research. This chapter examines the effects of such a trend and shows how interface terms can help us, once more, to understand and assess the impact and benefits of cross-fertilisation between domains.

The chapter begins with a review of the different approaches to integrative research, before going on to examine examples of cross-fertilisation between economics and other sciences, and discussing the question of interface terminology. It provides examples of three different categories of interface terms through the analysis of the fields of neurofinance, green management and the applications of chaos theory to various domains, including sub-fields of economics. Finally it suggests exploring the notion of interface terms further on the diachronic axis, as a means to trace the movement of intellectual trends through various disciplines, and to have a more holistic view of their influences.

7.1. From disciplinary autonomy to transdisciplinarity

In order to understand the present trend, it is necessary to go back in time and see how the different fields of knowledge have evolved. Originally, in very old universities such as Bologna, Cambridge or Oxford, knowledge was divided into four broad areas – medicine, philosophy, theology and law (Max-Neef 2005: 5), which would suggest that, in those days, academics were versatile. This situation can be considered as the "pre-disciplinary" stage. As pointed out in Chapter 3, economics started out as philosophy, before its scope was gradually narrowed to more specific questions with a view to gaining recognition as an autonomous scientific discipline, able to reach a consensus over widely-shared assumptions that became known as mainstream or orthodox economics. Its evolution seems to be representative of a more general trend from broad fields to narrower ones as scientific domains in the making construct their own methodologies and build their specific body of knowledge. It then became traditional for disciplines to live their own lives, to develop their own methods, language and terminology, to ask their own questions about the world, to have their own history of ideas, and to build their own communities (Newell & Green 1982: 25). The established disciplinary boundaries were often understood as barriers preventing intrusion from outsiders (Boyer Commission 1998: 23):

> In the earlier decades of the [twentieth] century, research was characteristically confined within traditional boundaries of disciplines that had themselves been defined only a few generations earlier. The anthropologist and the historian rarely ventured into each other's realms; nor did the chemist and the physicist.

In the 1950s, the University of Illinois published a book listing over 1,100 known scientific disciplines and the figure excluded humanities (Max-Neef 2005: 6). In 1996, as many as 4,000 disciplines were recorded (Mittelstrass 1996: 7). Obviously, as knowledge advanced and investigations became more sophisticated, greater specialisation was deemed necessary and was accompanied by division into sub-disciplines and narrower foci, with specialists dominating research. The advantages of specialisation cannot be ignored since it has resulted in great advances in some fields, but over-fragmented teams and research sometimes cause scientists to be unable to understand what their colleagues in another sub-field of research are doing and writing.

Paradoxically, alongside the trend towards hyper-specialised teams, another trend towards cross-disciplinary research has appeared. As Stigler (1984: 301) points out, the disciplinary landscape is likely to be reconsidered when the need to apply theory is felt or when scientists and researchers are confronted with new puzzles:

> The boundaries [between the various sciences] will shift, or become downright fuzzy, as a science uncovers new areas of study or new domains of application of the science. Physics and chemistry were much more easily distinguished in 1900 than they are today, and the traditional disciplines of zoology and botany have been swallowed up into biology.

Today, complex real-world problems require solutions that call for experts from different horizons and research areas. Admittedly, after decades of efforts to impose their science as a respectable one, it may not be easy for members of some disciplines such as economics to overcome their fear of being "contaminated" by the "softer disciplines of other social sciences" (Hulme & Toye, 2011: 3). Yet there are instances when topics and problems have much to gain from being approached from a cross-disciplinary perspective:

> If we are ultimately concerned with things like poverty, hunger, inequality, 'people's capabilities to be and do things', and so on, and with policies to make improvements, then we must recognize that economics is interdependent and cannot be isolated. (Knight 1991:26)

Disciplinary boundaries should then be understood as porous membranes, rather than barriers, so that concepts and the terms that denote them can travel from one scientific field to another. The new terms will therefore need monitoring if one is to assess the impact of such exchanges on the conceptual framework of each discipline involved in the exchanges. Cooperative, cross-disciplinary research[156] has in fact been envisaged in a number of ways, in the form of multidisciplinary, interdisciplinary and transdisciplinary relationships. Before considering how such blurring of disciplinary borders affects terminology and the way it can be approached, it is important to examine in turn the various types of cooperative research. They are presented below according to the degree of integration between disciplines they imply.

Multidisciplinary research seems to differ from the other forms of collaborative research mentioned, precisely because it does not involve any integration between disciplines: a multidisciplinary relationship is described as "a simple aggregation of different disciplines that preserve unchanged their specific perspectives" (Zaman & Goshin 2010: 5). Such cooperation "may be mutual and cumulative but not interactive" (Augsburg 2005: 56). By addressing the same issue from

156 Crossdisciplinary research is to be understood here in its broad definition "as any analysis or policy recommendation based on questions, concepts or methods of more than one academic discipline" (Hulme, D. and Toye, J.). <http://www.gprg.org>

different angles, each discipline will provide insights that could not have been gained from the approach of a single discipline, so that the overall analysis will be enriched. Such separate analyses are typically pasted together in multidisciplinary conferences or in fields that lie at the crossroads of several disciplines: for example, in the case of urban studies, insights from sociology, geography, planning, economics, municipal engineering, etc. are welcome.

Unlike multidisciplinary research, interdisciplinary research implies crossing traditional boundaries. "As science moves closer to applications, decision-making and policy-making, problems occur that cannot be confined to narrow disciplines or kept within the borders of specific departments. [It is then necessary to] go beyond disciplines and venture into territory commonly known as interdisciplinary research" (Karlqvist 1999: 379). The main difference between multi- and interdisciplinary research is best illustrated by the metaphors of the fruit salad and the smoothie (Nissani 1995: 125). The fruit salad of multidisciplinarity consists of a variety of fruits – i.e. disciplines – each fruit remaining identifiable and retaining its flavour even when chopped up, while enriching the whole. Interdisciplinarity is appropriately described through the image of fruits "finely blended so that the distinctive flavor of each is no longer recognizable, yielding instead the delectable experience of the smoothie". However, as Bennington (1999: 104) points out, interdisciplinarity is a slippery term: "It can suggest forging connections across the disciplines; but it can also mean establishing a kind of undisciplined space in the interstices between disciplines, or even attempting to transcend disciplinary boundaries altogether." Whatever the definitions and interpretations, let it be clear that interdisciplinary research does not mean the end of disciplinary fields; it simply refers to temporary collaboration consisting in combining methodologies in order to devise new tools that will help deal with intricate problems that a single discipline using its own assumptions and techniques might not be able to tackle. Hunt (1994: 3) defines interdisciplinarity as negotiation, in which disciplines must "learn to understand each other and give up some territory in the interest of long-term balance, without giving up their individual identities". In the field of economics, for example, complex topics such as inflation, credit, stock and labour markets require various approaches combining economics, mathematics, geography, politics, sociology, biology, physics and other fields. Economics of the firm, which requires insights from economics, psychology, sociology and politics, is another interdisciplinary context (Dietrich 2006). So is the recent branch of cognitive economics, interconnected with evolutionary economics and new institutional economics, but also with psychology, neurobiology and philosophy (Pelikan 2004). It is described as proposing:

> an interdisciplinary approach to the study of human problem-solving, choice, decision-making and change, to explain the nature and evolution of organizations and economic institutions, in a context characterized by structural uncertainty. Just like psychology, neurobiology and philosophy, cognitive economics has its micro-foundations in the understanding of human mental activities and it elaborates its models in relation to these disciplines and their advancements. As a consequence, the progress in the understanding of the activities of the mind that are relevant to explain economic actions will be crucial to allow the development of new micro-foundations. (Egidi & Rizzello 2004, online)

There are many instances of interdisciplinarity in economics, including management, where researchers are aware that the human factor calls for the cross-fertilisation of various disciplines in the human sciences, such as linguistics, cognitive and social psychology, sociology, psychoanalysis, anthropology and ethnology. Little by little, the range of disciplines and sciences destined to cooperate in interdisciplinary research is widening.

Transdisciplinarity was first defined as "the ultimate degree of coordination", leading to "the mutual enhancement of epistemologies in certain areas" (Jantsch 1972). When dealing with problems transgressing the boundaries of scientific disciplines, such as global warming or sustainability, scientists from various horizons as well as a number of other stakeholders and experts are understandably welcome. Unlike interdisciplinary research, where integration is restricted to disciplines, transdisciplinary research gathers both researchers from the academic world and non-academic participants: it is thus expected to provide a more holistic view of problems. Both interdisciplinary and transdisciplinary approaches, however, aim at developing integrated knowledge and theory. But because it "combines interdisciplinarity with a participatory approach" (Tress *et al* 2006: 17), transdisciplinary research opens a bridge between science and society. Interestingly, when reading the aims and scope of the *International Journal of Transdisciplinary Research* (IJTR)[157], it becomes clear that, beyond being "concerned with extending and integrating the study of economics with disciplines within the natural and social sciences, as well as the humanities", it is particularly interested in stimulating pioneering research in epistemological issues concerning "Sustainability, Social Multi-criteria Evaluations, Ecological Economics and the Biophysical Foundations of Economics, Systems Research, and Complexity and Post Normal Science". According to the IJTR, "a revolution" is needed "in the field of economics, to develop new approaches to real-world problems". It describes itself as "a journal where alternative frameworks can be disseminated and argued to develop a unifying vision of an economic paradigm that realistically portrays economic systems as a whole". Understandably, echoing the mini revolution that took place when advanced students in economics in France and in the United States started the post-autistic movement and called for the end of monism in economics, such a stance might frighten away some mainstream, traditional economists. Attached as they are to preserving the authenticity of their discipline and to distinguishing theoretical research from applied economics, they would rather economics were regarded as the "Imperial science" that infiltrates other sciences than vice versa (Stigler 1984).

Obviously, the notion of domain is being revisited: apart from being defined very strictly and even sub-divided into hyper-specialised units, a domain may also find itself at a crossroads of more than one discipline. Depending on the needs the research is carried out to meet, the domain will fluctuate and its geography may evolve as knowledge is in the making (Gambier 1991). The terminology of a given domain will fluctuate accordingly and will need to be adapted to facilitate communication and make concepts that are specific to one discipline clearer for the other disciplines involved. In the case of integrated research, it may imply revisiting concepts in order to agree on the terminology of the new integrated research and the resulting

157 <http://www.ijtr.org>

knowledge. Interestingly, the terminological issue is mentioned by Pelikan (2004: 2) in the context of combined research between cognitive economics, evolutionary economics and new institutional economics:

> […] to prevent misunderstandings, still frequent in all these fields, sufficient terminological clarity must be secured first. One of the greatest problems with all of them, which has slowed their development and supplied many arguments to their critics, is indeed that the key terms – "institutions", "evolutions" and "bounded cognition" – still lack generally adopted clear definitions; different authors use them in more or less different and more or less well-defined meanings. Let me therefore begin with their brief definitions. While the briefness prevents the definitions from being entirely precise, they appear to suffice for the present purposes.
>
> • "Institutions" are understood in the modern restricted sense of humanly devised formal and informal rules-constraints, or 'rules of the game', – such as written law and unwritten moral norms – and are strictly distinguished from organizations, seen as teams of agents playing the game.
>
> • "Evolutions" are understood as trial-and-error processes which create and change forms – such as genes, technologies, organisations and institutions – through a variety of imperfectly informed (possibly, but not necessarily, entirely random) trials and systematic elimination of errors (relative to certain success criteria), together with selection and retention of the usually small minority of successes; each type of the evolving forms will be considered to have an evolution of its own, which explains why this term is used in plural.
>
> • "Bounded cognition" means the limited abilities (competence) of human minds to perceive and process available information, which imply constraints on the difficulty of the problems that humans can solve optimally and of those that they can solve in a suboptimal, but nevertheless satisfactory way; it may also mean "bounded rationality", if this is understood to refer to imperfections of the ways of processing available information, and not to imperfections of this information.

The notion of "interface" when applied to terms may therefore refer to:

1) the set of terms that are exchanged, agreed upon and defined to facilitate understanding between disciplines; they can be described as an 'in-between' terminology bringing together terms

borrowed from each discipline participating in the interdisciplinary work as well as new terms, created as a result of the confrontation of ideas, that will be useful to all;

2) the terms signalling the influence of another discipline, while revisiting and enriching specialised domains; they clearly become part of the importing domain's terminology, but may be considered borderline terms as opposed to the core terminology of the field, until they find their way into the received terminology;
3) the terms that are common to different disciplines that have adopted them while adapting their definitions to their own fields; these "cross-disciplinary" terms evidence the influence of new concepts across scientific disciplines at a given period of time and may reveal paradigm shifts.

The first two categories of terms result from interdisciplinary or even transdisciplinary research, while the third one stems from a different phenomenon, as will be explained later. The first category of interface terms provides researchers from different fields with a common set of available terms, first resulting from the contribution of each field. If cooperation is to be successful, it is important for all the participants in the project to have a clear idea of what the terms they are going to use refer to. This may lead researchers in each field to think about the use of terms to denote concepts that they otherwise take for granted and to clarify their definitions; if need be, some terms are made more "transparent' and easier to grasp and use for researchers from the other field. In addition, working together, researchers may also create new terms to meet their new needs. Seen from the point of view of translators, such interface terminology is useful for understanding and translating texts pertaining to new interdisciplinary sub-fields, such as neurofinance, for example. This first category can be illustrated as follows:

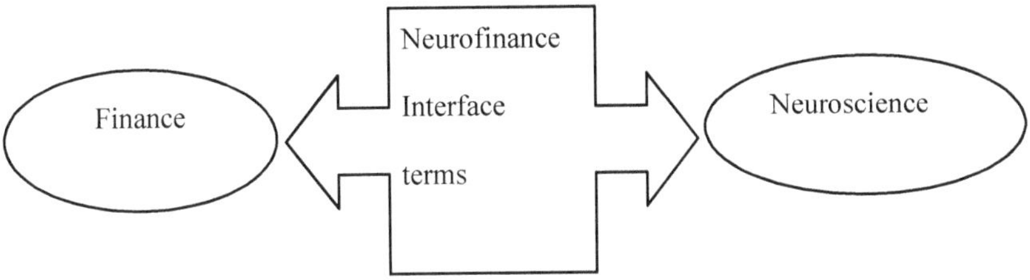

Fig. 6. Interface terminology as an in-between set of terms

Terms in the first category should not be confused with the terms in the second category, which clearly belong to specific domains: simply, as a result of awareness of new problems, a domain is led to widen its scope and to make room for new concepts inspired by other fields. The new terms may force experts to reconsider existing concepts: terms such as *GREEN ACCOUNTING*, *GREEN GDP*, *TRIPLE BOTTOM LINE* are representative of this category. Such terms show that considerations for the protection of the environment have made their way into accounting, management and more generally into economics and have introduced new concepts and methods. Of course, the same holds for the realm of ecology, where economic notions may have found their way into the more classical terminology. Here again, some of these new terms may be transparent enough to reveal the disciplines they have borrowed from: adding "green" to GDP, for example, immediately signals a shift in perspective and the influence of ecology on economics.

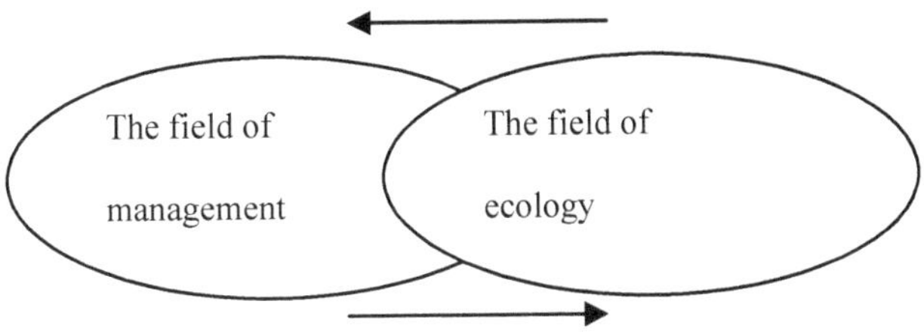

Fig. 7. Interface terminology as neonyms reflecting concepts borrowed from other fields and adapted to a given sphere of knowledge: the example of green management

Finally, the third category describes terms that have infiltrated various disciplines and been adapted by those disciplines to suit their purposes. The best example of this can be found in chaos theory, a sub-field of complexity theory, which has opened new vistas for a number of sciences, causing approaches to be questioned in different ways by hard and soft sciences, and by various sub-fields.

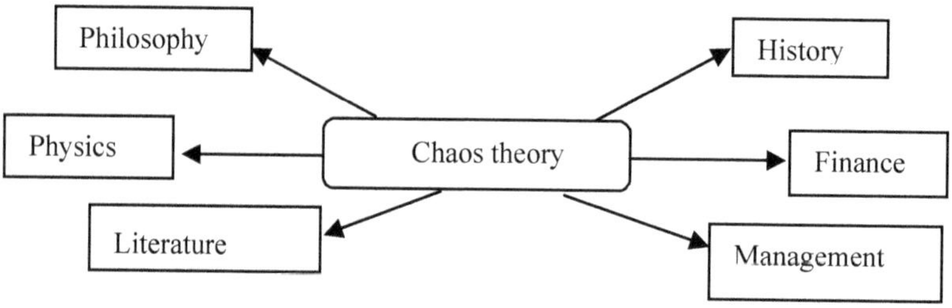

Fig. 8. Interface terminology as a shared set of terms revisited by a number of disciplines

Examples for the three categories of interface terms are developed in the course of this chapter when the various instances of interactions between economics and other disciplines are examined.

7.2. Cross-fertilisation between economics and other sciences

The past influences of physics and biology mentioned in the previous chapters cannot be considered as having contributed to interface terminology or as a sign of cross-fertilisation; the concepts that were borrowed and adapted evidenced one-way influences and were part of the process of basic theory-building, especially since some economists had been trained as engineers and could be considered as polymaths, well-versed in mathematics, mechanical physics and economics. The broadening of horizons and the interconnections of economics with other sciences stem from a different phenomenon and imply mutual influences between economics and other disciplines. Some of these interconnections seem to be more predictable than others, and as a social science, economics is naturally expected to be closer to other social sciences than it is to other broad categories of disciplines. As for its historical links with mathematics, physics and biology, they can be viewed differently as they seem to have evolved from one-way to reciprocal influences. One particular discipline where mutual influences have been at play is linguistics, and this is perhaps more of a surprise for outsiders to those fields and perhaps even for some specialists.

7.2.1. Interactions between economics and other social sciences

The exploration of the borderline territory between economics and other social sciences is not new. For example, geography is undeniably closely linked with economics since the geographic position of a country has an impact on its prosperity; a favourable climate and the existence of natural resources make a real difference in terms of economic opportunities. As for philosophy, which in ancient times was close to economics to such a degree that economics first emerged as social philosophy, its links with more modern economics are obvious: the choice of an economic system obviously translates an ideology. This explains why it is difficult to classify the writings of Karl Marx as pertaining to economics or to philosophy. In spite of the reluctance of some mainstream economists to really venture outside the realm of what is deemed to be economics proper, it seems that economists are increasingly crossing the borders of their own discipline. Experimental economics and behavioural economics are at the intersection of economics and psychology; political economics results from the mutual enrichment of economics and politics, and the paths of economics and law cross on such research topics as voting, contracts, etc. A number of economists such as Lionel Robbins (1932) or Gary Becker (1976) have clearly considered and asserted the links between economics and sociology, opening the way for interdisciplinary economics. According to Siegers (1992), the field of interdisciplinary economics offers a conceptual framework that facilitates analysis and is more balanced than narrow approaches strictly restricted to economics. Robbins's well-known definition of economics officially insists on the focus of economics on human behaviour, thus heralding the emergence of behavioural economics: "Economics is the science which studies human behaviour as a relationship between given ends and scarce means which have alternative uses" (1932: 16). Becker inquired into family size, marriage, divorce, crime and discrimination. He has shown that such social phenomena, which require choosing among alternatives, can be usefully submitted to economic analysis. A potential criminal, for example, will try to assess the costs and benefits of committing a crime; the same holds for a couple who decide to have a child after taking into consideration the advantages and disadvantages, including in terms of costs, of having an extra member in the family. Not only did Becker study social problems from an economist's point of view, but he also influenced sociologists by bringing the rational choice paradigm to their attention. The mutual influences of economics and sociology have led to social economic analysis, which offers a real interdisciplinary approach: it borrows the use of statistical models and quantitative skills from economics, for example, and such tools as surveys, interviews and field observations from sociology. Researchers in this field are required to be familiar with both economics and sociology, and to understand the principles and theories of both disciplines. Still, there exist different degrees of cooperation and exchanges between sociologists and economists, as evidenced by the existence of two competing professional associations: the Society for the Advancement of Socio-Economics (SASE) and the Association for Social Economics (ASE). The former is dominated by sociologists, even though economists are associated with it, while the latter is dominated by economists and works in conjunction with the American Economic Association (Rosser 2006: 226). This shows that cooperation is not always so easy, especially when it requires agreeing on methodology and assumptions.

Economic anthropology, sometimes also referred to as anthropological economics, is another scholarly field that illustrates the complex relations woven between the two fields by anthropologists who use the tools of both economics and anthropology in order to explain human economic decisions and behaviour. In his research and works, Marshall Sahlins, one of the greatest contemporary anthropologists, has crossed the boundaries of his disciplinary field, i.e. anthropology, to venture into the territories of history, philosophy, economics and the interface between biology and human sciences. Sahlins examined the links between economics and cultural and social factors from the perspective of anthropological economics which, he explains (1974), is "rather indebted to the nature of the primitive economies than to the categories of a bourgeois science".

Interestingly, when one reads the list of economists who have been awarded the Sveriges Riksbank Prize in Economic Sciences in Memory of Alfred Nobel, one realises that many were commended for broadening the scope of economic analysis to new areas. Prior to Gary Becker who became a Nobel laureate in 1992 for his research about the family and was praised "for having extended the domain of microeconomic analysis to a wide range of human behaviour and interaction, including nonmarket behavior"[158], James Buchanan got his Prize in 1986 "for his development of the contractual and constitutional basis for the theory of economic and political decision-making" (Levinowitz and Ringertz 2001: 204). With Gordon Tulloch, Buchanan is credited with founding modern public choice theory by using the tools of economics to examine the fabric of American politics (Buchanan and Tulloch 1962). Other economists have also conducted research on neighbouring territory: both Gunnar Myrdal and Friedrich von Hayek were congratulated in 1974 for "their penetrating analysis of the interdependence of economic, social and institutional phenomena". When he received the Swedish Central Bank's Prize in 1998, Amartya Sen was cited "for his contributions to welfare economics", another interdisciplinary field, which had been pioneered by Gunnar Myrdal whose citation had also mentioned research in the same field. The ultimate example of the benefits of cross-disciplinary research is that of Daniel Kahneman who, though he was a Princeton University psychologist, became a Nobel Laureate in economics in 2002 for his

158 <http://www.nobelprize.org/nobel_organisations/nobelfoundation/publications/lectures/WSC/econ-91-95.html>

contribution to behavioural economics. Such recognition of the real scientific contribution of economists or other researchers whose work has encompassed topics not yet analysed by a majority of their peers, only shows that the Prize committee seems to have given economics a wider interpretation and acknowledged the importance of interdisciplinary research.

Many new fields like cognitive economics, resource economics, socioeconomics, etc., require interdisciplinary approaches; it is also the case of consumer behaviour, and the sub-field of food consumption. The latter provides a good example of a research topic that calls for the integration of four broad sectors: physical sciences, psychology, economic sciences and social sciences. Quite strikingly, when the four broad sectors are subdivided further into specialised areas of research and expertise, as many as twenty-four sub-fields can be called upon to contribute their insights to the issue of food consumption (Becker[159] 2005). More precisely, as regards physical sciences, experts from the fields of medicine, physiology, toxicology, chemistry, physics, nutrition, food technology and sensories can be involved. Under the banner of psychology, researchers in behavioural science, biosocial psychology, psychology and medicine can be consulted. In the realm of economic sciences, specialists of marketing, consumer research, management, business, political sciences and economics are concerned. Finally, in the field of social sciences, insights from researchers in history, anthropology, sociology, geography, ecology and communication are welcome.

As for the mutual influences between politics and economics over time, they can easily be illustrated: Adam Smith is known to have borrowed many political ideas from John Locke, and, for a long time, economics was referred to as political economy; on the other side, Milton Friedman's pioneering views on economic liberalisation had an undeniable impact on President Reagan's policy choices. To illustrate the influence of economic theories on other fields and more particularly on policy-makers, it is tempting to refer to John Maynard Keynes's conclusion (1964: 383): "Practical men, who believe themselves to be quite exempt from any intellectual influence, are usually

159 Tilman Becker, not to be confused with Gary Becker.

the slaves of some defunct economist." However, those interested in economic history may well consider the problem from another angle and reply: "Practical economists, who believe themselves to be quite exempt from any humanistic influences, are usually the slaves of some defunct historian" (De Vries, 1999). These remarks are merely indicators of the mutual influences that can be exerted between research fields and the blurring and permeability of disciplinary borders: whether the influences are conscious and sought through interdisciplinary research or more subtle, as described by Keynes, ideas from one discipline will find their way into another.

7.2.2. Interactions between economics and physical or natural sciences

Ample evidence has been brought of the influence of physical sciences on economics in the past (Chapter 3), which resulted, for example, in elasticity theory, and in imported terms such as *MULTIPLIER*, *ACCELERATOR* and *OSCILLATOR*. But instead of thinking in terms of influence of one dominant science (physics then) over a softer science (economics), it is more useful to adopt the notion of mutual influence between economics and physics. In this respect, *ECONOPHYSICS* is a good example. The field is briefly described in Chapter 4 (Section 4.4). Characteristically, *ECONOPHYSICS* as a field of research was the initiative of physics specialists with an interest in economics, whose complex systems they found challenging to investigate, while former imports of physics into economics had been initiated by economists. In the fast-expanding field of *ECONOPHYSICS*, physicists apply "tools and methods developed in statistical mechanics and theoretical physics" to the field of finance, taking advantage of the fact that practically every financial transaction is recorded and that financial markets are monitored very closely (Mantegna and Stanley 2000: viii). The huge databases afforded by such monitoring provide physicists with a wonderful opportunity to analyse complex systems. Financial systems, which are open systems exhibiting many nonlinear interactions, can be analysed using "concepts such as power-law distributions, correlations, scaling, unpredictable time series and random processes" (Mantegna and Stanley

2000: 2). Other aspects of economics are also studied by physicists: "the income distribution of firms, [...] the statistical properties of their growth rates, [...] and the statistical properties of the economic performances of complex organisations such as universities or even entire countries have also been investigated" (Mantegna and Stanley 2000: 7). In addition, research is also conducted into price dynamics in a financial market, and the convergences with and divergences from physical processes like *TURBULENCE* are examined. The laws of *THERMODYNAMICS* and the concepts of *ENTROPY* and *RANDOMNESS* are also used by physicists to analyse economic phenomena. As regards randomness, however, it is worth noting that it did not originate in physics but in mathematics, among researchers investigating economic problems. As Mirowski (1999: 387) proudly points out, physics, then, is also indebted to economics:

> In the history of economics, there has existed a small but significant band of innovators of mathematical techniques and theories who drew their inspiration directly from social and economic phenomena, and whose mathematical techniques and models subsequently turned out to be useful in a physics context.

Bachelier, a French mathematician now considered as the father of financial mathematics, worked on stock prices as *RANDOM WALKS* in his doctoral dissertation and on the stochastic process that underlies Brownian motion (1900), predating Einstein's paper on *Brownian motion* (1905). It is also worth noting that seventy-three years before Black and Scholes devised their famous model in their 1973 paper, Bachelier had derived the price of what is now known as a *BARRIER OPTION*. And, of course, Mandelbrot's work on *FRACTALS* (1977), which was conducted to describe economic phenomena and gave rise to *FRACTAL FINANCE*, was applied a few years later in physics. Though one cannot consider that these examples are illustrations of interdisciplinary research, they do underline the spreading of ideas from one science to others and prefigure today's transgression of borders and interdisciplinary or transdisciplinary trends:

> It is not clear who preceded whom disciplinarily in these developments. Indeed, what we have is a truly complicated muddle of developments. What seem to be models of physics in some cases came from economics, and the

much-derided standard models of economics largely came from physics. "Econophysics" may well simply be a new name for something that has been going on for a long time. (Rosser 2006: 228)

The influence of biology on economics has also been mentioned (Chapter 3). Here again, as was the case for econophysics, a new field has appeared, i.e. *NEUROECONOMICS*, which is characteristic of a biological field investigating topics that used to be considered the realm of economics. "Neuroeconomics is the study of how the embodied brain interacts with its external environment to produce economic behaviour. Research in this field will allow social scientists to better understand individuals' decision-making and consequently to better predict economic behaviour" (McCabe 2003: 294). *NEUROECONOMICS* takes advantage of the technological breakthrough of Magnetic Resonance Imaging (MRI) to investigate further what is going on in the head of *homo oeconomicus*: MRI makes it possible to visualise the chemical processes going on in the brain and to analyse people's reactions to different situations. *NEUROECONOMICS* blends insights from psychology, neuroscience, and economics to try to devise a model about decisions, interactions, risks, and rewards thanks to a more integrative approach. The first step towards *NEUROECONOMICS* was made by *BEHAVIOURAL ECONOMICS*, which established that economic decision-making was not rational but influenced by emotion or unconscious cognitive biases. It is also important to remember Edgeworth's quest for measuring utility through his *HEDONIMETER*, or Frank Ramsey's *PSYCHOGALVANOMETER*, intended to achieve the same goal. Benefits are expected from cross-disciplinary research in *NEUROECONOMICS*: insights from neuroscience could provide economists and psychologists with a much better understanding of people's decisions and reactions[160], while economics could contribute by introducing neuroscientists to more sophisticated aspects of game theory. Eventually, optimists think that a broader range of disciplines interested in behavioural sciences – economics, psychology, anthropology, sociology, political science,

160 Though neuroeconomics gives rise to theoretical research, its findings can also be applied in neuromarketing for example, where people's reactions to advertising can be closely monitored, studied and taken into account for persuasion purposes.

and some sub-fields in biology – could be brought together to conduct integrated research thanks to the expected breakthroughs in neuroscience. Recent advances in neuroscience have led to the emergence of a new field, *NEUROFINANCE*, which seeks to predict investor behaviour, identify environmental markers of investor irrationality in financial markets and devise ways to aid decision-making.

NEUROFINANCE can serve as an illustration of our first category of interface terms, defined as a set of terms facilitating understanding between disciplines. For specialists of finance and neuroscience to understand one another, it is necessary to consider an interface terminology tailored to their needs. In other words, specialists of finance will need definitions for terms belonging to neuroscience, while specialists of neuroscience will need to get acquainted with terms pertaining to finance. The following table provides an example of what the interface terminology of neurofinance could be like[161]. Needless to say, the interface terminology would include all the terms listed below but, for reasons of clarity, they are presented in two columns, the left column more particularly aimed at finance specialists and the right column at neuroscience specialists. All those involved in neurofinance research will need to be familiar with all these terms:

Terms intended to help the finance specialists	Terms intended to help the neuroscience specialists
AFFECT	ANALYST (FINANCIAL)
AMPHETAMINES	ARBITRAGE
AMYGDALIA	ASSET PRICING
ANTERIOR CINGULATED CORTEX (ACC)	BOOK VALUE
ANTERIOR INSULA	BUBBLE
ATTENTION-DEFICIT-HYPERACTIVITY DISORDER (ADHA)	CRASH (MARKET)
BENZODIAZEPINES	DAY TRADING
BIG FIVE	DISUTILITY
COMPARATOR	EQUITY RATE PREMIUM
DEFENCE MECHANISM (EMOTIONAL)	EQUITY PREMIUM PUZZLE
DOPAMINE	EXPECTED VALUE
DORSOLATERAL PREFRONTAL CORTEX	IMPLIED VOLATILITY
EPINEPHINE (ADRENALIN)	LOSS AVERSION
	MOMENTUM INVESTING

161 The terms have been selected from Peterson's glossary (2007).

HOMINID BRAIN HYPOTHALAMIC-PITUITARY-ADRENAL AXIS (HPA) LIMBIC SYSTEM MAMALIAN BRAIN ORBITAL FRONTAL CORTEX (OFC) PLASTICITY POSITRON EMISSION TOPOGRAPHY (PET) PREFRONTAL CORTEX REPTILIAN BRAIN REWARD SYSTEM VALENCE	OPTION PRICE-TO-EARNINGS RATIO PRISONER'S DILEMMA RISK PREFERENCE TECHNICAL ANALYSIS TIME PREFERENCE TRADER ULTIMATUM GAME UTILITY VALUE

Table 20. An example of interface terminology in neurofinance

Some of the interface terms in Table 20 might sound familiar to some researchers from the other discipline, but their technical definition would still be needed in order to avoid any misunderstanding or approximation. Two terms in the left-hand side column – *BIG FIVE* and *DEFENCE MECHANISM* – deserve our attention, for they have altogether different meanings for economists, which might lead to misunderstandings in their dealings with neurologists; it is therefore important to compare the following definitions for these terms in economics or finance and in neuroscience:

- Economics/accounting: *THE BIG FIVE* refer to the five biggest accounting firms that used to dominate the market until Arthur Andersen vanished in mid-2002, implicated in the Enron scandal. There remain the Big Four now: PricewaterhouseCoopers (PwC), Ernst & Young (EY), KPMG (Klynveld Peat Marwick Goerdeler) and Deloitte (Deloitte Touche Tohmatsu or DTT). They offer their services to the largest companies in the world, acting as auditors, consultants, tax advisors, administrators, etc.
- Neuroscience: *THE BIG FIVE* refer to the broad categories of personality traits: neuroticism, extraversion, agreeableness, conscientiousness and openness to experience. (adapted from Peterson 2007)
- Economics: *DEFENCE MECHANISM* describes any means devised to thwart any unsolicited or hostile takeover attempts.

- Neuroscience/psychology: *DEFENCE MECHANISM* refers to an "automatic psychological process that protects the individual against anxiety". (Peterson 2007: 371)

Clearly, a set of interface terms of this kind is bound to evolve to meet the needs of the participants in cross-disciplinary research; should economists, for example, contribute a greater share to enlarging the knowledge of neurofinance, then neuroscientists would have to become familiar with even more sophisticated concepts in finance, and *vice versa*.

7.2.3. Interactions between economics and linguistics

As disciplines, economics and linguistics may seem to stand further apart than economics and sociology or philosophy: actually, the science of wealth does not seem to have much in common with the science of language if one considers the former as dealing with material goods and the latter with ideas. One may rightly wonder how these two different worlds can be reconciled. However, for over two centuries now, the two disciplines have repeatedly crossed paths, as pointed out by Jakobson (1970: 425-428):

> One may recall that economists of the Enlightenment period used to attack linguistic problems as, for example, Anne-Robert-Jacques Turgot, who compiled a study on etymology for the *Encyclopédie* (1756), or Adam Smith, who wrote on the origin of language (1770). G. Tarde's influence on Saussure's doctrine in such matters as circuit, exchange, value, output-input, and producer-consumer is well-known. Many common topics as, for instance, "dynamic synchrony", contradictions within the system, and its continual motion, undergo similar developments in both fields. Fundamental economic concepts are repeatedly subjected to semiotic interpretation. [...] At present, Talcot Parsons [1967/1968] systematically treats money as "a very highly specialised language", economics transactions as "certain types of conversations", the circulation of money as "the sending of messages", and the monetary system as "a code in the grammatical-symbolical sense". He avowedly applies to the economics interchange the theory of code and message developed in linguistics.

Saussure's example is most revealing because he considered linguistics and economics as sciences of value: " both sciences are concerned with a system for equating things of different orders – labour and wages in one and a signified and signifier in the other" (Saussure 1916: 79). Table 21 offers a comparison of definitions of different kinds of value in economics and in Saussurean linguistics:

Economics	*Saussurean linguistics*
EXCHANGE VALUE: a quarter can be used for buying goods or commodities or can be exchanged for two dimes and a nickel.	LINGUISTIC VALUE: synonyms have the same meaning or linguistic value: for example, the word "bachelor" can be "exchanged" for the term "unmarried man". This is, in many ways, an *equal exchange*.
INTRINSIC VALUE: The actual value of an asset or a company based on an underlying perception of its true value including all aspects of the business, in terms of both tangible and intangible factors. This value may or may not be the same as the current market value.	Signs have NO INTRINSIC VALUE. "Language is a system based entirely on the opposition of its concrete units", that have value only "from the simultaneous presence of other units". Convinced that nothing has intrinsic value, Saussure chose the example of "chess pieces [that] change in value according to the moves that are made".
MARKET VALUE, also called market price: the price determined dynamically by buyers and sellers in an open market.	
USE VALUE: this economic concept holds that "the value of a good or service is related only to its mode of use, or to an equivalent value in cash, and not to any intrinsic value. <www.businessdictionary.com>	Signs have FUNCTIONAL VALUE within the system of language understood as a set of relations between differentially connected terms.

Table 21. Value in economics and in Saussurean linguistics

Without pretending to assert the validity of the parallel between economics and linguistics, it is worth noting that Saussure refers to economics at very crucial moments of his building his structuralist theory: for example, whether he seeks to justify his distinction between synchrony and diachrony (i), to explain that the value of a term depends on the other terms in the system (ii), to establish the arbitrary character of a sign (iii), he resorts to examples borrowed from economics:

> (i) Very few linguists suspect that the intervention of the factor of time creates difficulties peculiar to linguistics and opens to their science two completely divergent paths. Most other sciences are unaffected by this radical duality; time produces no special effect on them. [...] On the contrary, that duality is already forcing itself upon the economic science. Here, in contrast to the other sciences, political economy and economic history constitute two clearly separate disciplines within a single science; the works that have recently appeared on these subjects point up the distinction. Proceeding as they have, economists are – without being well aware of it – obeying an inner necessity. A similar necessity obliges us to divide linguistics into two parts, each with its own principle. Here, as in political economy, we are confronted with the notion of value. (Saussure 1916: 79)

> (ii) To determine what a five-franc piece is worth one must therefore know: (1) that it can be exchanged for a fixed quantity of a different thing, e.g. bread; and (2) that it can be compared with a similar value of the same system, e.g. a one-franc piece, or with coins of another system (a dollar, etc.). In the same way, a word can be exchanged for something dissimilar, an idea; besides, it can be compared with something of the same nature, another word. Its value is therefore not fixed so long as one simply states that it can be "exchanged" for a given concept, i.e. that it has this or that signification: one must also compare it with similar values, with other words that stand in opposition to it. Its content is really fixed only by the concurrence of everything that exists outside it. Being part of a system, it is endowed not only with a signification but also and especially with a value, and this is something quite different. (Saussure 1916: 115)

> (iii) All our conventional values have the characteristic of not being confused with the tangible element which supports them. For instance, it is not the metal in a piece of money that fixes its value. A coin nominally worth five francs may contain less than half its worth of silver. Its value will vary according to the amount stamped upon it and according to its use inside or outside a political boundary. This is even truer of the linguistic signifier which is not

> phonic but incorporeal – constituted not by its material substance but by the differences that separate its sound-image from all others. (Saussure 1916:118-119)

Researchers have tried to establish the sources of Saussure's inspiration and the names of Walras and Pareto have most often been quoted. It is true that Walras was in Lausanne from 1870 to 1892, which could account for his influence on Saussure. McCloskey (1998: 29) points out that Saussure was influenced by neoclassical economists (Jevons and Walras) and by Austrian economists as well (Menger, for example). The essential point lies, however, in the fact that both Walras and Pareto were interested in the theory of general equilibrium, and that the concept of synchrony used by Saussure indicates a state of equilibrium rather than a brief moment in time. If the influence of general equilibrium theory on linguistic structuralism is undeniable, it might also be worth raising the question of the influence of structuralism on some economists in return, especially as Walras's theory is still influential today, and as a number of researchers are interested in structural economics. More generally speaking, since both linguistics and economics have evolved since Saussure's and Walras's days, new interdisciplinary research bringing together economists and specialists of linguistics would certainly yield useful information on common topics of interest in the two disciplines.

7.3. Interface terminology revisiting domains

Whenever researchers are led to investigate problems whose answers require crossing disciplinary boundaries, they inevitably introduce new concepts born of the confrontation of ideas suggested by researchers from other horizons, which results in the creation of new terms in their initial domain of research and discipline. These new terms that enrich the terminology of a domain or discipline draw our attention to the changes and the broadening of views taking place. In the field of corporate management, for example, theories as well as practices evidence a trend towards greater considerations for environmental issues, which is signalled by a number of new terms that have emerged from the exchanges with researchers in ecology and with environmentalists. As green economics has already been dealt with in Chapter 4, the focus here will be on the corporate world's considerations for environmental matters. The example of the greening of corporate management[162] will serve to illustrate the second category of interface terms described in Section 7.1.

7.3.1. Interface terms as added value: the greening of corporate management

The shift that has taken place in the corporate world, both in management theory and practice, and in manufacturing, can be measured by the number of new terms that have appeared as a result of the sensitisation to environmental issues. The awareness of the need for emergency action to preserve our planet has given rise to a green wave that has had two effects. Firstly, it has flooded everyday language with vague, broad concepts like *CLEAN*[163], *GREEN*[164], *SMART*[165] and *SUSTAINABLE*[166]; secondly, it has caused economists and managers to reconsider

---

162 All the terms quoted as examples in section 6.3.1 were extracted from a corpus of articles and reports in the *McKinsey Quarterly*, *Strategy+Business* and *Knowledge@Wharton* in addition to a book on Green management: *Green to Gold* (Esty, D. C. and Winston A. S. (2006). Also see Resche (2007).

163 According to Clean Tech Group "clean" describes any technology that "addresses the roots of ecological problems with new science, emphasizing natural approaches such as biomimicry and biology". <http://www.clantech.com/about/cleantechdefinition.cfm>

164 "Green" is generally used for referring to any product or business that aims at minimising the harm that could be done to the environment. Green policies and laws are meant to prevent such harm.

165 "Smart" is usually used when electricity and digital technology are combined to ensure that systems and products are more energy efficient and able to adapt to fluctuating energy demands and supplies. Examples of frequent uses are smart grid, smart cars, smart homes, smart appliances.

166 "Sustainable development" was defined by the World Commission on Environment and Development in what is known as the Brundtland Report (1987:

some of their assumptions and habits. Though one may wonder whether the changes in viewpoint are always genuinely motivated by the desire to act in favour of the environment, or simply to comply with the new rules and with the demands of consumers and economic agents, it is undeniable that changes have taken place in management, in manufacturing, and in national and corporate accounting. The new terms that have been introduced all point to a shift in habits and attitudes.

The change in attitudes is also noticeable among a number of investors who are now referred to as *SOCIALLY RESPONSIBLE INVESTORS*: as their investment decisions are motivated by the efforts made by business leaders to take measures in favour of the natural and human environment, they are courted by companies that do their best to implement virtuous practices such as environmental stewardship, consumer protection, respect for human rights, respect for diversity and to behave ethically in all circumstances. The companies that are selected by official indices such as the Dow Jones Sustainability Index Series (DJSI) or FTSE4Good[167] are proud of being labelled as virtuous companies: the challenge for them, however, is to remain on the lists that are reconsidered on a yearly basis.

The terms in Table 22, which highlight the change that has taken place in corporate practices as well as in management theory, through a broader focus on stakeholders, have now entered the terminology of economics and even finance.

---

43): "development that meets the needs of the present without compromising the ability of future generations to meet their own needs". However, as mentioned in Chapter 5, sustainability is a much-debated issue and defining it seems to be a challenging task. If one compares the use of sustainable in a number of terms such as sustainable agriculture, sustainable building or sustainable business, one realises the instability of the concept, which needs to be understood according to the context in which it is used.

167 An ethical index jointly created by the *Financial Times* and the London Stock Exchange.

CORPORATE CITIZENSHIP	In addition to making profits for its shareholders, a company is expected to contribute to making life better for the communities in which it operates; it should therefore maintain sustainable partnerships with governments at national, state and local levels. It must be conscious that it can play a major role through its presence in the developing world and in many countries.
CORPORATE SOCIAL RESPONSIBILITY (CSR)	According to the European Commission, it is "A concept whereby companies integrate social and environmental concerns in their business operations and in their interaction with their stakeholders on a voluntary basis".
CRADLE-TO-CRADLE MANUFACTURING (C2C)	It refers to a new methodology for the design of processes, products and services, "by looking at raw materials both in terms of their intrinsic value and how, at the end of that product's useful life, they can be taken apart and recycled or "upcycled" into products that may have a value and sophistication beyond that of their original use. Simply, it's a philosophy of birth-to-rebirth." <http://business-ethics.com/>
DOW JONES SUSTAINABILITY INDEXES	"Thanks to the best-in-class approach, a vibrant competition among companies for inclusion in the Dow Jones Sustainability Indexes has ensued. To be included or remain in the index, companies have to continually intensify their sustainability initiatives." <http://www.sustainability-index.com/07_htmle/assessment/overview.html>
ECO-ENTREPRENEUR/ ECO-ENTREPRENEURSHIP	The practice of starting new businesses in response to an identified opportunity to earn a profit and provide (minimize) a positive (negative) environmental externality. (Kotcher 2009: 25)
ENVIRONMENT, SOCIAL JUSTICE AND CORPORATE GOVERNANCE (ESG)	These areas of concern are given priority by socially responsible investors, whether individuals or mutual funds.
FTSE4GOOD	"The FTSE4Good Index Series has been designed to objectively measure the performance of companies that meet globally recognised corporate responsibility standards." <http://www.ftse;com/indices>
GENUINE PROGRESS INDICATOR (GPI)	The Genuine Progress Indicator (GPI) measures how well we are doing as individuals, families, communities and as a province using 51 economic, social and environmental indicators. Traditional economic indicators of progress such as

	the Gross Domestic Product (GDP) measure only one factor – the flow of money through the economy. The GPI includes indicators such as volunteerism, timber sustainability, and even traditional economic measures such as the GDP. It provides a more balanced picture of progress. <http://www.pembina.org/ economics/gpi>
GLOBAL REPORTING INITIATIVE (GRI)	Also known as "ecological footprint reporting", it provides standards for sustainability reporting; disclosure concerns the environment, as well as social and governance performance. The ultimate goal is for sustainability reporting to become as common as financial reporting.
GREEN ACCOUNTING	Also referred to as "resource accounting", "environmental accounting" or "integrated economic and environmental accounting", it modifies the System of National Accounts that now incorporate the use or depletion of natural resources. <http://www.unpri.org>
GREEN GDP	It is a measure of economic growth that factors in the environmental consequences of such growth; its popularity has continued to grow since the 1992 Rio Earth Summit.
GREEN LOGISTICS	Supply chain management practices and strategies that reduce the environmental and energy footprint of freight distribution. It focuses on material handling, waste management, packaging and transport. <http://people.hofstra.edu/geotrans/eng/ch8en/appl8en/ch8a4en.html>
GREEN SUPPLY CHAIN	A green supply chain is meant to reduce a company's carbon footprint and environmental impact through decreased paper use, improved product availability, reduced waste and optimised transportation.
LIFE-CYCLE ANALYSIS (LCA)	Also referred to as Life Cycle Assessment, it can help companies to understand the environmental impact associated with their products, processes and activities. It consists of life-cycle inventory, impact assessment and improvement analysis.
SOCIALLY, ENVIRONMENTALLY, ETHICALLY, RESPONSIBLE BUSINESS PRACTICES (SEER)	SEER concepts as applied to business are based on four macro-values: CSR, environmental stewardship, financial strength and product/service quality.
SOCIALLY RESPONSIBLE INVESTING (SRI)	Also referred to as sustainable, socially conscious or ethical investing, its areas of concern are ESG. This investment strategy seeks to maximise both financial return and social

	good (to "do well by doing good").
SUSTAINABLE AND RESPONSIBLE INVESTING (SRI)	It defines the same attitude to investment as Socially Responsible Investing, integrating environmental, social and governance factors into investment decisions.
SUSTAINABLE BUSINESS	A business that is committed to environmental principles in all its operations.
SUSTAINABLE ECONOMICS	A new approach to economics that expands the three traditional factors of production (land, labour and capital) into "five reservoirs of wealth": environmental capital (EC), human capital (HC), social and organisational capital (SOC), manufactured capital (MC) and credit capital (CC). <http://www.context.org/ICLIB/IC32/Gilman.htm>
SUSTAINABLE RESPONSIBLE BUSINESS (SRB)	It refers to a company that implements SEER practices.
TRIPLE BOTTOM LINE	The term is often explained by referring to People, Planet, Profit; it means that accounting now takes into consideration a company's financial results as well as its impact on people and on the environment.

Table 22 New economic and managerial terms evidencing the impact of ecology on economics

These terms, which were extracted from a corpus athered for a previous paper (Resche 2007), can be considered as interface terms because they result from the combination of ecological considerations and principles applied to economics, finance and management. However, they cannot be considered as an "in-between" set of terms compiled for the purpose of promoting fruitful dialogue among scientists belonging to different disciplines; though their origin is exogenous, they belong to the terminology of economics and corporate management, which they have enriched. Therefore, whenever a number of new terms obviously inspired by concepts borrowed from another sphere of scientific research come ti enrich a given domain or discipline, they are worth our attention because they can signal new approaches and directions; so are terms belonging to the third type of interface mentioned in Section 7.1, that translate the impact of a sweeping paradigm influencing several disciplinary fields over a given period of time, i.e. chaos theory.

7.3.2. *Cross-disciplinary interface terms: chaos theory across domains*

By observing how a given discipline's new findings are appropriated by other disciplines and alter their conceptual framework, it is possible to track the influence of major ideas and shifts in scientific approaches across disciplines. Chaos theory, which is the study of non-linear dynamic systems and therefore a sub-field of complexity theory, affords us the opportunity to illustrate the third category of cross-disciplinary interface terms. Although chaos theory was initially developed in the physical sciences, it is also relevant to any system – whether social, ecological or economic – that is characterised by non-linear relationships and numerous interactions evolving over time (Radzicki 1990; Butler 1990). As a result, chaos theory has aroused interest among a number of researchers from various horizons, who sought to apply it to such fields as ecology, medicine, international relations, policy planning, urban development, populations dynamics and economics; it has also been explored in the fields of literary criticism and history (Levy 1994).

Chaos theory dates back to the early sixties when a number of researchers, intrigued by the odd behaviour of complex systems, started investigating the potential causes for the anomalies displayed by such systems; this led them to think along new lines and to come up with a series of findings that questioned the conventional representation of the world as a well-regulated machine. In 1961, Edward Lorenz, a meteorologist from the Massachusetts Institute of Technology (MIT), discovered the "butterfly effect" by chance as he was working on computational models to try to forecast the weather. The butterfly effect is one of the fundamental principles of chaos theory; it refers to the idea that, for example, a butterfly flapping its wings in Tokyo could impact the weather conditions in Toronto. In more general terms, it means that apparently unimportant details can have a tremendous, unforeseen impact, as described in the well-known nursery rhyme:

> For want of a nail, the shoe was lost;
> For want of a shoe, the horse was lost;

For want of a horse, the rider was lost;
For want of a rider, the battle was lost;
For want of a battle, the kingdom was lost!

For meteorologists, the butterfly effect underlines the difficulty of predicting the weather over a long period of time, especially when small events risk escaping attention. For historians, now sensitised to the risk of disregarding seemingly insignificant details when interpreting any historical event, application of the butterfly effect principle has opened up new vistas. A broader consequence of the butterfly effect has been to point out that the apparent randomness in systems may not be due to external factors, but can result from small internal fluctuations. In the early seventies Robert May, working in ecology, contributed to the new field of chaos theory by establishing two new concepts: *BIFURCATION* and *PERIOD DOUBLING*. *BIFURCATION* is rather self-explanatory and refers to a split into two, but *PERIOD DOUBLING* requires some explanation. A period can be defined as the time required for any cyclic system to resume its original state; obviously, *PERIOD DOUBLING* can warn us against problems and oncoming chaos for different systems. The notion was applied to medical research, for example, and helped a research team at MIT led by Richard Cohen to establish that *PERIOD DOUBLING* was associated with the onset of a heart attack and could therefore be monitored to signal a major problem. In 1982, Benoit Mandelbrot demonstrated that the irregular shapes that can be observed in nature are only random and chaotic on the surface, but display some kind of order. What he called *FRACTALS* are actually characterised by infinite depth and self-similarity: zooming in on ever-smaller details reveals ever more details with similar shapes, as is the case with a cauliflower, Romanesco broccoli, or snowflakes. The geometrical presentation of *FRACTALS* was made possible by the sophistication of computer programs, which were also able to display images of *STRANGE ATTRACTORS*, i.e. whatever shape a system's activity settles down to (Stewart 1997: 99). By the mid-1980s, the terminology of chaos theory, including *EMERGING ORDER, FEEDBACK LOOPS, COMPLEXITY* and *SELF-ORGANISATION*, was born and started spreading across disciplines (Table 23).

BIFURCATION POINT	A critical or sensitive decision point, corresponding to a sudden change causing a system to take a new direction or branch into a new type of behaviour. <www.schuelers.com/ChaosPsyche/part_1_7.htm>
CHAOTIC ATTRACTORS	A stable, nonperiodic state or behavior exhibited by some dynamic systems, especially turbulent ones, that can be represented as a nonrepeating pattern in the system's phase space. Syn: strange attractor. < http://dictionary.reference.com/browse/chaotic+attractor>
COMPLEXITY	It describes nonlinear systems such as ecologies, markets, social systems or neural networks, in which parts interact. Such systems cannot be approached through linear or reductionist analysis because their nonlinearity implies circular causation and feedback effects. < http://www.calresco.org/glossary.htm>
DISCONTINUITY	Unpredictable, unforeseen natural or man-made sudden change, consequence, event or force that confounds or disrupts earlier expectations or estimates. <http://www.businessdictionary.com/definition/discontinuity.html>
EDGE OF CHAOS (EOC)	The tendency of dynamic systems to self-organise to a state roughly midway between globally static (unchanging) and chaotic (random) states. This can also be regarded as the liquid phase, half way between solid (static) and gas (random) natural states. In information theory this is the state containing the maximum information. < http://www.calresco.org/glossary.htm>
EMERGENT PROPERTIES/PATTERNS	When dealing with complex systems, it is essential to keep in mind that the system is more than the sum of its component parts. Emergent properties can be considered as any unexpected properties exhibited by a complex system, whether beneficial or harmful. Those properties cannot be identified through functional decomposition.
FEEDBACK LOOPS	In every feedback loop, information about the result of a transformation or an action is sent back to the input of the system in the form of input data. If these new data facilitate and accelerate the transformation in the same direction as the preceding results, they are positive feedback: their effects are cumulative. If the new data produce a result in the opposite direction to previous results, they are negative feedback: their effects stabilise the system. <http://pespmc1.vub.ac.be/FEEDBACK.html>
FRACTAL	A fractal is a "rough or fragmented geometric shape that can

	be split into parts, each of which is (at least approximately) a reduced-size copy of the whole" (Mandelbrot 1982).
ORDERLY DISORDER	A paradoxical notion pointing at the emergence of order on the edge of chaos.
NONLINEARITY	Property of chaotic systems, characterised by approximation, random behaviour, and unpredictability. It is the feature of natural (real world) or other systems which cannot be decomposed into parts and reassembled into the same thing, and do not change in proportion to a change in an input. <http://www.businessdictionary.com/definition/nonlinearity.html>
PERIOD DOUBLING	A scenario for the transition of a natural process from regular periodic motion to chaos, in which the time required for the motion of the system to repeat itself doubles again and again as a parameter describing the system is increased. (*McGraw-Hill Dictionary of Scientific & Technical Terms* 2003)
SELF-ORGANISATION	Self-organisation is basically a process of evolution where the effect of the environment is minimal, i.e. where the development of new, complex structures takes place primarily in and through the system itself. <http://pespmc1.vub.ac.be/SELFORG.html>
SELF-SIMILARITY	A characteristic property of fractals.
SENSITIVITY TO INITIAL CONDITIONS	This refers to the fact that small changes in the initial state of a complex system can drastically alter the final outcome.
STRANGE ATTRACTORS	Also known as chaotic attractors.
TURBULENCE	Turbulence is connected with fluid dynamics and refers to any condition where orderly motion is broken up into random or chaotic motion. <http://www.schuelers.com/ChaosPsyche/part_1_3.htm>

Table 23. Chaos theory terminology as a common denominator for many fields of research

The terms in Table 23 have become familiar to a number of researchers from various horizons, and the theory they stem from has been adapted to various fields of inquiry. In this respect, one can refer to a shared, interface terminology that is reinterpreted depending on the field's context, and on the researchers' objectives and viewpoints. As chaos theory aroused increasing interest in the 1980s and 1990s, the number of papers, conferences and scientific as well as popularisation books on the topic grew substantially. The abundant literature, however, underlines the idea that "there is no unified field of complexity theory, but rather a number of different fields with intriguing points of resemblance, overlap or complementarity" (Rosenhead 1998 online). Each science or domain will select or stress one particular aspect of the concepts in question.

Literary scholars were also influenced by chaos theory, which found an echo in the cultural environment of the time. It is true that the themes of unpredictability, fractal diffusion and reflexivity were well in place in postmodern works of literature by the time chaos theory was articulated in the sciences, thus making the theory an attractive analogy for literary scholars (Polvinen 2008 :10). Yet, though science and literature may share the terminology of chaos theory, they differ in their perception of chaos. A major difference is highlighted by Hayles (1990: 184) who remarks that "for deconstructionists, chaos repudiates order; for scientists, chaos makes order possible"; in fact, for poststructuralists, chaos theory became a narrative of anti-order, a means to support their politically subversive discourse. As far as literary criticism is concerned, according to Hayles it is possible to consider texts as disordered systems from which complex order can emerge by means of interpretation. Literary critic McKusick points out the advantage of considering intellectual circles as dynamic ecosystems (2000: 18):

> [...] the old-fashioned study of the "history of ideas" may be usefully reconceived for our time as a study of the dynamics of intellectual ecosystems. Whatever its merits as a description of what actually occurs in the unruly ferment of a new intellectual movement, such an ecocritical approach offers some distinctive possibilities for a new approach to the study of literary history. It suggests that the linear analysis of "sources and influences" should be enlarged and perhaps even supplanted by a study of the dialogical exchange of ideas among a community of writers. Such a community should be regarded as a dynamic entity, sometimes verging upon utter chaos, and always in the process of becoming something other than itself.

In the field of economics, chaos theory has found a number of applications, which is understandable if one considers that, at the core of chaos theory, one finds the idea that a higher form of order is to be found beneath the apparent *RANDOMNESS* of *NONLINEAR DYNAMIC SYSTEMS*. Although predictability remains a challenge, the idea that a degree of predictability could be achieved is of course tempting. A lot has been written about *FRACTAL FINANCE* and *FRACTAL MARKET ANALYSIS*, where chaos theory seems to be able to provide tools for analysing the dynamics of uncertainty and to locate hidden order. Chaos theory has also been applied to price fluctuations, as well as cycles, and to evolutionary economics, but one particular arena where it has proved useful is that of business and management. Companies are organisations, i.e. nonlinear systems that "evolve in a dynamic way over time as a result of complex interactions among firms, government, labour, consumers, financial institutions and other elements of the environment" (Levy 1994: 167). In this context, chaos theory may provide a useful conceptual famework enabling researchers to identify distinctive patterns in contexts that are essentially unpredictable (Cartwright 1991). It is relevant to strategic aspects, planning and forecasting and may help to better assess the impact of change on firms and entire industries. Models are just models, as is widely acknowledged by economists, business people and anyone involved in planning: they cannot incorporate small disturbances that may nevertheless cause unexpectedly large changes over time. What this means for business strategy is that any seemingly minor change may have an unexpected impact: a new entrant on the market may substantially disrupt the competitive landscape and a new, but rather small technological change may greatly question a firm's position in a given industry. A good illustration of the relevance of chaos theory to corporate management can be found in the conception of an international supply chain as a *COMPLEX DYNAMIC SYSTEM* where many different agents interact. In this context, uncertainty exists at each stage, with potential disruptions rippling backwards and forwards along the chain. Management should not underestimate the impact of such disruptions. To avoid substantial costs, guidelines and decision rules can be developed to cope with complexity; in addition, the new framework may help to consider "nonobvious and indirect means to achieving goals" (Levy 1994: 176).

More generally speaking, complexity and chaos theory question the received ideas about organisation viewed as a piece of clockwork, a view that led to a rationalist conception of management. For theorists and practitioners, well-managed businesses were seen as places where the responsibility of managers was to announce the mission of the firm, to set clear targets and to devise the overall strategy to meet those targets; any deviation from the main lines was to be avoided and stability was a key notion. From the perspective of complexity and chaos theory, such a view of management is counter-productive and managers should endeavour to position their firm "in a region of bounded instability, to seek the edge of chaos" (Rosenhead 1998[168]). Interestingly, one of the features of complex adaptive systems is *PUNCTUATED EQUILIBRIUM*, in other words, periods of stability interrupted by more agitated periods called *PUNCTUATION POINTS*. The argument is that the strategies and skills that are efficient in stable periods cease to be relevant at *PUNCTUATION POINTS*, which may be unsettling for a company struggling to survive. Therefore, two different types of situations should be distinguished: one that justifies *ORDINARY MANAGEMENT* and one that requires *EXTRAORDINARY MANAGEMENT* (Stacey 1993). As the term implies, *ORDINARY MANAGEMENT*, based on data analysis, goal setting, monitoring and rational choice, can help the company meet the purpose of solving problems on a daily basis in "normal" times. By contrast, *EXTRAORDINARY MANAGEMENT* is called for when the company faces *DISRUPTIVE CHANGE* and must adapt quickly. It goes without saying that openness to change should not mean constantly introducing radical changes. Rather, the goal is to strike the right balance between stasis and chaos, and to aim at the *EDGE OF CHAOS*, "where fitness is maximised. Being at the edge of chaos means something more subtle than pursuing a moderate level of change. At the edge of chaos, one is simultaneously conservative and radical" (Beinhocker 2000: 116). In order to do so, it is essential to use instability in a positive way, to encourage creative disorder through the ferment of ideas – within limits, of course, if one is to avoid complete anarchy – so that the organisation can re-invent itself. When an organisation is in equilibrium and everything is planned, people are imprisoned in fixed patterns and habits; by contrast, it is easier to introduce change when the organisation is far from equilibrium. Concretely, this can be achieved by en-

168 Online LSE working paper; no page number available.

couraging informal, self-organising teams gathered around particular issues or reflecting on particular processes, from which group learning emerges.

Meyer (2001) summarises the new approach to the firm as part of an adaptive system, using such key notions as *INTERACTIONS*, *ADAPTIVE SYSTEMS, EMERGING PROPERTIES* and *CYCLICALITY*:

> An economy is an adaptive system of agents (firms and individuals) interacting. Under certain environmental conditions (a legal system, capital availability), properties such as growth, cyclicality and distribution of income emerge. Likewise, a company can be reframed not as a machine in equilibrium, but as an adaptive system of individuals. Success, however measured, is an emergent outcome, not the product of a machine[169].

A number of terms already mentioned in Chapter 4 as neonyms should be considered as evidence of the impact of chaos theory on corporate management theory and practice: *DISRUPTIVE INNOVATION* or technology, *LEARNING ORGANISATION, THE LEFT-BRAIN ORGANISATION, ORGANISATIONAL AGILITY, RESILIENCE* or *SCENARIO PLANNING*. Paying attention to these terms and the concepts they denote automatically means investigating the field of complexity and chaos theory and tracking the evolution of positions in various circles of scientists, researchers and practitioners.

7.4. Concluding remarks

This chapter has shown that interface terms are a barometer of cross-disciplinary research as well as a means to assess how influential a discipline can be. A more systematic diachronic approach to cross-disciplinary terms, considered as a reflection of intellectual trends impregnating various disciplines, should make it possible to feel the pulse of influential intellectual movements and better understand the prevailing philosophy and set of beliefs at particular periods of time. For example, as has been mentioned in former chapters, both termi-

169 <http://www.leader-values.com/Content/detail.asp?ContentDetailID=270>

nology and economics seem to have evolved from an orthodox, mainstream body of assumptions towards a number of more diversified approaches, now that the core beliefs have been questioned. In physics, relativity theory and quantum physics have swept away the deeply-rooted beliefs of classical physics, replacing absoluteness and predictability with notions of uncertainty. In linguistics, structuralism has been superseded by cognitive linguistics and generative grammar. These changes could be interpreted as the reflection of the evolution that has taken place at large in the scientific world, from positivism to post-modernist currents. A wide-ranging research project consisting in detecting the concepts and terms that have infiltrated those fields and given rise to a number of new trends and approaches at specific periods would certainly yield most interesting results.

8. Conclusion

> Great steps in human progress are made by things
> that don't work the way philosophy thought they should.
> If things always worked the way they should, you could
> write the history of the world from now on. But they don't,
> and it is those deviations from the normal that make human progress.
>
> Charles F. Kettering (1876-1958)

It is now time to take stock of the lessons that can be drawn from the various paths that have been followed in this book to investigate a specialised domain from the point of view of a linguist, using terms as an entry point. Following in Kettering's footsteps, I can truly say that it is, indeed, the deviations from the "normal" that have helped me progress along the path towards a better understanding of the domains of economics, finance and management; in other words, it was the atypical terms I encountered which triggered questions and led to further investigation.

The stance adopted here is thus based on the idea that discontinuities, disharmony, complex and ambiguous phenomena should not be disregarded, but on the contrary sought as a treasure that has many riches to offer. Wüster's positions on language and the linguistic sign were obviously influenced by positivist views and a logicist systemic vision of terminology (Gambier 1991: 49), hence his purpose to eliminate ambiguity and terminological inconsistencies from scientific and technical communication. Postmodernism, however, has brought new approaches to many fields of knowledge, including terminology. Terminologists are now well aware that terms must be considered against the background of discourse and in their situational context. It is now acknowledged that terms may vary and that a domain's conceptual system is not set forever. Linguistic and sociological evolution is inherent not only in any language, but also in every field (Gaudin 2003), including that of any specialised area of knowledge. Thus, variability and indeterminacy need not be considered as negative aspects, but as a sign of openness and dynamism (Beaugrande 1997; Myking 2007:74). In addition, the textual and communicative environment must be taken into consideration (Cabré). Sociocognitive concerns (Temmerman 2000) also point to the need to take a broader context into account.

The domain of economics is a case in point as "economic knowledge is culturally inscribed and socially constructed" (Brown 2002: 64). Concepts and the terms that denote them obviously have to be placed in the context of the time and circumstances in which they emerged. New findings in other sciences – natural sciences, physics, mathematics and other social sciences – have clearly influenced the development of economics, and vice versa. As historical circumstances changed, they affected the scope and methods of economic analysis. Social demands, new challenges and the evolution of techniques generally require rethinking theoretical postures, and reconsidering approaches to meet new needs and find answers to ever more complex problems. For all these reasons, economic terms offer an ideal testing ground to show how a Specialised Variety of English can be approached by researchers and teachers of English as a foreign language in higher education seeking to investigate a specialised domain they were not initially trained in.

As scientific theory and findings are expressed through language, the researcher in the field of SVE, as a linguist, is in an ideal position to investigate specialised disciplines, domains and communities on the basis of language and terminology. In the circles of SVE research, however, too many colleagues seem to have a biased attitude towards terminology. Those who are interested in discourse analysis tend to devote too little attention to terms, for they consider that terms are merely the minimal units of specialised discourse, and thus cannot help them to gain an accurate idea of discourse as a whole; in so thinking, they fail to realise the wealth of information they miss by not inquiring further into these units. As for those who concentrate on terminology *per se* for translation purposes or for creating terminological data banks, they are logically limited in their need to consider the discursive and cultural contexts, as their focus is not specialised discourse in the broader sense. Besides, translators are obviously pressed for time. It seems, however, that investigating specialised domains requires a more holistic approach if one is to render as accurate as possible a picture of the language, discourse, habits, culture and people representative of those domains. SVE should then be seen as an area of research that is at a crossroads between linguistics, genre and discourse analyses, sociology, cultural studies and even anthropology when it comes to inquiring into a specific community through field work; therefore, it can and should be approached from various angles. In this context, terminological investigation can serve several purposes. The cement that holds all the members of a community together is a common language and, for a specialised community, it is also the shared knowledge based on a number of concepts – expressed by terms – and conceptual networks. Therefore, terms are an essential part of the researcher's investigation. But the message I would like to convey here is that, over and above their definitions and positions in conceptual networks within a domain, terms can yield a great deal of information about the theory, history and principal players of a specific domain – provided they are not taken out of their textual, situational, cultural and historical contexts. What holds for disciplines can also be applied to techniques or specialised activities where skills are transmitted either orally or through texts. The linguist can certainly play a role in investigating such communities and their discourse, starting with the analysis of the basic concepts that gave birth to the field and its activities, inquiring into the history of the specialised milieu, and observing the evolution of the terminology of the field, and of its customs and practices, thus helping preserve and record the cultural heritage of different occupations and professions.

As illustrated by the examples provided in the various chapters in this book, there are many ways in which researchers can rely on terminology to gain insight into a specialised domain. A diachronic perspective can help to identify the evolution of concepts and theoretical stances, and to detect important turning points in approaches and attitudes. A synchronic approach can be an opportunity to take a snapshot of a given event or phenomenon. Apart from these two broad perspectives, which are to be seen as complementary and not mutually exclusive, various other angles can be adopted when considering a specialised domain. Looking at the birth certificate of terms and those who coined them can tell us about well-known figures in the field, and about prevailing scientific or social concerns and trends at various points in time; focusing on new terms is a means to keep track of current, ongoing change in processes, techniques or in a scientific domain. Metaphorical terms invite the researcher to inquire further into the history of the ideas that have shaped a discipline or a specialised group's activities and practices, and once a clear map of the main metaphorical veins has been established, it becomes easier to understand the influences that have been at play. It is then easier to deal with metaphorical networks and observe any sudden departure from the original ones, which may well signal a paradigm shift. Concepts and the terms that denote them may also cross disciplinary boundaries and fertilise other fields. Observing and understanding how some concepts and terms travel across disciplines, open up new vistas, are adapted and finally enrich new fields offers an opportunity to trace the itinerary of theories and ideas and to bear testimony to scientific and social evolution. Indeterminate terms also deserve careful analysis. When trying to understand what has prompted the emergence of euphemisms, oxymora and the use of vague or ambiguous terms, the researcher will need to take into account the discursive context, the norms prevailing in a given discipline or domain, and the constraints that bear on discursive and terminological choices. In other words, through all the questions raised by the categories of terms dealt with in this book, it is possible to gain insight into specialised domains and communities, their cultural environment, standards, and shared knowledge.

This approach may sound unorthodox for those researchers in terminology who may not be interested in discourse analysis or in the study of specialised discourse communities and their traditions and norms. However, if one considers the evolution that has taken place in approaches to terminology, in addition to the fact that terminology is a discipline at a crossroads, it should not be surprising to see that terms, as multifaceted units, can meet different needs. The approach presented here capitalises on the three dimensions of terms that are now recognised: the cognitive, the linguistic and the socio-communicative aspects. Back in 1990, Sager had identified three dimensions for a theory of terminology:

> Since it is semantically based, terminology can be studied from three different points of view, i.e. from the point of view of the referent, from the point of view of the designation given the referent, and finally from the point of view of the use the equation of referent and designation can be put to. Consequently we identify three dimensions of a theory of terminology; a cognitive one which relates the linguistic forms to conceptual content, i.e. the referents in the real world; a linguistic one which examines the existing and potential forms of the representation of terminologies; a communicative one which looks at the use of terminologies and has to justify the human activity of terminology compilation and processing. (1990: 13)

Adapting this approach and broadening the scope of terms, it is possible to consider that each dimension can be prioritised in turn. In some instances, terms will be considered as an end in themselves, when inquiring into the conceptual framework of a specific sub-domain. In other instances, the cognitive dimension will prevail, and in others still, the socio-communicative one will be preferred (Cabré 2000). Bringing together all the information obtained when considering each dimension is like assembling the pieces of a gigantic jigsaw puzzle in order to see the big picture and have a more accurate idea of the specificity of specialised domains and their players.

As stated at the beginning of this book, the approach suggested here for the domain of economics can be adapted for other disciplines, as well as non-disciplinary occupations or activities. And there seems to be no end to the research work that can be conducted in the field:

> There is no theoretical limit to the number of special purposes to which language can be put. As society develops new facets, so language is devised to express them. In recent times, whole new areas of expression have emerged, in relation to such domains as computing, broadcasting, commercial advertising and popular music. Over a longer time-scale, special styles have developed associated with religion, law, politics, commerce, the press, medicine and science. A detailed linguistic account of any one of these areas would itself require an encyclopedia, as the analysis of the language used would require an exposition of the conceptual system that gave rise to it. (Crystal 1987: 378)

Obviously, Crystal's remarks need to be explicited and updated to fit today's context, while his point that it would ideally take an encyclopedia to provide a detailed account of each specialised area is extremely pertinent and seems to square with the approach to SVE that is advocated here. Much work thus awaits linguists working along those lines since progress in each area will lead to the creation of new terms; cooperation between disciplines will evolve, generating new interface terms; new types of discourse will emerge, and the new conventions will make it necessary for terms to be adapted to the new discursive environment.

> Knowledge does not come "*off the shelf, prepackaged, ready for use*" (Hayes-Roth 1987: 293). As already mentioned, it can be inconsistent and contradictory. [...] It may be hard to "*capture*", since it is constantly changing, and since emergent knowledge can be incomplete and unclear. (Meyer, Skuce, Bowker & Eck 1992: 957)

For these reasons, researchers in SVE would gain much from setting up various monitoring committees that would help them collect, analyse and synthesise data on neonyms, metaphorical and interface terms. They would thus be able to observe the evolution of a domain, to keep up with the dynamics of progress, to detect any shift in theory-constitutive metaphors and to assess how influential a domain may be over others as well as how open it may be to cross-border exchanges. The linguist's lens would most certainly be useful for monitoring changing scientific traditions, as well as evolving social trends and for accounting for successive worldviews over time. Linguists may also have a role to play alongside the specialists of a given field, since their investigations of linguistic phenomena that may escape insiders' attention make them more sensitive to puzzles, internal contradictions and deviations and enable them to record and signal change. Undoubtedly, research conducted by linguists in the field of SVE, based on *in situ, in vivo* terminological investigation, can prove most useful in so far as, in their position as careful observers, they hold a mirror up to the members of various specific communities, whether scientific or professional, and to society at large.

References

Abbey, Edward 1991. *The Journey Home: Some Words in Defense of the American West*. London: Plume.

Adkins, Roy 2005. *Nelson's Trafalgar, the Battle That Changed the World*. New York: Viking Penguin.

Agrawal, Vivek / Manyika, James M. / Richards, John E. 2003. Matching people and jobs. *The McKinsey Quarterly*, Special edition: the value in organisation, 71-79.

Alborn, Timothy L. 1994. Economic man, economic machine: images of circulation in the Victorian money market. In Mirowski, Philip (ed.) *Natural Images in Economic Thought*. Cambridge: Cambridge University Press, 173-196.

Alchian, Armen A. 1950. Uncertainty, Evolution and Economic Theory. *Journal of Political Economy*. 58, 211-221.

Algeo, John 1991. *Fifty years among the new words: A dictionary of neologisms, 1941-1991*. Cambridge: Cambridge University Press.

Allen, Keith / Burridge, Kate 1991. *Euphemism and Dysphemism: Language Used as Shield and Weapon*. New York: Oxford University Press.

Andersen, Øivin 2002. Terminology and pragmatics. In Koskela, Merja / Laurén, Christer / Nordman, Marianne / Pilke Nina (eds.) *Porta Scientiae 1. Lingua Specialis*. Vaasa: Proceedings of the University of Vaasa, 136-146.

Antia, Bassey E. 2001. Metadiscourse in Terminology: Thesis, Antithesis, Synthesis. *Terminology Science and Research*. 12/1-2, 65-84.

Antia, Bassey E. 2002. Wüster and Applied Linguistics Research. *LSP & Professional Communication*. 2/1, 102-111.

Antia, Bassey E. (ed.). 2007. *Indeterminacy in Terminology and LSP. Studies in Honour of Heribert Picht*. Amsterdam/Philadelphia:

John Benjamins, Terminology and Lexicography Research and Practice 8.
Argyris, Chris / Schön, Donald A. 1978. *Organisational learning: A theory of action perspective*. Reading, MA: Addison Wesley.
Argyris, Chris / Schön, Donald A. 1996. *Organisational learning II: Theory, method and practice*. Reading, MA: Addison Wesley.
Aristotle, *Rhetoric*. 1991. (Trans). George A. Kennedy. New York: Oxford University Press.
Aristotle, *Poetics*. (Trans). S. H. Butcher. <http://classics.mit.edu/Aristotle/poetics.html>.
Arthur, W.Brian 1999. The end of economic certainty. In J.H. Clippinger (eds.) *The biology of business – decoding the natural laws of enterprise*. San Francisco: Jossey-Bass Publishers, 31-46.
Augsburg, Tania 2005. *Becoming Interdisciplinary: An Introduction to Interdisciplinary Studies*, Kendall Hunt Publishing Company.
Bachelier, Louis 1900. *Théorie de la spéculation*. Paris: Gauthier-Villiers.
Backhouse, Roger E. / Dudley-Evans, Tony / Henderson, Willie [1993] 2002. Exploring the language and rhetoric of economics. In Henderson, Willie / Dudley-Evans, Tony / Backhouse, Roger E (eds.) *Economics & Language*. London: Routledge, 1-20.
Beaugrande (de), Robert 1997. *New Foundations for a Science of Text and Discourse: Cognition, Communication and the Freedom of Access to Knowledge and Society*. Norwood: Ablex.
Becker, Gary [1964] 1993. *Human Capital: a Theoretical and Empirical Analysis, with Special Reference to Education.* Chicago: The University of Chicago Press.
Becker, Gary 1971. *Economic Theory*. New York: Knopf.
Becker, Gary 1976 *a*. The Economic Approach to Human Behavior. In, Becker, Gary (ed.) *The Economic Approach to Human Behavior*. Chicago: University of Chicago Press, 3-14.
Becker, Gary 1976*b*. Altruism, Egoism and Genetic Fitness: Economics and Sociobiology. *Journal of Economic Literature*. 14, 817-826.
Becker, Tilman C. 2005. Consumer behavior research in the advent of the twenty-first century. In Mattas, Konstadinos / Tsakiridou,

Efthimia (eds.) *Food quality products in the advent of the 21st century: production, demand and public policy.* Cahiers Options Méditerranéennes. 64, 5-16.

Beinhocker, Eric D. 2000. Strategy at the Edge of Chaos. *The McKinsey Quarterly,* 109-118. <www.mckinseyquarterly.com/strategy/sted97.asp>.

Bell, Daniel 1881. Models and Reality in Economic Discourse. In Bell Daniel / Kristol, Irving (eds.) *The Crisis in Economic Theory.* New York: Basic Books, 46-80.

Bennington, Geoffrey 1999. Inter-. In McQuillan, Martin / MacDonald, Graeme / Purves, Robin / Thomson, Stephen (eds.) *Post-Theory: New Directions in Criticism.* Edinburgh: Edinburgh University Press,103-119.

Bergenholtz, Henning 1995. Wodurch unterscheidet sich Fachlexikographie von Terminologie? *Lexicographica.* 11, 50-59.

Bicchieri, Cristina 1988. Should a Scientist Abstain from a Metaphor? In Klamer, Arjo / McCloskey, Donald N. / Solow, Robert (eds.) *The Consequences of Economic Rhetoric.* Cambridge: Cambridge University Press, 100-114.

Black, Max 1962. *Models and Metaphors.* Ithaca, MA: Cornell University Press.

Blanchon, Elisabeth 2004. Report on the Second International Terminology Conference - CIT 2003. Terminology: The State of the Theories. *Terminology.* 10/2, 337-340.

Borg, Erik 2003. Key Concepts in ELT: Discourse Community. *ELT Journal.* 57/4, Oxford: Oxford University Press, 398-400.

Borges, Jorge L. 1964. The fearful sphere of Pascal. In, Yates, Donald A. / James E. Irby (eds.), André. Maurois, Pref. *Labyrinths: Selected stories and other writings.* New York: New Directions, 189-192.

Boulding, Kenneth E. 1950. *A Reconstruction of Economics.* New York: John Wiley & Sons.

Boulding, Kenneth E. 1958. *Principles of Economic Policy.* Englewood Cliffs, NJ: Prentice-Hall.

Boulding, Kenneth E. 1966. The Economics of the Coming Spaceship Earth, in H. Jarret (ed.) *Environmental Quality in a Growing Economy*. Johns Hopkins University Press, 3-14.

Boulding, Kenneth E. 1969. Economics as a moral science. *American Economic Review*. 59/1, 1-12.

Bourdieu, Pierre 1983. The Forms of Capital. In Richardson, John G. (ed.) *Handbook of Theory and Research for the Sociology of Education*. New York: Greenwood Press, 241-258.

Bourigault, Didier / Jacquemin, Christian / L'Homme, Marie-Claude 2001. *Recent Advances in Computational Terminology*. Amsterdam/Philadelphia: John Benjamins.

Bourigault, Didier / Slodzian, Monique 1999. Pour une terminologie textuelle. *Terminologies Nouvelles* Special TIA99. 19, 29-32.

Boyd. Richard[1979] 1993. Metaphor and theory change: What is 'metaphor' a metaphor for? In Ortony, Andrew (ed.) *Metaphor and Thought*. Cambridge: Cambridge University Press, 481-532.

Boyer Commission on Educating Undergraduates in the Research University. 1998. *Reinventing Undergraduate Education.*

Brook, William / Magee, Stephen P. 1985. The Invisible Foot and the Waste of Nations / Redistribution and Economic Growth. In Colander, David C. (ed.) *Neoclassical Political Economy.* Cambridge, MA: Ballinger Publishing Company,177-186.

Brown, Arnold 1999. The Invisible Fist. *The Futurist*. 33.

Brown, Vivienne 2002. Decanonising discourses: textual analyses and the history of economic thought. In Henderson, Willie / Dudley-Evans, Tony / Backhouse, Roger E. (eds.) *Economics & Language.* London: Routledge, 64-84.

Buchanan, James M. 1964. What Should Economists Do? *Southern Economic Journal*. 30/3, 213-222.

Buchanan, James M. / Tullock, Gordon 1962. *The Calculus of Consent*. Ann Arbor: University of Michigan Press.

Budin, Gerhard 1998. The Wüster Archive – a special node in a European digital archive network. In Oeser, Erhard / Galinski, Christian (eds.) *Eugen Wüster (1898-1977). Leben und Werk. Ein österreichischer Pionier der Informationsgesellschaft.* Vienna: Termnet Publisher, 169-173.

Burns, Arthur F. and Mitchell, Wesley C. 1946. *Measuring Business Cycles*. New York: National Bureau of Economic Research.
Burridge, Keith 1996. Political Correctness: Euphemism with Attitude. *English Today*. 12/3, 42-49.
Butler, Alison 1990. A Methodological Approach to Chaos: Are Economists Missing the Point? *Federal Reserve Bank of St. Louis*. 72/13, 36-48.
Cabré, Maria Teresa [1992] 1998. *La terminologie, Théorie, méthode et applications*. Translated and adapted by M.C. Cormier and J. Humbley. Ottawa/Paris: Les Presses de l'Université d'Ottawa/Armand Colin.
Cabré, Maria Teresa 1999. *La terminología: Representación y comunicación. Elementos para una teoría de base comunicativa y otros artículos*, Barcelona: Institut Universitari de Lingüística Aplicada.
Cabré, Maria Teresa 2000. Elements for a Theory of Terminology. Towards an Alternative Paradigm. *Terminology. International Journal of Theoretical and Applied Issues in Specialised Communication*. 6/1, 35-57.
Cabré, Maria Teresa 2003. Theories of Terminology: their Description, Prescription and Explanation. *Terminology*. 9/2, 163-19.
Candel, Daniel 2004. Wüster par lui-même. *Des Fondements théoriques de la terminologie*, Paris: Cahier du C.I.E.L, UP7/ULCO, 15-31.
Cannon, Walter F. 1961. John Herschel and the Idea of Science. *Journal of the History of Ideas*. 22, 215-239.
Carter, David 1983. Some Propositions about ESP. *English for Specific Purposes*. 2, 131-137.
Cartwright, Tim J. 1991. Planning and Chaos Theory. *Journal of the American Planning Association*. 57/1, 44-56.
Chandler, Alfred D. 1977. *The Visible Hand: the Managerial Revolution in American Business*. Cambridge, MA: Harvard University Press.
Charteris-Black, Jonathan 2000. Metaphor and Vocabulary Teaching in ESP Economics. *English for Specific Purposes*. 19/2, 149-165.

Christensen, Paul P. 1994. Fire, Motion, and Productivity: the Proto-energetics of Nature and Economy in François Quesnay. In Mirowski, P. (ed.) *Natural Images in Economic Thought*. Cambridge: Cambridge University Press, 249-288.

Clark, Barry 1998. *Political Economy: A Comparative Approach*. Westport, CT: Preager.

Coats, Alfred W. 1990. Economic rhetoric: the social and historical context. In Klamer, Arjo / McCloskey, Donald N. / Solow Robert M. (eds.) *The Consequences of Economic Rhetoric* Cambridge: Cambridge University Press, 64-84.

Coddington, Alan 1983. *Keynesian Economics: The Search for First Principles*. London: George Alien & Unwin.

Colander, David C. 2000. The Death of Neoclassical Economics. *Journal of the History of Economic Thought*. 22/2, 127-143.

Colander, David C. 2006. *Economics*. Boston: McGraw-Hill Irwin.

Commons, John R. 1934. *Institutional economics – its place in political economy*. New York: Macmillan.

Cortezzi, Martin / Jin, Lixian 1999. Bridges to Learning. In Cameron, Lynne / Low, Graham (eds.) *Researching and Applying Metaphor*. Cambridge: Cambridge University Press,149-176.

Crespo Fernández, Eliecer 2005. Euphemistic Strategies in Politeness and Face Concerns. *Pragmalinguistica*. 13, 77-86.

Croft, William / Cruse, David A. 2005. *Cognitive Linguistics*. Cambridge: Cambridge University Press.

Crossan, Mary M. / Lane, Henry W. / White, Roderick E. / Klus, Leo 1996. The Improvising Organisation: Where Planning Meets Opportunity. *Organisational Dynamics*. 24 /4, 20-35.

Crystal, David 1987. *The Cambridge Encyclopedia of Language*. Cambridge: Cambridge University Press.

Detourbe, Marie-Agnès 2011. *Contribution à la caractérisation des pratiques d'évaluation dans le monde de l'enseignement supérieur britannique envisagé comme domaine spécialisé*. Doctoral dissertation defended September 15th, 2011, Bordeaux Segalen University.

De Vries, Jan 1999. Comments. <http://www.econ.yale.edu/alumni/reunion99/devries.htm>.

Dietrich, Michael 2006. *Economics of the Firm: Analysis, Evolution and History*. Studies in Global Competition Series, London: Routledge.

Domenec, Fanny 2011. 'Monsanto's claims' au Royaume-Uni et aux Etats-Unis: les communiqués de presse de Monsanto, entre unité générique et hétérogénéïté culturelle. *Asp*. 59, 65-93.

Donaldson, Lex 1990. The Ethereal Hand: Organisational Economics and Management Theory. *The Academy of Management Review*. 15/3, 369-381.

Donzelli, Franco 1997. Pareto's mechanical dream. Paper presented at the *Third National Scientific Meeting of the Italian Association for the History of Economic Thought* (AISPE), held in Pisa, Italy, on May 16th-18th, 1996. <http://air.unimi.it/bitstream/2434/25222/1/pareto%27s_mechanical_dream.pdf>.

Dudley-Evans, Tony / St John, Maggie Jo 1998. *Developments in English for Specific Purposes*. Cambridge: Cambridge University Press.

Dury, Pascaline 1999. Étude comparative et diachronique des concepts 'ecosystem' et 'écosystème'. *Meta: Translators' Journal*. 44 /3, 485-499.

Edgeworth, Francis.Y. [1881] 1967. *Mathematical Psychics: An Essay on the Application of Mathematics to the Moral Sciences*. New York: Augustus M. Kelley.

Egidi, Massimo / Rizzello, Salvatore 2004. Cognitive Economics: Foundations and Historical Evolution. Working paper No. 04/2003, Dpt. of Economics, University of Turin. <http://www.cesmep.unito.it/WP/2003/4_WP_Cesmep.pdf>.

Einstein, Albert 1905. On the motion of small particles suspended in liquids at rest required by the molecular-kinetic theory of heat. (Brownian motion paper) *Annalen der Physik*. 17, 549-560. <https://lyle.smu.edu/ee/5375/downloads/Lectures/Lecture11/einstein-bm.pdf>.

Emblemsvåg, Jan 2003. The Green Invisible Hand. *Foresight*. 5/1, 11-19.

Esty, Daniel C. / Winston, Andrew S. 2006. *Green to Gold*. Hoboken, NJ: Wiley & Sons.

Fairclough, Norman 1992. *Discourse and Social Change*. Cambridge: Polity Press.

Farb, Peter 1973. *Word play*. London: Jonathan Cape.

Fauconnier, Gilles / Turner, Mark 1998. Conceptual integration networks. *Cognitive Science*. 22/2, 133-187.

Fetter, Frank A. 1924. The Economic Law of Market Areas. *The Quarterly Journal of Economics*. 38/3, 520-529.

Feyerabend, Paul 1975. *Against method: outline of an anarchistic theory of knowledge*. London: New Left Books.

Fisher, Irving [1897] 1906. *A Brief Introduction to the Infinitesimal Calculus*. New York: The Macmillan Company. <http://www.archive.org/stream/abriefintroduct05fishgoog#page/n7/mode/2up>.

Fisher, Irving 1918*a*. Is 'Utility' the Most Suitable Term for the Concept it is Used to Denote? *American Economic Review*. 8, 335-337. <http://socserv.mcmaster.ca/econ/ugcm/3ll3/fisher/utility.htm>.

Fisher, Irving 1918*b*. Precedents for Defining Capital. *Quarterly Journal of Economics*. 18, 386-408. <http://socserv.mcmaster.ca/econ/ugcm/3ll3/fisher/capital4>.

Fisher, Irving [1926] 1965. *Mathematical Investigations into the Theory of Value and Prices*. New York: A.M. Kelley.

Florini, Ann M. 1999. Does the Invisible Hand Need a Transparent Glove? The Politics of Transparency. Paper prepared for the *Annual World Bank Conference on Development Economics*, Washington, D.C. <http://derechoasaber.org.mx/documentos/pdf0042.pdf>.

Forman, David C. 2004. *Harnessing the Elusive Asset: Developing Intangible Organisational Capital*. Human Capital Institute. <www.humancapitalinstitute.org>.

Foster, John 1997. The analytical foundations of evolutionary economics: from biological analogy to economic self-organisation. *Structural Change and Economic Dynamics*. 8, 427-451.

Foster, Richard / Kaplan, Sarah 2001. Creative Destruction. *The McKinsey Quarterly*. 3, 41-51.

Fraser, Lindley M. 1937. *Economic Thought and Language*. London: A. & C. Black.

Frege, Gottlob [1903] 1952. Grundgesetze der Arithmetik, begriffsschriftlich abgeleitet. In Geach, Peter T. / Black, Max (eds.) *Translations from the Philosophical Writings of Gottlob Frege*. Oxford: Blackwell, 21-41.

Friedman, Milton 1953. The methodology of positive economics. In Friedman, Milton (ed.) *Essays in Positive Economics*. Chicago: University of Chicago Press, 3-34.

Friedman, Milton 1970. The Social Responsibility of Business is to Increase its Profits. *The New York Times Magazine*, September 13th.

Fries, Marie-Hélène 2011. Playing God in nanotechnologies : metaphors as an interface between science and spirituality, talk given at a Conference in Nice (France) in June 2011. *Approches transdisciplinaires de la spiritualité dans les arts et les sciences*.

Frisch, Ragnar [1926] 1971. On a problem in pure economics. In Chipman, John S. / Hurwicz, Leonid / Richter, Marcel K. / Sonnenschein Hugo F. (eds.) *Preferences, Utility, and Demand* New York: Harcourt Brace Jovanovich, 386-423.

Frisch, Ragnar 1933. Introduction. *Econometrica*. 1, 1-2,

Frisch, Ragnar 1970. Econometrics in the world of today. In Eltis, Walter A. / Scott, Maurice F. / Wolfe, James N. (eds.) *Induction, Growth and Trade, Essays in honour of Sir Roy Harrod*. Oxford: Clarendon Press, 152-166.

Frye, Timothy / Schleifer, Andrei 1998. The Invisible Hand and the Grabbing Hand. *American Economic Review*, papers and proceedings, 354-358.

Funtowicz, Silvio O. / Ravetz, Jerry R. 2003. Post-normal science. In International Society for Ecological Economics (ed.) *Online Encyclopedia of Ecological Economics*. < http://www.ecoeco.org/publica/encyc.htm>.

Galbraith, John K. 1990. The grammar of political economy. In Klamer, Arjo / McCloskey, Donald N. / Solow, Robert M. (eds.) *The Consequences of Economic Rhetoric*. Cambridge: Cambridge University Press, 221-239.

Gambier, Yves 1991. Travail et vocabulaire spécialisés: prolégomènes à une socio-terminologie. *Meta*. 36/1.
GAO. 1999. *Major Management Challenges and Program Risks: A Governmentwide Perspective.* US Government Accounting Office.
Gaudin, François 1993. *Pour une socioterminologie. Des problèmes sémantiques aux pratiques institutionnelles*. Rouen: Université de Rouen.
Gaudin, François 2003. *Socioterminologie: une approche sociolinguistique de la terminologie*, Manuels champs linguistiques, Brussels: De Boeck & Larcier et Duculot.
Georgescu-Roegen, Nicholas. 1971. *The Entropy Law and the Economic Process*. Cambridge, MA: Harvard University Press.
Gibbons, Robert / Waldman, Michael 2004. Task-specific human capital. *American Economic Review*. 94/2, 203-207.
Goodwin, Crawford D. 1990. The heterogeneity of the economists' discourse: philosopher, priest, and hired gun. In Klamer, Arjo / McCloskey, Donald N. / Solow, Robert M. (eds.) *The Consequences of Economic Rhetoric*. Cambridge: Cambridge University Press, 207-220.
Goodwin, Neva R. 1995. Series Introduction, xxi-xxxiii. In Krishnan, Rajavam / Harris, Jonathan M. / Goodwin, Neva R. (eds.) *A Survey of Ecological Economics*. Washington, DC: Island Press.
Gorz, André 2005. La personne devient une entreprise. Note sur le travail de production de soi. *Ecorev' (Revue critique d'écologie politique*.
< http://ecorev.org/spip.php?article382>.
Gotti, Maurizio. 2003. *Specialized Discourse. Linguistic Features and Changing Conventions*. Bern: Peter Lang.
Gowdy, John M. 1987. Bio-economics: social economy versus the Chicago School. *International Journal of Social Economics*. 14/1, 32-42.
Grey, William 2000. *Metaphor and Meaning*.
< http://www.ul.ie/~philos/ vol4/metaphor.HTML>.
Halliday, Michael / Martin James 1993. *Writing Science: Literacy and Discursive Power*. London: The Falmer Press.

Harré, Rom 1986. *Varieties of Realism*. Oxford: Blackwell.

Hartley, Peter / Porter, Michael G. 1990. *A green thumb for the invisible hand*. Melbourne: Tasman Institute.

Hawken, Paul, Lovins, L. Hunter and Lovins, Amory. 2000. *Natural Capitalism*. New York, Boston, London: Little, Brown & Company.

Hayek, Friedrich A. 1960. *The Constitution of Liberty*. London: Routledge & Kegan Paul / Chicago: University of Chicago Press.

Hayek, Friedrich A. 1976. *Law, Legislation, and Liberty*. vol. 2.

Hayek, Friedrich A. 1988. *The fatal conceit: The errors of socialism*. Chicago: University of Chicago Press.

Hayes-Roth, Frederick 1987. Expert Systems. In Shapiro, Stuart (ed.) *Encyclopedia of Artificial Intelligence*. New York: Wiley & Sons.

Hayles, Katherine N. 1990. *Chaos Bound: Orderly Disorder in Contemporary Literature and Science*. Ithaca, NY: Cornell University Press.

Heilbroner, Robert L. Rhetoric and identity. In Klamer, Arjo / McCloskey, Donald N. / Solow, Robert M. (eds.) *The Consequences of Economic Rhetoric*. Cambridge: Cambridge University Press, 38-43.

Hench, Thomas J. 1999. Rediscovering entrepreneurship in a complex world: a nonlinear framework for organizing. *Journal of Business and Entrepreneurship*. 11, 1-26.

Henderson, James P. 1994. The place of economics in the hierarchy of the sciences: section F from Whewell to Edgeworth. In Mirowski, Philip (ed.) *Natural Images in Economic Thought*. Cambridge: Cambridge University Press, 484-535.

Henderson, Willie 1982. Metaphor in Economics. *Economics*. 18/4, 147-157.

Henderson, Willie 1994. Metaphor and Economics. In Backhouse, Roger E. (ed.) *New Approaches to Economics Methodology*, London: Routledge, 343-367.

Henderson, Willie / Dudley-Evans, Tony / Backhouse, Roger E. [1993] 2002. *Economics & Language*. London and New York: Routledge.

Hesse, Mary B. 1966. *Models and Analogies in Science*. London: Sheed & Ward.

Hicks, John 1937. Mr. Keynes and the 'Classics': A Suggested Interpretation. *Econometrica*. 5/2,147-159.

Hicks, John 1981. *Wealth and Welfare: Collected Essays on Economic Theory*. Vol.1, Cambridge, MA: Harvard University Press.

Hindle, Tim 2008. *Guide to Management Ideas and Gurus*. London: Profile Books Ltd.

Hirshleifer, Jack 1976. Economics and sociobiology. *Working paper* 87, Economics Department, UCLA.

Hobbes, Thomas [1651] 1962. *Leviathan*. J. Plamenetz (ed.), London: Collins.

Hock, Dee W. 1995. The Chaordic Organisation: Out of Control and into Order. *World Business Academy Perspectives*. 9/1, 5-18.

Hodgson, Geoffrey M. 1993. The Mecca of Alfred Marshall. *The Economic Journal* 103, Oxford (UK)/Cambridge (US): Blackwell Publishers. 406-415.

Hodgson, Geoffrey M. 2002. Darwinism in economics: from analogy to ontology. *Journal of Evolutionary Economics*. 12, 259–281.

Hodgson, Geoffrey M. 2005. Decomposition and growth: biological metaphors in economics from the 1880s to the 1980s. In Dopfer, Kurt (ed.) *The Evolutionary Foundations of Economics*. Cambridge: Cambridge University Press, 105-149.

Hoffmann, Lothar 1979. Towards a Theory of LSP: Elements of a methodology of LSP analysis. *Fachsprache*. 1/1-2, 12-17.

Hofstede, Geert 1991. *Cultures and Organizations: Software of the Mind*. New York: McGraw-Hill.

Holton, Gerald 1984. Metaphors in Science and Education. In Taylor, William (ed.) *Metaphors of Education*. London: Heinemann, 91-113.
<http://www.econ.ucla.edu/workingpapers/wp087.pdf>.

Hopkin, Jonathan / Rodríguez-Pose, Andrés 2007. 'Grabbing Hand' or 'Helping Hand'? Corruption and the Economic Role of the State. *Governance*. 20/2, 187-208.

Howey, Richard S. 1972. The Origins of Marginalism. *History of Political Economy*. 4/2, 281-302.

Hulme, David / Toye, John 2006. The case for cross-disciplinary social science research on poverty, inequality and well-being. *Journal of Development Studies*. 42/7, 1085-1107.
Humbley, John 1997. Is terminology specialised lexicography? The experience of French-speaking countries. *Hermes, Journal of Linguistics*. 18, 13-31.
Humbley, John 2004. La réception de l'œuvre d'Eugen Wüster dans les pays de langue française. *Des Fondements théoriques de la terminologie*. Paris: Cahiers du C.I.E.L, UP7/ULCO, 33-51.
Humbley, John 2005. La traduction des métaphores dans les langues de spécialité : le cas des virus informatiques. *Linx*. <http://linx.revues.org/186>.
Hunt, Lynn 1994. The Virtues of Disciplinarity. *Eighteenth Century Studies*. 28/1, 8.
Hutchinson, Tom / Waters, Alan. 1987. *English for Specific Purposes: A Learning-centred Approach*. Cambridge: Cambridge University Press.
Hyland, Ken 1994. Hedging in academic textbooks and EAP. *English for Specific Purposes*. 13/3, 239-256.
Jakobson, Roman 1970. *Main Trends in the Science of Language*. New York: Harper & Row.
Jantsch, Erich 1970. Inter-and trans-disciplinary university: a systems approach to education and innovation. *Policy Sciences*. 1, 403-428.
Jennings, Reg / Cox, Charles / Cooper, Cary L. 1994. *Business Elites: the Psychology of Entrepreneurs and Intrapreneurs*. London: Routledge.
Jevons, William S. [1879] 1965. *The Theory of Political Economy*. London: Macmillan.
Johnstone, Barbara 2008. *Discourse analysis*. Malden: Blackwell.
Kageura, Kyo 1997. Multifaceted/Multidimensional concept systems. In Wright, Sue E. / Budin, Gerhard. (eds.) *Handbook of Terminology Management*, vol.1. Amsterdam/Philadelphia: John Benjamins,119-132.
Karlqvist, Anders 1999. Going beyond disciplines. *Policy Sciences*, 32/4, Dordrecht, NL: Kluwer Academic Publishers, 379-383.

Kauffman, Stuart A. 1993. *The Origins of Order: Self-organisation and Selection in Evolution.* Oxford, New York: Oxford University Press.

Keynes, John M. 1964. *The General Theory*. New York: Harcourt Brace and World.

Klamer, Arjo 1984. *Conversations with Economists: New Classical Economists and Opponents Speak Out on the Current Controversy in Macroeconomics*, Totowa, NJ: Rowman and Allanheld.

Klamer, Arjo 2003. *The Art of Economic Persuasion: about Rhetoric and All That.* < http://www.klamer.nl/ch-draft.doc>.

Kleiner, Arjo 2008. *The Age of Heretics*? San Francisco: Jossey-Bass.

Knight, Etheridge [1987] 1988. On the oral nature of poetry. A talk at Colorado State University, *The Painted Bride Quarterly*. 32/33, 79-83.

Knight, Frank H. [1921] 1964. *Risk, Uncertainty, and Profit*. New York: Sentry Press.

Knight, John B., 1991. The Evolution of Development Economics. In Balasubramanyam, Vudayagiri / Lall Sanjaya (eds.) *Current Issues in Development Economics*. Basingstoke: Macmillan Education Ltd, 10-22.

Kotchen, Matthew J. 2009. Some microeconomics of eco-entrepreneurship. *Frontiers in Eco-Entrepreneurship Research (Advances in the Study of Entrepreneurship, Innovation and Economic Growth)*. 20: 25-32.

Krishnan, Rajaram / Harris, Jonathan M. / Goodwin, Neva R. (eds.). 1995. *A Survey of Ecological Economics*. Washington D.C.: Island Press.

Kronenberg, Eric 2011. How to Prevent Self-Inflicted Disasters. *Strategy+business*, August issue.

Kuhn, Thomas [1962] 1970. *The Structure of Scientific Revolutions*. Chicago: University of Chicago Press.

Kuhn, Thomas S. 1993. Metaphor in Science. In Ortony, Andrew (ed.) *Metaphor and Thought.* Cambridge: Cambridge University Press, 533-542.

Laffont, Hélène 2005. *Contribution à la caractérisation de l'anglais pour l'ingénieur.* Doctoral dissertation, Bordeaux Segalen University.

Laffont, Hélène 2006. Un ingénieur est-il bien 'an engineer'? Contribution à l'analyse contrastive du milieu professionnel de l'ingénieur en France, au Royaume-Uni et aux Etats-Unis. *Asp.* 49/50, 9-21.

Lakoff, George / Johnson, Mark 1984. *Metaphors We Live By.* Chicago: The University of Chicago Press.

Langlois, Richard N. 2003. The Vanishing Hand: the Changing Dynamics of Industrial Capitalism. *Industrial and Corporate Change.* 12/2, 351-385

Laroche, Mireille / Mérette, Marcel / Ruggieri, Giuseppe C. 1998. On the Concept and Dimensions of Human Capital in a Knowledge-Based Economy Context. *Journal of Canadian Public Policy.* 25/1, 87-100.

Larsson, Rikard 1993. The handshake between visible and invisible hands: toward a Tripolar Institutional Framework. *International Studies in Management and Organisation.* 23/1, 87-106.

Latouche, Serge 2011. *Vers une société d'abondance frugale: Contresens et controverses sur la décroissance.* Paris: Fayard, Mille et une nuits.

Lauwers, Luc 2009. Ordering infinite utility stream: maximal anonymity. Discussion paper, Faculty of Economics and Applied Economics, Leuven, Belgium. <http://www.econ.kuleuven.be/ces/discussionpapers/default.htm>.

Lazear, Edward P. 2000. Economic Imperialism. *Quarterly Journal of Economics.* 115: 99-146.

Leech, Geoffrey N. [1974] 1981. *Semantics.* Harmondsworth: Penguin Books.

Lempert, Robert J. / Nakicenovic, Nebojsa / Sarewitz, Daniel / Schlesinger, Michael E. 2004. Characterising climate-change uncertainties for decision makers. *Climatic Change.* 65, 1-9.

Lesser, Jonathan A. / Dodds, Daniel E. / Zerbe, Richard O. Jr. 1997. *Environmental Economics and Policy.* New York: Addison-Wesley.

Levinowitz, Agneta W. / Ringertz, Nils (eds.) 2001. *The Nobel Prize, the First 100 Years*. Stockholm: Nobel Foundation. World Scientific Public Company Inc.

Levy, David 1994. Chaos Theory and Strategy: Theory, Application, and Managerial Implications. *Strategic Management Journal*. 15, 167-178.

L'Homme, Marie-Claude 2004a. *La terminologie: principes et techniques*. Montréal: Les Presses de l'Université de Montréal (Paramètres).

L'Homme, Marie-Claude 2004b. A Lexico-Semantic Approach to the Structuring of Terminology. *Computerm 2004*, University of Geneva, 7–14.

Liebert, Mary A. 1995. Metaphor Domains of Virological AIDS Research-Metaphernbereiche der Virologischen Aidsforschung. *Lexicology*. 1/l, 142-182.

Lindsey, Brink 2002. *Against the Dead Hand – the Uncertain Struggle for Global Capitalism*. New York: John Wiley & Sons.

Lipsey, Richard G. / Chrystal, K.Alec 1999. *Principles of Economics*. Oxford: Oxford University Press.

Locke, John 1690. *An Essay Concerning Human Understanding*. <http://oregonstate.edu/instruct/phl302/texts/locke/locke1/Book 3b.html >.

Luenberger, David G. 1994. "Dual Pareto efficiency." *Journal of Economic Theory* 62 (1), New York and London: Academic Press Inc.

Machlup, Fritz 1937. On the Meaning of Marginal Product. In *Explorations in Economics*, in honour of Franck W. Taussig, New York: McGraw Hill, 250-263.

Machlup, Fritz 1943. Forced or Induced Saving: an Exploration into its Synonyms and Homonyms. *The Review of Economics and Statistics*. 25/1, 26-39.

Machlup, Fritz 1950. Three Concepts of the Balance of Payments and the so-called Dollar Shortage. *Economic Journal*. 60, 46-68.

Machlup, Fritz 1958. Equilibrium and Disequilibrium: Misplaced Concreteness and Disguised Politics. *Economic Journal*. 68, 1-24.

Machlup, Fritz 1959. Statics and Dynamics: Kaleidoscopic Words. *Southern Economic Journal*. 26/2, 91-110.

Mahon, James E. 1999. Getting your sources right. What Aristotle did not say. In Cameron, Lynne / Low Graham (eds.) *Researching and Applying Metaphor*. Cambridge: Cambridge University Press, 69-80.

Malthus, Thomas 1827. *Definitions in Political Economy: Preceded by an inquiry into the rules which ought to guide political economists in the definition and use of their terms; with remarks on the derivation from these rules in their writings*. London: John Murray. <http://oll.libertyfund.org/?option=com_staticxt&staticfile=show.php%3Ftitle=2255>.

Mandelbrot, Benoit 1977. *Fractals: Form, Chance and Dimension*. San Francisco: W.H Freeman & Co.

Mandelbrot, Benoit 1982. *The Fractal Geometry of Nature*. San Francisco: W.H Freeman & Co.

Mankiw, N.Gregory 2001. *Principles of Economics*. Fort Worth, TX: Harcourt Publishers.

Mankiw, N.Gregory 2004. *Principles of Economics*. Mason, OH: Thomson South-Western.

Mantegna, Rosario N. / Stanley, H.Eugene 2000. *An Introduction to Econophysics: Correlations and Complexity in Finance*. Cambridge: Cambridge University Press.

Manville, Brook 2001. *Talking Human Capital with Professor Gary S. Becker, Nobel Laureate*. <http://www.linezine.com>.

Marshall, Alfred [1920] 1961. *Principles of Economics*. London: Macmillan. <http://socserv.mcmaster.ca/econ/ugcm/3ll3/marshall/prin/prinbk4>.

Max-Neef, Manfred A. 2005. Foundations of trans-disciplinarity. *Ecological Economics*. 53, 5-16.

McCabe, Kevin 2003. Neuroeconomics. In Nadel, Lynn (ed.) *Encyclopedia of Cognitive Science*. New York: Nature Publishing Group / Macmillan Publishing, 294-298.

McCloskey, Donald 1992. *If You're So Smart*. Chicago: The University of Chicago Press.
McCloskey, Deirdre 1998. *The Rhetoric of Economics*. Madison, WI: The University of Wisconsin Press.
McCloskey, Deirdre [1994] 2000. *Knowledge and persuasion in economics*. Cambridge: Cambridge University Press.
McKusik, James C. 2000. *Green Writing: Romanticism and Ecology*. New York: Palgrave MacMillan.
Menger, Carl 1979. *Selected Papers in Logic and Foundations, Didactics, Economics*. Dordrecht & Boston: Reidel Publishing Co.
Meyer, Christopher 2001. The Connected Economy: Beyond the Information Age. <http://www.leader-values.com/Content/detail.asp?ContentDetailID=270>.
Meyer, Ingrid / Mackintosh, Kristen 2000. L'étirement du sens terminologique : aperçu du phénomène de la déterminologisation. In Béjoint, Henri / Thoiron, Philippe (eds.) *Le sens en terminologi*. Lyons: Presses universitaires de Lyon, 198-217.
Meyer, Ingrid / Skuce, Douglas / Bowker, Lynne / Eck, Karen 1992. Towards a new generation of terminological resources: An experiment in building a terminological knowledge base. In *Proceedings of the 16th International Conference on Computational Linguistics*. 956-957.
Meyer, Ingrid / Zaluski, Victoria / Mackintosh, Kristen 1997. Metaphorical Internet terms: A conceptual and structural analysis. *Terminology*. 4/1, 1-33.
Mill, John S. [1848] 1909. *The Principles of Political Economy*. William J. Ashley (ed.). London: Longmans, Green & Co. <http://www.econlib.org/library/Mill/mlP1.html#PreliminaryRemarks>.
Mill, John S. 1941. *A System of Logic*. London: Longmans, Green, & Co.
Mincer, Jacob 1958. Investment in Human Capital and Personal Income Distribution. *Journal of Political Economy*. 66/4, 281-302.

Mirowski, Philip 1988. *Against Mechanism: Protecting Economics from Science*. Totowa, NJ: Rowman & Littlefield.

Mirowski, Philip [1989] 1999. *More Heat than Light*. Cambridge: Cambridge University Press.

Mittelstrass, Jürgen 1996. Stichwort Interdisziplinarität. Mit einem Anschliessenden Werkstattgespräch. *Basler Schriften zur Europäischen Integration*. 22. Basel: Europainstitut an der Universität Basel.

Møller, Bernt 1998. À la recherche d'une terminochronie. *Meta: Translators' Journal*. 43/3, 426-438.

Moore, Henry L. 1906. Paradoxes of Competition. *Quarterly Journal of Economics*. 20, 211-230.

Morgan, Gareth [1986] 2006. *Images of Organisation*. London: Sage Publications.

Morrell, Jack / Thackray, Arnold 1981. *Gentlemen of Science: Early Years of the British Association for the Advancement of Science*. Oxford: Clarendon Press.

Mouton, Nicolaas T.O. Metaphor and economic thought: A historical perspective. In Herrera-Soler, Honesto / White, Michael (eds.) *Metaphor and Mills*. Berlin: De Gruyter Mouton, 49-76.

Myking, Johan 2001. Against Prescriptivism. The 'Social-Critical' challenge to Terminology. *Terminology Science and Research*. 12/1-2, 49-64.

Nadeau, Robert L. 2003. *The Wealth of Nature: How Mainstream Economics Has Failed the Environment*. New York: Columbia University Press.

Neilson, Gary / Pasternak, Bruce A. / Mendes, Decio 2003. The Four Bases of Organisational DNA. *Strategy+Business* <http://www.strategy-business.com/media/file/03406.pdf>.

Nelson, Richard R. / Winter, Sidney G. 1982. *An Evolutionary Theory of Economic Change*. Cambridge, MA: Harvard University Press.

Newell, William H. / Green, William J. 1982. Defining and teaching interdisciplinary studies. *Improving College and University Teaching*. 30/1, 23-30.

Nissani, Moti 1995. Fruits, salads, and smoothies: a working definition of inter-disciplinarity. *Journal of Educational Thought*. 26/2. <http://www.is.wayne.edu/mnissani/pagepub/smoothie.htm>.

Nystrand, Martin 1982. *What Writers Know: The Language, Process, and Structure of Written Discourse*. New York: Academic.

Okun, Arthur M. 1980. The Invisible Handshake and the Inflationary Process. *Challenge*. 23, 5-12.

Oresme, Nicholas 1956. De Moneta. In *The De Moneta of Nicholas Oresme and English Mint Documents*, translated with introduction and notes by Johnson, Charles, London/New York/Paris: Thomas Nelson and Sons Ltd. <http://www.constitution.org/mon/oresme.pdf.>.

Pearson, Jennifer 1998. *Terms in Context*. Amsterdam/Philadelphia: John Benjamins.

Pelikan, Pavel 2004. Interconnecting Evolutionary, Institutional and Cognitive Economics: Six Steps towards Understanding the Six Links. Contribution to the 10th Meeting of J.A. Schumpeter International Society in Milan, June 9th-12th.

Penrose, Edith 1952. Biological analogies in the theories of the firm. *The American Economic Review*. 42/5, 804-819. <htpp://www.jstor.org/stable/ 1812528>.

Pepper, Stephen C. 1942. *World Hypotheses*. Berkeley: University of California Press.

Peters, Tom 1988. *Thriving on Chaos: Handbook for a Management Revolution*. New York: Harper.

Peterson, Richard L. 2007. *Inside the Investor's Brain: the Power of Mind over Money*. Hoboken, NJ: John Wiley & Sons.

Petit, Michel 2010. Le discours spécialisé et le spécialisé du discours: repères pour l'analyse du discours en anglais de spécialité. *E-rea* [online review] <http://erea.revues.org/1400>.

Peynaud, Caroline 2011. Parole rapportée et positionnement discursif dans la presse américaine: analyse de l'utilisation des citations dans des commentaires politiques. *ASp*. 59, 43-64.

Phelps, Edmund 2007. Pas de bonne vie sans travail. *Le Monde*, February 25th.

Picht, Heribert / Draskau, Jennifer 1985. *Terminology: An Introduction*. Guildford: University of Surrey.
Picht, Heribert / Schmitz, Klaus D. (eds). 2001. *Terminologie und Wissenordnung. Ausgewählte Schriften aus dem Gesamtwerk von Eugen Wüster*. Vienna: Termnet Publisher.
Pigou, Arthur C. 1925. *Memorials of Alfred Marshall*. London: Macmillan.
Pigou, Arthur C. 1952. *The Economics of Welfare*. London: MacMillan.
Pindi, Makaya / Bloor, Thomas 1987. Playing safe with predictions: hedging, attribution and conditions in economic forecasting. In Bloor, Thomas / Norrish, John (eds.) *Written Language*. London: CILT/BAAL, 55-69.
Pinker, Steven 2007. *The Stuff of Thought: Language as a Window into Human Nature*. London: Penguin.
Polvinen, Merja 2008. *Reading the Texture of Reality. Chaos Theory, Literature and the Humanistic Perspective*. Helsinki: Helsinki University Press.
Popper, Karl R. 1963. *Conjectures and Refutations: The Growth of Scientific Knowledge*. New York: Routledge & Kegan Paul.
Porter, James E. 1992. *Audience and Rhetoric: An Archaeological Composition of the Discourse Community*. Englewood Cliffs, NJ: Prentice Hall.
Quirion, Jean 2003. La mesure de l'implantation terminologique: proposition d'un protocole. Étude terminométrique du domaine des transports au Québec. *Langues et sociétés 40*, Montréal: Office québécois de la langue française.
Quirk, Randolph / Greenbaum, Sidney / Leech, Geoffrey / Svartvik, Jan 1972. *A Grammar of Contemporary English*. London: Longman.
Radzicki, Michael J. 1990. Institutional Dynamics, Deterministic Chaos and Self-organising Systems. *Journal of Economic Issues*. 24/1, 57-102.
Ramsay, Colin M. 2009. The distribution of compound sums of Pareto-distributed losses. *Scandinavian Actuarial* Journal. 1, 27-37.

Rawls, John 2007. *Lectures on the History of Political Philosophy*. S. Freeman (ed.), Cambridge, MA: Harvard University Press.

Read, Rupert 2007. Economics is philosophy, economics is not science. *International Journal of Green Economics*. 1/3-4, 307–325.

Reinhart, Carmen / Rogoff, Ken 2009. *This Time is Different: Eight Centuries of Financial Folly*. Princeton, NJ: Princeton University Press.

Resche, Catherine 1999. Equivocal Economic Terms or Terminology Revisited. *Meta: Translators' Journal*. 44 /4, 617-632.

Resche, Catherine 2004*a*. Approche 'terminométrique' du cycle économique : implications et prolongements. *Meta: Translators' Journal*. 49 /2, 343-359.

Resche, Catherine 2004*b*. Investigating 'Greenspanese': from hedging to 'fuzzy transparency'. *Discourse & Society* 15 /6, 723-744.

Resche, Catherine 2007*a*. *Human capital* : l'avers et le revers d'un terme métaphorique. *ESP and Professional Communication*. 7/2, 23-48.

Resche, Catherine 2007*b*. L'implicite dans le discours des grandes entreprises sur leur responsabilité sociale. *Les Cahiers de l'ILCEA*. 9, 7-47.

Resche, Catherine 2012. Towards a better understanding of metaphorical networks in the language of economics: the importance of theory-constitutive metaphors. In Herrera-Soler, Honesto / White, Michael (eds.) *Metaphor and Mills*. Berlin: De Gruyter Mouton, 77-102.

Resche, Catherine 2013. Les anthroponymes en économie : une autre voie d'accès à un domaine de spécialité et à sa culture. *Neologica*. *7*, Paris : Editions Garnier, 137-155.

Resche, Catherine Forthcoming. Étude de diverses appellations pour le concept d'utilité en économie : les termes comme témoins de l'évolution de la théorie. *Domaines linguistiques*, Paris : Editions Garnier.

Richards, Ivor A. [1936] 1971. *The Philosophy of Rhetoric*. Oxford: Oxford University Press.

Robbins, Lionel [1932]1935. *An Essay on the Nature and Significance of Economic Science*. London: Macmillan.

Robinson, Pauline C. 1991. *ESP Today: A Practitioner's Guide.* London: Prentice Hall.

Roche, Christophe / Calbert-Challot, Marie / Damas, Luc / Rouard, Philippe 2009. Ontoterminology: a new paradigm for terminology. *KEOD* 2009, Madeira. <http://ontology.univ-savoie.fr/condillac/files/docs/articles/Ontoterminology-a-new-paradigm-for-terminology.pdf>.

Roscher, William 1878. *Principles of Political Economy.* New York: Holt & Co.

Rosenberg, Alexander 1994. Does evolutionary theory give comfort or inspiration to economics? In Mirowski, Philip (ed.) *Natural Images of Economic Thought.* Cambridge: Cambridge University Press, 384-407.

Rosenhead, Jonathan 1998. Complexity theory and management practice. *Operational Research working papers*, LSEOR 98.25. Department of Operational Research, London School of Economics and Political Science, London, UK. <http://human-nature.com/science-as-culture/rosenhead.html>.

Rosser, J. Barkley 2006. The Nature and Future of Econophysics. In Chatterjee Arnab / Chakrabarti Bikas K. (eds.) *Econophysics of Stock and Other Markets.* Milan: Springer Verlag, 225-238.

Rothschild, Michael 1990. *Preface to Bionomics.* <http:// bionomics.org/text/resource/preface.html>.

Rothschild, Michael 1995. *Bionomics. Economy as Ecosystem Outline* <http:// bionomics.org >.

Russell. David R. [1992] 1994. American Origins of the Writing-across-the-Curriculum Movement. In Bazerman, Charles / Russell, David R. (eds.) *Landmark Essays.* Davis: Hermagoras Press, 3-22. <http://www.archive.org/stream/principlesofpoli00roscuoft/principlesofpoli00roscuoft_djvu.txt >.

Saber, Anthony 2006. Tradition, mémoire et préconstruit chez les militaires américains. *ASp* 49 /50. <http://asp.revues.org/642>.

Sager, Juan C. 1981. Criteria for measuring the Functional Efficacy of Terms. *Infoterm Series 6*, Munich: K.G.Saur Verlag KG, 194-217.

Sager, Juan C. 1990. *A practical course in terminology processing.* Amsterdam/Philadelphia: John Benjamins.

Sager, Juan C. / Dungworh, David / McDonald, Peter F. 1980. *English Special Languages: Principles and Practice in Science and technology*. Wiesbaden: O. Brandstetter.

Sahlins, Marshall D. 1974. *Stone Age Economics*. New York: Aldine de Gruyter.

Samuelson, Paul A. / Temin, Peter 1976. *Economics*. New York: McGraw Hill.

Samuelson, Paul A. / Nordhaus, William D. 2005. *Economics*. New York: McGraw Hill.

Sandbothe, Mike 2000. Interactivity, Hypertextuality, Transversality. A media-philosophical analysis of the Internet. *Hermes, Journal of Linguistics*. 24, 81-108.

Saussure (de) Ferdinand 1916. *Course in General Linguistics*. Ch. Bally and A. Sechehaye (eds.). New York: McGraw Hill.

Say, Jean-Baptiste [1821] 2010. *Catéchisme d'économie politique*. Legacy reprint series, Whitefish, MT: Kessinger Publishings.

Schabas, Margaret 1994. The greyhound and the mastiff: Darwinian themes in Mill and Marshall. In Mirowski, Philippe (ed.) *Natural Images of Economic Thought*. Cambridge: Cambridge University Press, 322-335.

Schiffer, Stephen 1998. Two Issues of Vagueness. *The Monist*. 88, 193-214.

Schleifer, Andrei / Vishny, Robert W. 1999. *The Grabbing Hand/Government Pathologies and their Cures*. Cambridge MA: Harvard University Press.

Schultz, Theodore W. 1961. Investment in Human Capital. *The American Economic Review*. 1/2, 1-17.

Scott, David L. 2003. *Wall Street Words: An A to Z Guide to Investment Terms for Today's Investor*. Boston: Houghton Mifflin Company.

Scott Cato, Molly 2009. *Green Economics: An Introduction to Theory, Policy and Practice*. London: Earthscan.

Segura, Julio / Braun, Carlos R. 2004. *An Eponymous Dictionary of Economics: A Guide to Laws and Theorems named after*

Economists. Cheltenham, UK/Northampton, MA (US): Edward Elgen.
Senge, Peter M. 1990. *The Fifth Discipline. The Art and Practice of the Learning Organisation*. London: Random House.
Senior, Nassau W. [1850] 1854. *Political Economy*. London: Richard Griffin & Co. <http://www.econlib.org/library/Senior/snP1.html>.
Senior, Nassau W. [1872] 1938. *An Outline of the Science of Political Economy*. London: Allen and Unwin.
Sidgwick, Henry 1891. *The Principles of Political Economy*. London: Macmillan. <http://www.archive.org/stream/elementspolitic00sidggoog#page/n6/mode/2up>.
Siegers, Jacques J. 1992. Interdisciplinary Economics. *De Economist*.140 /4, 531-547.
Singh Katar / Shishodia, Anil. 2007. *Environmental Economics: Theory and Applications*. Los Angeles, London, New Delhi: Singapore SAE Publication.
Slodzian, Monique 1994. La doctrine terminologique, nouvelle théorie du signe au carrefour de l'universalisme et du logicisme. ALFA, *Terminologie et linguistique de spécialité*. 7/8, 121-136.
Slodzian, Monique 1995. Comment revisiter la doctrine terminologique aujourd'hui ? *La Banque des mots : Terminologie et Intelligence Artificielle*. 7, 11-18.
Slodzian, Monique. 2000. L'émergence d'une terminologie textuelle et le retour du sens. In Béjoint, Henri / Thoiron, Philippe (eds.) *Le sens en terminologie*. Lyons: Presses universitaires de Lyon, 61-85.
Smith, Adam 1776. *An Inquiry into the Nature and Causes of the Wealth of Nations*. <http://www.econlib.org/library/Smith/smWN1.html#B.ICh.1>.
Spencer, Herbert 1891. *Essays: Scientific, Political, and Speculative*. London: Williams & Norgate. <http://files.libertyfund.org/files/335/0620-01_Bk.pdf>.
Sprat, Thomas 1667. *The History of the Royal Society*. <http://www.wwnorton.com/college/english/nael/noa/pdf/27636_17th_U38_Sprat-1-6.pdf>.

Stacey, Ralph D. 1993. *Strategic Management and Organisational Dynamics*. London: Pitman Publishing.
Steen, Gerald 1999. Metaphor and discourse. Towards a linguistic checklist for metaphor analysis. In Cameron, Lynne / Low, Graham (eds.) *Researching and Applying Metaphor*. Cambridge: Cambridge University Press, 81-104.
Stewart, Ian 1997. *Does God Play Dice? The New Mathematics of Chaos*. Harmondsworth: Penguin.
Stigler, George 1946. *The Theory of Price*. New York: Macmillan.
Stigler, George 1964. Statistical Studies in the History of Economic Thought. In *Essays in the History of Economics*. Chicago: University of Chicago Press, 31-50.
Stigler, George 1984. Economics – The Imperial Science. *The Scandinavian Journal of Economics*. 86/3, 301-313.
Stiglitz, Joseph E. 1982. Self-selection and Pareto Efficient Taxation. *Journal of Public Economics*. 17/2, 231-240.
Strevens, Peter 1988. ESP after twenty years: a reappraisal. In M. L. Tickoo (ed.) *ESP: State of the art*. Anthology Series. 21, Singapore: SEAMEO Regional Language Centre, 1-13.
Sull, Donald N. 2005. Strategy as Active Waiting. *Harvard Business Review*. 120-129.
Sutton, Clive 1994. 'Nullius in verba' and 'nihil in verbis': Public understanding of the role of language in science. *British Journal of the History of Science*. 27, 55-64.
Swales, John M. 1988. *Episodes in ESP*. Hemel Hempstead: Prentice Hall International.
Swales, John M. 1990. *Genre Analysis*. Cambridge: Cambridge University Press.
Swales, John M. 2004. *Research Genres: Explorations and Applications*. Cambridge: Cambridge University Press.
Taleb, Nassim N. 2007. *The Black Swan: The Impact of the Highly Improbable*. New York: Random House and Penguin.
Tatsuki, Donna 2001. The Place of Pragmatics in the Teaching / Learning of Language and Culture. *Jalt Pragmatics SIG Newsletter*. 3/1, 3-4.

Temmerman, Rita 2000a. *Towards New Ways of Terminology Description. The sociocognitive approach.* Amsterdam/Philadelphia: John Benjamins.

Temmerman, Rita 2000b. Une théorie réaliste de la terminologie: le socio-cognitivisme. *Terminologies nouvelles.* 21, 58-64.

Temmerman, Rita / Kerremans, Koen 2003. Termontography: Ontology Building and the Sociocognitive Approach to Terminology Description. *Prague CIL17 conference.* <http://www.hf.uib.no/forskerskole/temmerman_art_prague03.pdf>.

Thomas, Craig 2009. *The Econosphere: What Makes the Economy Really Work, How to Protect it and Maximize Your Opportunity for Financial Prosperity.* London: Financial Times / Prentice Hall.

Tocqueville (de), Alexis 1840. *Democracy in America.* Vol. 1, Book 1, Chapter 16.

Toft, Bertha 2001. Towards New Ways of Terminology Description: the Sociocognitive Approach. Book review by Rita Temmerman, 2000, *Terminology.* 7/1, 125-128. <http://xroads.virginia.edu/~HYPER/DETOC/ch1_16.htm >.

Toulmin, Stephen 1953. *The Philosophy of Science.* Watford, Herts: The Mayflower Press. <http://www.scribd.com/doc/10084082/TOULMIN-Stephen-The-Philosophy-of-Science-Copia-virtual>.

Tress, Barbel / Tress, Gunther / Fry, Gary / Paul Opdam (eds.). 2005. *From Landscape Research to Landscape Planning. Aspects of integration, education and application.* Heidelberg: Springer.

Trouillon, Jean-Louis 2006. Introduction au langage des forces armées anglophones. *Asp.* 49/50, 23-34.

Turbayne, Colin M. 1962. *Myth and Metaphor.* New Haven, CT: Yale University Press.

Van Campenhoudt, Marc 2006. Que nous reste-t-il d'Eugen Wüster?. *International Conference on Eugen Wüster and the Vienna school of terminology*, Paris 7 University, 3rd-4th February.

Van der Yeught, Michel 2007. The Metaphors of Financial Bubbles in British and American Discourses. *ESP Across Cultures.* 4, 66-79.

Van der Yeught, Michel 2009a. *Une histoire de Wall Street*. Paris: Editions ESKA.

Van der Yeught, Michel 2009b. Les premiers essais de spécialisation des langues: les cas de l'anglais de l'économie, de la médecine, du droit et de la bourse. Paper presented at the *SVE/ESP workshop during the 49th annual SAES Conference in Bordeaux*, 8th-10th May.

Veblen, Thorstein 1898. Why is Economics Not an Evolutionary Science? *The Quarterly Journal of Economics*. 12, 373-397. <http://socserv2.mcmaster.ca/~econ/ugcm/3ll3/veblen/econevol.txt>.

Vecchi (de), Dardo 2009. Pragmaterminologie: une terminologie de l'entreprise en évolution. *A one-day symposium at Università Cattolica*, Milan, June 9th, 2009. < http://realiter.net/spip.php?article1763>.

Wagner, Richard B. 2003. Financial metaphors: mechanic, organic, or…? *Financial Advisor Magazine*, April issue.

Ward, Lester F. 1897. Review of 'Organisme et Société' (René Worms); La pathologie sociale (Paul de Lilienfeld). *The American Journal of Sociology*. 3/2, 258-265.

Weatherly, Leslie A. 2003. Human capital: the elusive asset. *SHRM Research Quarterly*. 1, 1-7.

Webber, Allen M. 2001. How Business Is a Lot Like Life. Online interview with R. Pascale. <http://www.fastcompany.com/42660/how-business-lot-life>.

Weber, Bruce H. / Depew, David J. 1996. Natural selection and self-organisation: dynamical models as clues to a new evolutionary synthesis. *Biology and Philosophy*. 11, 33-65.

Weber, Max [1904] 1949. Objectivity in Social Science and Social Policy. In Shils, Edward A. / Finch, Henry A. (eds./trans.) *The Methodology of the Social Sciences*. New York: Free Press, 49-112.

Wenger, Etienne 1998. *Communities of Practice: Learning, Meaning and Identity*. Cambridge: Cambridge University Press.

Whately, Richard [1826] 1838. *Elements of Logic*, revised edition with an appendix "On Certain Terms which are Particularly Liable to be Used Ambiguously in Political Economy". London: Allen & Unwin.

Whewell, William 1833. *Report of the Third Meeting of the British Association for the Advancement of Science*. Held at Cambridge in July 1833. <http://www.archive.org/stream/reportofthirdmee34lond/reportofthirdmee34lond_djvu.txt>.

White, Michael 2004. Turbulence and turmil in the market or the language of a financial crisis. *Iberica*. 7, 71-86.

Wicken, Jeffrey S. 1987. *Evolution, thermodynamics, and information: extending the Darwinian paradigm*. Oxford/New York: Oxford University Press.

Williamson, Tim 1994. *Vagueness*, London: Routledge.

Wittgenstein, Ludwig [1953] 2009. *Philosophical Investigations*. translated by P.M.S. Hacker and J. Schulte, Oxford: Wiley-Blackwell.

Wittgenstein, Ludwig 1961. *Tractatus Logico-Philosophicus*. D.F. Pears & B.F. McGuiness (trans.), London: Routledge & Kegan Paul.

Wozniak, Séverine 2011. *Contribution à la caractérisation de l'anglais de l'alpinisme, par l'étude du domaine spécialisé des guides de haute montagne états-uniens*. Doctoral dissertation defended November 25th, 2011, Bordeaux Segalen University.

Wright, Crispin 2006. Vagueness-related Partial Belief and the Constitution of Borderline Cases. *Philosophy and Phenomenological Research*. 72, 225-32.

Wüster, Eugen 1931. *Internationale Sprachnormung in der Technik: besonders in der Elektrotechnik*. Berlin: VDI-Verlag.

Wüster, Eugen. 1974. Die allgemeine Terminologielehre – Ein Grenzgebiet zwischen Sprachwissenschaft, Logik, Ontologie, Informatik und den Sachwissenschaften. *Linguistics*. 119, 61-106.

Wüster, Eugen 1981. L'étude scientifique générale de la terminologie, zone frontalière entre la linguistique, la logique, l'ontologie, l'informatique et les sciences des choses. In Rondeau, Guy / Felber, Helmut (eds.) *Textes choisis de terminologie. Fondements théoriques de la terminologie*. 55-114. Quebec: GIRSTERM.

Zaman, Gheorghe. / Goshin, Zizi 2010. Multidisciplinarity, Interdisciplinarity and Transdisciplinarity: Theoretical Approaches and Implications for the Strategy of Post-crisis Sustainable Development. *Theoretical and Applied Economics.* 17/12, 5-20.

Subject index

Author index

Linguistic Insights

Studies in Language and Communication

This series aims to promote specialist language studies in the fields of linguistic theory and applied linguistics, by publishing volumes that focus on specific aspects of language use in one or several languages and provide valuable insights into language and communication research. A cross-disciplinary approach is favoured and most European languages are accepted.

The series includes two types of books:

- **Monographs** – featuring in-depth studies on special aspects of language theory, language analysis or language teaching.
- **Collected papers** – assembling papers from workshops, conferences or symposia.

Each volume of the series is subjected to a double peer-reviewing process.

Vol. 1 Maurizio Gotti & Marina Dossena (eds)
Modality in Specialized Texts. Selected Papers of the 1st CERLIS Conference.
421 pages. 2001. ISBN 3-906767-10-8 · US-ISBN 0-8204-5340-4

Vol. 2 Giuseppina Cortese & Philip Riley (eds)
Domain-specific English. Textual Practices across Communities and Classrooms.
420 pages. 2002. ISBN 3-906768-98-8 · US-ISBN 0-8204-5884-8

Vol. 3 Maurizio Gotti, Dorothee Heller & Marina Dossena (eds)
Conflict and Negotiation in Specialized Texts. Selected Papers of the 2nd CERLIS Conference.
470 pages. 2002. ISBN 3-906769-12-7 · US-ISBN 0-8204-5887-2

Vol. 4 Maurizio Gotti, Marina Dossena, Richard Dury, Roberta Facchinetti & Maria Lima
Variation in Central Modals. A Repertoire of Forms and Types of Usage in Middle English and Early Modern English.
364 pages. 2002. ISBN 3-906769-84-4 · US-ISBN 0-8204-5898-8

Editorial address:

Prof. Maurizio Gotti
Università di Bergamo, Facoltà di Lingue e Letterature Straniere,
Via Salvecchio 19, 24129 Bergamo, Italy
Fax: 0039 035 2052789, E-Mail: m.gotti@unibg.it

Vol. 5 Stefania Nuccorini (ed.)
Phrases and Phraseology. Data and Descriptions.
187 pages. 2002. ISBN 3-906770-08-7 · US-ISBN 0-8204-5933-X

Vol. 6 Vijay Bhatia, Christopher N. Candlin & Maurizio Gotti (eds)
Legal Discourse in Multilingual and Multicultural Contexts.
Arbitration Texts in Europe.
385 pages. 2003. ISBN 3-906770-85-0 · US-ISBN 0-8204-6254-3

Vol. 7 Marina Dossena & Charles Jones (eds)
Insights into Late Modern English. 2nd edition.
378 pages. 2003, 2007.
ISBN 978-3-03911-257-9 · US-ISBN 978-0-8204-8927-8

Vol. 8 Maurizio Gotti
Specialized Discourse. Linguistic Features and Changing Conventions.
351 pages. 2003, 2005.
ISBN 3-03910-606-6 · US-ISBN 0-8204-7000-7

Vol. 9 Alan Partington, John Morley & Louann Haarman (eds)
Corpora and Discourse.
420 pages. 2004. ISBN 3-03910-026-2 · US-ISBN 0-8204-6262-4

Vol. 10 Martina Möllering
The Acquisition of German Modal Particles. A Corpus-Based Approach.
290 pages. 2004. ISBN 3-03910-043-2 · US-ISBN 0-8204-6273-X

Vol. 11 David Hart (ed.)
English Modality in Context. Diachronic Perspectives.
261 pages. 2003. ISBN 3-03910-046-7 · US-ISBN 0-8204-6852-5

Vol. 12 Wendy Swanson
Modes of Co-reference as an Indicator of Genre.
430 pages. 2003. ISBN 3-03910-052-1 · US-ISBN 0-8204-6855-X

Vol. 13 Gina Poncini
Discursive Strategies in Multicultural Business Meetings.
2nd edition. 338 pages. 2004, 2007.
ISBN 978-3-03911-296-8 · US-ISBN 978-0-8204-8937-7

Vol. 14 Christopher N. Candlin & Maurizio Gotti (eds)
Intercultural Aspects of Specialized Communication.
2nd edition. 369 pages. 2004, 2007.
ISBN 978-3-03911-258-6 · US-ISBN 978-0-8204-8926-1

Vol. 15 Gabriella Del Lungo Camiciotti & Elena Tognini Bonelli (eds)
Academic Discourse. New Insights into Evaluation.
234 pages. 2004. ISBN 3-03910-353-9 · US-ISBN 0-8204-7016-3

Vol. 16 Marina Dossena & Roger Lass (eds)
Methods and Data in English Historical Dialectology.
405 pages. 2004. ISBN 3-03910-362-8 · US-ISBN 0-8204-7018-X

Vol. 17 Judy Noguchi
The Science Review Article. An Opportune Genre in
the Construction of Science.
274 pages. 2006. ISBN 3-03910-426-8 · US-ISBN 0-8204-7034-1

Vol. 18 Giuseppina Cortese & Anna Duszak (eds)
Identity, Community, Discourse. English in Intercultural Settings.
495 pages. 2005. ISBN 3-03910-632-5 · US-ISBN 0-8204-7163-1

Vol. 19 Anna Trosborg & Poul Erik Flyvholm Jørgensen (eds)
Business Discourse. Texts and Contexts.
250 pages. 2005. ISBN 3-03910-606-6 · US-ISBN 0-8204-7000-7

Vol. 20 Christopher Williams
Tradition and Change in Legal English. Verbal Constructions in Prescriptive Texts.
2nd revised edition. 216 pages. 2005, 2007. ISBN 978-3-03911-444-3.

Vol. 21 Katarzyna Dziubalska-Kolaczyk & Joanna Przedlacka (eds)
English Pronunciation Models: A Changing Scene.
2nd edition. 476 pages. 2005, 2008. ISBN 978-3-03911-682-9.

Vol. 22 Christián Abello-Contesse, Rubén Chacón-Beltrán, M. Dolores López-Jiménez & M. Mar Torreblanca-López (eds)
Age in L2 Acquisition and Teaching.
214 pages. 2006. ISBN 3-03910-668-6 · US-ISBN 0-8204-7174-7

Vol. 23 Vijay K. Bhatia, Maurizio Gotti, Jan Engberg & Dorothee Heller (eds)
Vagueness in Normative Texts.
474 pages. 2005. ISBN 3-03910-653-8 · US-ISBN 0-8204-7169-0

Vol. 24 Paul Gillaerts & Maurizio Gotti (eds)
Genre Variation in Business Letters. 2nd printing.
407 pages. 2008. ISBN 978-3-03911-681-2.

Vol. 25 Ana María Hornero, María José Luzón & Silvia Murillo (eds)
Corpus Linguistics. Applications for the Study of English.
2nd printing. 526 pages. 2006, 2008. ISBN 978-3-03911-726-0

Vol. 26 J. Lachlan Mackenzie & María de los Ángeles Gómez-González (eds)
Studies in Functional Discourse Grammar.
259 pages. 2005. ISBN 3-03910-696-1 · US-ISBN 0-8204-7558-0

Vol. 27 Debbie G. E. Ho
Classroom Talk. Exploring the Sociocultural Structure of Formal ESL Learning.
2nd edition. 254 pages. 2006, 2007. ISBN 978-3-03911-434-4

Vol. 28 Javier Pérez-Guerra, Dolores González-Álvarez, Jorge L. Bueno-Alonso & Esperanza Rama-Martínez (eds)
'Of Varying Language and Opposing Creed'. New Insights into Late Modern English.
455 pages. 2007. ISBN 978-3-03910-788-9

Vol. 29 Francesca Bargiela-Chiappini & Maurizio Gotti (eds)
Asian Business Discourse(s).
350 pages. 2005. ISBN 3-03910-804-2 · US-ISBN 0-8204-7574-2

Vol. 30 Nicholas Brownlees (ed.)
News Discourse in Early Modern Britain. Selected Papers of CHINED 2004.
300 pages. 2006. ISBN 3-03910-805-0 · US-ISBN 0-8204-8025-8

Vol. 31 Roberta Facchinetti & Matti Rissanen (eds)
Corpus-based Studies of Diachronic English.
300 pages. 2006. ISBN 3-03910-851-4 · US-ISBN 0-8204-8040-1

Vol. 32 Marina Dossena & Susan M. Fitzmaurice (eds)
Business and Official Correspondence. Historical Investigations.
209 pages. 2006. ISBN 3-03910-880-8 · US-ISBN 0-8204-8352-4

Vol. 33 Giuliana Garzone & Srikant Sarangi (eds)
Discourse, Ideology and Specialized Communication.
494 pages. 2007. ISBN 978-3-03910-888-6

Vol. 34 Giuliana Garzone & Cornelia Ilie (eds)
The Use of English in Institutional and Business Settings.
An Intercultural Perspective.
372 pages. 2007. ISBN 978-3-03910-889-3

Vol. 35 Vijay K. Bhatia & Maurizio Gotti (eds)
Explorations in Specialized Genres.
316 pages. 2006. ISBN 3-03910-995-2 · US-ISBN 0-8204-8372-9

Vol. 36 Heribert Picht (ed.)
Modern Approaches to Terminological Theories and Applications.
432 pages. 2006. ISBN 3-03911-156-6 · US-ISBN 0-8204-8380-X

Vol. 37 Anne Wagner & Sophie Cacciaguidi-Fahy (eds)
Legal Language and the Search for Clarity / Le langage juridique et la quête de clarté.
Practice and Tools / Pratiques et instruments.
487 pages. 2006. ISBN 3-03911-169-8 · US-ISBN 0-8204-8388-5

Vol. 38 Juan Carlos Palmer-Silveira, Miguel F. Ruiz-Garrido &
Inmaculada Fortanet-Gómez (eds)
Intercultural and International Business Communication.
Theory, Research and Teaching.
2nd edition. 343 pages. 2006, 2008. ISBN 978-3-03911-680-5

Vol. 39 Christiane Dalton-Puffer, Dieter Kastovsky, Nikolaus Ritt &
Herbert Schendl (eds)
Syntax, Style and Grammatical Norms. English from 1500–2000.
250 pages. 2006. ISBN 3-03911-181-7 · US-ISBN 0-8204-8394-X

Vol. 40 Marina Dossena & Irma Taavitsainen (eds)
Diachronic Perspectives on Domain-Specific English.
280 pages. 2006. ISBN 3-03910-176-0 · US-ISBN 0-8204-8391-5

Vol. 41 John Flowerdew & Maurizio Gotti (eds)
Studies in Specialized Discourse.
293 pages. 2006. ISBN 3-03911-178-7

Vol. 42 Ken Hyland & Marina Bondi (eds)
Academic Discourse Across Disciplines.
320 pages. 2006. ISBN 3-03911-183-3 · US-ISBN 0-8204-8396-6

Vol. 43 Paul Gillaerts & Philip Shaw (eds)
The Map and the Landscape. Norms and Practices in Genre.
256 pages. 2006. ISBN 3-03911-182-5 · US-ISBN 0-8204-8395-4

Vol. 44 Maurizio Gotti & Davide Giannoni (eds)
New Trends in Specialized Discourse Analysis.
301 pages. 2006. ISBN 3-03911-184-1 · US-ISBN 0-8204-8381-8

Vol. 45 Maurizio Gotti & Françoise Salager-Meyer (eds)
Advances in Medical Discourse Analysis. Oral and Written Contexts.
492 pages. 2006. ISBN 3-03911-185-X · US-ISBN 0-8204-8382-6

Vol. 46 Maurizio Gotti & Susan Šarcević (eds)
Insights into Specialized Translation.
396 pages. 2006. ISBN 3-03911-186-8 · US-ISBN 0-8204-8383-4

Vol. 47 Khurshid Ahmad & Margaret Rogers (eds)
Evidence-based LSP. Translation, Text and Terminology.
584 pages. 2007. ISBN 978-3-03911-187-9

Vol. 48 Hao Sun & Dániel Z. Kádár (eds)
It's the Dragon's Turn. Chinese Institutional Discourses.
262 pages. 2008. ISBN 978-3-03911-175-6

Vol. 49 Cristina Suárez-Gómez
Relativization in Early English (950-1250). the Position of Relative Clauses.
149 pages. 2006. ISBN 3-03911-203-1 · US-ISBN 0-8204-8904-2

Vol. 50 Maria Vittoria Calvi & Luisa Chierichetti (eds)
Nuevas tendencias en el discurso de especialidad.
319 pages. 2006. ISBN 978-3-03911-261-6

Vol. 51 Mari Carmen Campoy & María José Luzón (eds)
Spoken Corpora in Applied Linguistics.
274 pages. 2008. ISBN 978-3-03911-275-3

Vol. 52 Konrad Ehlich & Dorothee Heller (Hrsg.)
Die Wissenschaft und ihre Sprachen.
323 pages. 2006. ISBN 978-3-03911-272-2

Vol. 53 Jingyu Zhang
The Semantic Salience Hierarchy Model. The L2 Acquisition of Psych Predicates
273 pages. 2007. ISBN 978-3-03911-300-2

Vol. 54 Norman Fairclough, Giuseppina Cortese & Patrizia Ardizzone (eds)
Discourse and Contemporary Social Change.
555 pages. 2007. ISBN 978-3-03911-276-0

Vol. 55 Jan Engberg, Marianne Grove Ditlevsen, Peter Kastberg & Martin Stegu (eds)
New Directions in LSP Teaching.
331 pages. 2007. ISBN 978-3-03911-433-7

Vol. 56 Dorothee Heller & Konrad Ehlich (Hrsg.)
Studien zur Rechtskommunikation.
322 pages. 2007. ISBN 978-3-03911-436-8

Vol. 57 Teruhiro Ishiguro & Kang-kwong Luke (eds)
Grammar in Cross-Linguistic Perspective.
The Syntax, Semantics, and Pragmatics of Japanese and Chinese.
304 pages. 2012. ISBN 978-3-03911-445-0

Vol. 58 Carmen Frehner
Email – SMS – MMS
294 pages. 2008. ISBN 978-3-03911-451-1

Vol. 59 Isabel Balteiro
The Directionality of Conversion in English. A Dia-Synchronic Study.
276 pages. 2007. ISBN 978-3-03911-241-8

Vol. 60 Maria Milagros Del Saz Rubio
English Discourse Markers of Reformulation.
237 pages. 2007. ISBN 978-3-03911-196-1

Vol. 61 Sally Burgess & Pedro Martín-Martín (eds)
English as an Additional Language in Research Publication and Communication.
259 pages. 2008. ISBN 978-3-03911-462-7

Vol. 62 Sandrine Onillon
Pratiques et représentations de l'écrit.
458 pages. 2008. ISBN 978-3-03911-464-1

Vol. 63 Hugo Bowles & Paul Seedhouse (eds)
Conversation Analysis and Language for Specific Purposes.
2nd edition. 337 pages. 2007, 2009. ISBN 978-3-0343-0045-2

Vol. 64 Vijay K. Bhatia, Christopher N. Candlin & Paola Evangelisti Allori (eds)
Language, Culture and the Law.
The Formulation of Legal Concepts across Systems and Cultures.
342 pages. 2008. ISBN 978-3-03911-470-2

Vol. 65 Jonathan Culpeper & Dániel Z. Kádár (eds)
Historical (Im)politeness.
300 pages. 2010. ISBN 978-3-03911-496-2

Vol. 66 Linda Lombardo (ed.)
Using Corpora to Learn about Language and Discourse.
237 pages. 2009. ISBN 978-3-03911-522-8

Vol. 67 Natsumi Wakamoto
Extroversion/Introversion in Foreign Language Learning.
Interactions with Learner Strategy Use.
159 pages. 2009. ISBN 978-3-03911-596-9

Vol. 68 Eva Alcón-Soler (ed.)
Learning How to Request in an Instructed Language Learning Context.
260 pages. 2008. ISBN 978-3-03911-601-0

Vol. 69 Domenico Pezzini
The Translation of Religious Texts in the Middle Ages.
428 pages. 2008. ISBN 978-3-03911-600-3

Vol. 70 Tomoko Tode
Effects of Frequency in Classroom Second Language Learning.
Quasi-experiment and stimulated-recall analysis.
195 pages. 2008. ISBN 978-3-03911-602-7

Vol. 71 Egor Tsedryk
Fusion symétrique et alternances ditransitives.
211 pages. 2009. ISBN 978-3-03911-609-6

Vol. 72 Cynthia J. Kellett Bidoli & Elana Ochse (eds)
English in International Deaf Communication.
444 pages. 2008. ISBN 978-3-03911-610-2

Vol. 73 Joan C. Beal, Carmela Nocera & Massimo Sturiale (eds)
Perspectives on Prescriptivism.
269 pages. 2008. ISBN 978-3-03911-632-4

Vol. 74 Carol Taylor Torsello, Katherine Ackerley & Erik Castello (eds)
Corpora for University Language Teachers.
308 pages. 2008. ISBN 978-3-03911-639-3

Vol. 75 María Luisa Pérez Cañado (ed.)
English Language Teaching in the European Credit Transfer System. Facing the Challenge.
251 pages. 2009. ISBN 978-3-03911-654-6

Vol. 76 Marina Dossena & Ingrid Tieken-Boon van Ostade (eds)
Studies in Late Modern English Correspondence. Methodology and Data.
291 pages. 2008. ISBN 978-3-03911-658-4

Vol. 77 Ingrid Tieken-Boon van Ostade & Wim van der Wurff (eds)
Current Issues in Late Modern English.
436 pages. 2009. ISBN 978-3-03911-660-7

Vol. 78 Marta Navarro Coy (ed.)
Practical Approaches to Foreign Language Teaching and Learning.
297 pages. 2009. ISBN 978-3-03911-661-4

Vol. 79 Qing Ma
Second Language Vocabulary Acquisition.
333 pages. 2009. ISBN 978-3-03911-666-9

Vol. 80 Martin Solly, Michelangelo Conoscenti & Sandra Campagna (eds)
Verbal/Visual Narrative Texts in Higher Education.
384 pages. 2008. ISBN 978-3-03911-672-0

Vol. 81 Meiko Matsumoto
From Simple Verbs to Periphrastic Expressions: The Historical Development of Composite Predicates, Phrasal Verbs, and Related Constructions in English.
235 pages. 2008. ISBN 978-3-03911-675-1

Vol. 82 Melinda Dooly
Doing Diversity. Teachers' Construction of Their Classroom Reality.
180 pages. 2009. ISBN 978-3-03911-687-4

Vol. 83 Victoria Guillén-Nieto, Carmen Marimón-Llorca & Chelo Vargas-Sierra (eds)
Intercultural Business Communication and Simulation and Gaming Methodology.
392 pages. 2009. ISBN 978-3-03911-688-1

Vol. 84 Maria Grazia Guido
English as a Lingua Franca in Cross-cultural Immigration Domains.
285 pages. 2008. ISBN 978-3-03911-689-8

Vol. 85 Erik Castello
Text Complexity and Reading Comprehension Tests.
352 pages. 2008. ISBN 978-3-03911-717-8

Vol. 86 Maria-Lluisa Gea-Valor, Isabel García-Izquierdo & Maria-José Esteve (eds)
Linguistic and Translation Studies in Scientific Communication.
317 pages. 2010. ISBN 978-3-0343-0069-8

Vol. 87 Carmen Navarro, Rosa Mª Rodríguez Abella, Francesca Dalle Pezze & Renzo Miotti (eds)
La comunicación especializada.
355 pages. 2008. ISBN 978-3-03911-733-8

Vol. 88 Kiriko Sato
The Development from Case-Forms to Prepositional Constructions in Old English Prose.
231 pages. 2009. ISBN 978-3-03911-763-5

Vol. 89 Dorothee Heller (Hrsg.)
Formulierungsmuster in deutscher und italienischer Fachkommunikation. Intra- und interlinguale Perspektiven.
315 pages. 2008. ISBN 978-3-03911-778-9

Vol. 90 Henning Bergenholtz, Sandro Nielsen & Sven Tarp (eds)
Lexicography at a Crossroads. Dictionaries and Encyclopedias Today, Lexicographical Tools Tomorrow.
372 pages. 2009. ISBN 978-3-03911-799-4

Vol. 91 Manouchehr Moshtagh Khorasani
The Development of Controversies. From the Early Modern Period to Online Discussion Forums.
317 pages. 2009. ISBN 978-3-3911-711-6

Vol. 92 María Luisa Carrió-Pastor (ed.)
Content and Language Integrated Learning. Cultural Diversity.
178 pages. 2009. ISBN 978-3-3911-818-2

Vol. 93 Roger Berry
Terminology in English Language Teaching. Nature and Use.
262 pages. 2010. ISBN 978-3-0343-0013-1

Vol. 94 Roberto Cagliero & Jennifer Jenkins (eds)
Discourses, Communities, and Global Englishes
240 pages. 2010. ISBN 978-3-0343-0012-4

Vol. 95 Facchinetti Roberta, Crystal David, Seidlhofer Barbara (eds)
From International to Local English – And Back Again.
268 pages. 2010. ISBN 978-3-0343-0011-7

Vol. 96 Cesare Gagliardi & Alan Maley (eds)
EIL, ELF, Global English. Teaching and Learning Issues
376 pages. 2010. ISBN 978-3-0343-0010-0

Vol. 97 Sylvie Hancil (ed.)
The Role of Prosody in Affective Speech.
403 pages. 2009. ISBN 978-3-03911-696-6

Vol. 98 Marina Dossena & Roger Lass (eds)
Studies in English and European Historical Dialectology.
257 pages. 2009. ISBN 978-3-0343-0024-7

Vol. 99 Christine Béal
Les interactions quotidiennes en français et en anglais. De l'approche comparative à l'analyse des situations interculturelles.
424 pages. 2010. ISBN 978-3-0343-0027-8

Vol. 100 Maurizio Gotti (ed.)
Commonality and Individuality in Academic Discourse.
398 pages. 2009. ISBN 978-3-0343-0023-0

Vol. 101 Javier E. Díaz Vera & Rosario Caballero (eds)
Textual Healing. Studies in Medieval English Medical, Scientific and Technical Texts.
213 pages. 2009. ISBN 978-3-03911-822-9

Vol. 102 Nuria Edo Marzá
The Specialised Lexicographical Approach. A Step further in Dictionary-making.
316 pages. 2009. ISBN 978-3-0343-0043-8

Vol. 103 Carlos Prado-Alonso, Lidia Gómez-García, Iria Pastor-Gómez &
David Tizón-Couto (eds)
New Trends and Methodologies in Applied English Language Research.
Diachronic, Diatopic and Contrastive Studies.
348 pages. 2009. ISBN 978-3-0343-0046-9

Vol. 104 Françoise Salager-Meyer & Beverly A. Lewin
Crossed Words. Criticism in Scholarly Writing?
371 pages. 2011. ISBN 978-3-0343-0049-0.

Vol. 105 Javier Ruano-García
Early Modern Northern English Lexis. A Literary Corpus-Based Study.
611 pages. 2010. ISBN 978-3-0343-0058-2

Vol. 106 Rafael Monroy-Casas
Systems for the Phonetic Transcription of English. Theory and Texts.
280 pages. 2011. ISBN 978-3-0343-0059-9

Vol. 107 Nicola T. Owtram
The Pragmatics of Academic Writing.
A Relevance Approach to the Analysis of Research Article Introductions.
311 pages. 2009. ISBN 978-3-0343-0060-5

Vol. 108 Yolanda Ruiz de Zarobe, Juan Manuel Sierra &
Francisco Gallardo del Puerto (eds)
Content and Foreign Language Integrated Learning.
Contributions to Multilingualism in European Contexts
343 pages. 2011. ISBN 978-3-0343-0074-2

Vol. 109 Ángeles Linde López & Rosalía Crespo Jiménez (eds)
Professional English in the European context. The EHEA challenge.
374 pages. 2010. ISBN 978-3-0343-0088-9

Vol. 110 Rosalía Rodríguez-Vázquez
The Rhythm of Speech, Verse and Vocal Music. A New Theory.
394 pages. 2010. ISBN 978-3-0343-0309-5

Vol. 111 Anastasios Tsangalidis & Roberta Facchinetti (eds)
Studies on English Modality. In Honour of Frank Palmer.
392 pages. 2009. ISBN 978-3-0343-0310-1

Vol. 112 Forthcoming.

Vol. 113 Mihhail Lotman & Maria-Kristiina Lotman (eds)
Frontiers in Comparative Prosody. In memoriam: Mikhail Gasparov.
426 pages. 2011. ISBN 978-3-0343-0373-6

Vol. 114 Merja Kytö, John Scahill & Harumi Tanabe (eds)
Language Change and Variation from Old English to Late Modern English.
A Festschrift for Minoji Akimoto
422 pages. 2010. ISBN 978-3-0343-0372-9

Vol. 115 Giuliana Garzone & Paola Catenaccio (eds)
Identities across Media and Modes. Discursive Perspectives.
379 pages. 2009. ISBN 978-3-0343-0386-6

Vol. 116 Elena Landone
Los marcadores del discurso y cortesía verbal en español.
390 pages. 2010. ISBN 978-3-0343-0413-9

Vol. 117 Maurizio Gotti & Christopher Williams (eds)
Legal Discourse across Languages and Cultures.
339 pages. 2010. ISBN 978-3-0343-0425-2

Vol. 118 David Hirsh
Academic Vocabulary in Context.
217 pages. 2010. ISBN 978-3-0343-0426-9

Vol. 119 Yvonne Dröschel
Lingua Franca English. The Role of Simplification and Transfer.
358 pages. 2011. ISBN 978-3-0343-0432-0

Vol. 120 Tengku Sepora Tengku Mahadi, Helia Vaezian & Mahmoud Akbari
Corpora in Translation. A Practical Guide.
135 pages. 2010. ISBN 978-3-0343-0434-4

Vol. 121 Davide Simone Giannoni & Celina Frade (eds)
Researching Language and the Law. Textual Features and Translation Issues.
278 pages. 2010. ISBN 978-3-0343-0443-6

Vol. 122 Daniel Madrid & Stephen Hughes (eds)
Studies in Bilingual Education.
472 pages. 2011. ISBN 978-3-0343-0474-0

Vol. 123 Vijay K. Bhatia, Christopher N. Candlin & Maurizio Gotti (eds)
The Discourses of Dispute Resolution.
290 pages. 2010. ISBN 978-3-0343-0476-4

Vol. 124 Davide Simone Giannoni
Mapping Academic Values in the Disciplines. A Corpus-Based Approach.
288 pages. 2010. ISBN 978-3-0343-0488-7

Vol. 125 Giuliana Garzone & James Archibald (eds)
Discourse, Identities and Roles in Specialized Communication.
419 pages. 2010. ISBN 978-3-0343-0494-8

Vol. 126 Iria Pastor-Gómez
The Status and Development of N+N Sequences in
Contemporary English Noun Phrases.
216 pages. 2011. ISBN 978-3-0343-0534-1

Vol. 127 Carlos Prado-Alonso
Full-verb Inversion in Written and Spoken English.
261 pages. 2011. ISBN 978-3-0343-0535-8

Vol. 128 Tony Harris & María Moreno Jaén (eds)
Corpus Linguistics in Language Teaching.
214 pages. 2010. ISBN 978-3-0343-0524-2

Vol. 129 Tetsuji Oda & Hiroyuki Eto (eds)
Multiple Perspectives on English Philology and History of Linguistics.
A Festschrift for Shoichi Watanabe on his 80th Birthday.
378 pages. 2010. ISBN 978-3-0343-0480-1

Vol. 130 Luisa Chierichetti & Giovanni Garofalo (eds)
Lengua y Derecho. líneas de investigación interdisciplinaria.
283 pages. 2010. 978-3-0343-0463-4

Vol. 131 Paola Evangelisti Allori & Giuliana Garzone (eds)
Discourse, Identities and Genres in Corporate Communication.
Sponsorship, Advertising and Organizational Communication.
324 pages. 2011. 978-3-0343-0591-4

Vol. 132 Leyre Ruiz de Zarobe & Yolanda Ruiz de Zarobe (eds)
Speech Acts and Politeness across Languages and Cultures.
402 pages. 2012. 978-3-0343-0611-9

Vol. 133 Thomas Christiansen
Cohesion. A Discourse Perspective.
387 pages. 2011. 978-3-0343-0619-5

Vol. 134 Giuliana Garzone & Maurizio Gotti
Discourse, Communication and the Enterprise. Genres and Trends.
451 pages. 2011. ISBN 978-3-0343-0620-1

Vol. 135 Zsuzsa Hoffmann
Ways of the World's Words.
Language Contact in the Age of Globalization.
334 pages 2011. ISBN 978-3-0343-0673-7

Vol. 136 Cecilia Varcasia (ed.)
Becoming Multilingual.
Language Learning and Language Policy between Attitudes and Identities.
213 pages. 2011. ISBN 978-3-0343-0687-5

Vol. 137 Susy Macqueen
The Emergence of Patterns in Second Language Writing.
A Sociocognitive Exploration of Lexical Trails.
325 pages. 2012. ISBN 978-3-0343-1010-9

Vol. 138 Maria Vittoria Calvi & Giovanna Mapelli (eds)
La lengua del turismo. Géneros discursivos y terminología.
365 pages. 2011. ISBN 978-3-0343-1011-6

Vol. 139 Ken Lau
Learning to Become a Professional in a Textually-Mediated World.
A Text-Oriented Study of Placement Practices.
261 pages. 2012. ISBN 978-3-0343-1016-1

Vol. 140 Sandra Campagna, Giuliana Garzone, Cornelia Ilie & Elizabeth Rowley-Jolivet (eds)
Evolving Genres in Web-mediated Communication.
337 pages. 2012. ISBN 978-3-0343-1013-0

Vol. 141 Edith Esch & Martin Solly (eds)
The Sociolinguistics of Language Education in International Contexts.
263 pages. 2012. ISBN 978-3-0343-1009-3

Vol. 142 Forthcoming.

Vol. 143 David Tizón-Couto
Left Dislocation in English. A Functional-Discoursal Approach.
416 pages. 2012. ISBN 978-3-0343-1037-6

Vol. 144 Margrethe Petersen & Jan Engberg (eds)
Current Trends in LSP Research. Aims and Methods.
323 pages. 2011. ISBN 978-3-0343-1054-3

Vol. 145 David Tizón-Couto, Beatriz Tizón-Couto, Iria Pastor-Gómez & Paula Rodríguez-Puente (eds)
New Trends and Methodologies in Applied English Language Research II.
Studies in Language Variation, Meaning and Learning.
283 pages. 2012. ISBN 978-3-0343-1061-1

Vol. 146 Rita Salvi & Hiromasa Tanaka (eds)
Intercultural Interactions in Business and Management.
306 pages. 2011. ISBN 978-3-0343-1039-0

Vol. 147 Francesco Straniero Sergio & Caterina Falbo (eds)
Breaking Ground in Corpus-based Interpreting Studies.
254 pages. 2012. ISBN 978-3-0343-1071-0

Vol. 148 Forthcoming.

Vol. 149 Vijay K. Bhatia & Paola Evangelisti Allori (eds)
Discourse and Identity in the Professions. Legal, Corporate and Institutional Citizenship.
352 pages. 2011. ISBN 978-3-0343-1079-6

Vol. 150 Maurizio Gotti (ed.)
Academic Identity Traits. A Corpus-Based Investigation.
363 pages. 2012. ISBN 978-3-0343-1141-0

Vol. 151 Priscilla Heynderickx, Sylvain Dieltjens, Geert Jacobs, Paul Gillaerts &
Elizabeth de Groot (eds)
The Language Factor in International Business.
New Perspectives on Research, Teaching and Practice.
320 pages. 2012. ISBN 978-3-0343-1090-1

Vol. 152 Paul Gillaerts, Elizabeth de Groot, Sylvain Dieltjens, Priscilla Heynderickx &
Geert Jacobs (eds)
Researching Discourse in Business Genres. Cases and Corpora.
215 pages. 2012. ISBN 978-3-0343-1092-5

Vol. 153 Yongyan Zheng
Dynamic Vocabulary Development in a Foreign Language.
262 pages. 2012. ISBN 978-3-0343-1106-9

Vol. 154 Carmen Argondizzo (ed.)
Creativity and Innovation in Language Education.
357 pages. 2012. ISBN 978-3-0343-1080-2

Vol. 155 David Hirsh (ed.)
Current Perspectives in Second Language Vocabulary Research.
180 pages. 2012. ISBN 978-3-0343-1108-3

Vol. 156 Seiji Shinkawa
Unhistorical Gender Assignment in Laȝamon's *Brut*. A Case Study of a Late Stage
in the Development of Grammatical Gender toward its Ultimate Loss.
186 pages. 2012. ISBN 978-3-0343-1124-3

Vol. 157 Forthcoming.

Vol. 158 Bárbara Eizaga Rebollar (ed.)
Studies in Linguistics and Cognition.
301 pages. 2012. ISBN 978-3-0343-1138-0

Vol. 159 Giuliana Garzone, Paola Catenaccio, Chiara Degano (eds)
Genre Change in the Contemporary World. Short-term Diachronic Perspectives.
329 pages. 2012. ISBN 978-3-0343-1214-1

Vol. 160 Carol Berkenkotter, Vijay K. Bhatia & Maurizio Gotti (eds)
Insights into Academic Genres.
468 pages. 2012. ISBN 978-3-0343-1211-0

Vol. 161 Forthcoming.

Vol. 162 Patrizia Anesa
Jury Trials and the Popularization of Legal Language. A Discourse Analytical Approach.
247 pages. 2012. ISBN 978-3-0343-1231-8

Vol. 163-165 Forthcoming.

Vol. 166 Rita Salvi & Janet Bowker (eds)
Space, Time and the Construction of Identity.
Discursive Indexicality in Cultural, Institutional and Professional Fields.
324 pages. 2013. ISBN 978-3-0343-1254-7

Vol. 167 Shunji Yamazaki & Robert Sigley (eds)
Approaching Language Variation through Corpora. A Festschrift in Honour of Toshio Saito.
421 pages. 2013. ISBN 978-3-0343-1264-6

Vol. 168 Franca Poppi
Global Interactions in English as a Lingua Franca. How written communication is changing under the influence of electronic media and new contexts of use.
249 pages. 2012. ISBN 978-3-0343-1276-9

Vol. 169-170 Forthcoming.

Vol. 171 Aleksandra Matulewska
Legilinguistic Translatology. A Parametric Approach to Legal Translation.
279 pages. 2013. ISBN 978-3-0343-1287-5

Vol. 172 Maurizio Gotti & Carmen Sancho Guinda (eds)
Narratives in Academic and Professional Genres.
513 pages. 2013. ISBN 978-3-0343-1371-1

Vol. 173-175 Forthcoming.

Vol. 176 Catherine Resche
Economic Terms and Beyond: Capitalising on the Wealth of Notions.
How Researchers in Specialised Varieties of English Can Benefit from Focusing on Terms.
332 pages. 2013. ISBN 978-3-0343-1435-0

Vol. 177 Forthcoming.

Vol. 178 Cécile Desoutter & Caroline Mellet (dir.)
Le discours rapporté: approches linguistiques et perspectives didactiques.
270 pages. 2013. ISBN 978-3-0343-1292-9

www.ingramcontent.com/pod-product-compliance
Ingram Content Group UK Ltd.
Pitfield, Milton Keynes, MK11 3LW, UK
UKHW021853100926
8556IPUK00020B/1196

9 783034 314350